T0320063

Markets for Carbon and Power Pricing in Europe

NEW HORIZONS IN ENVIRONMENTAL ECONOMICS

Series Editors: Wallace E. Oates, *Professor of Economics, University of Maryland, College Park and University Fellow. Resources for the Future, USA and* Henk Folmer, *Professor of Research Methodology, Groningen University and Professor of General Economics, Wageningen University, The Netherlands*

This important series is designed to make a significant contribution to the development of the principles and practices of environmental economics. It includes both theoretical and empirical work. International in scope, it addresses issues of current and future concern in both East and West and in developed and developing countries.

The main purpose of the series is to create a forum for the publication of high quality work and to show how economic analysis can make a contribution to understanding and resolving the environmental problems confronting the world in the twenty-first century.

Recent titles in the series include:

The Impact of Climate Change on Regional Systems
A Comprehensive Analysis of California
Edited by Joel Smith and Robert Mendelsohn

Explorations in Environmental and Natural Resource Economics
Essays in Honor of Gardner M. Brown, Jr.
Edited by Robert Halvorsen and David Layton

Using Experimental Methods in Environmental and Resource Economics
Edited by John A. List

Economic Modelling of Climate Change and Energy Policies
Carlos de Miguel, Xavier Labandeira and Baltasar Manzano

The Economics of Global Environmental Change
International Cooperation for Sustainability
Edited by Mario Cogoy and Karl W. Steininger

Redesigning Environmental Valuation
Mixing Methods within Slated Preference Techniques
Neil A. Powe

Economic Valuation of River Systems
Edited by Fred J. Hitzhusen

Scarcity, Entitlements and the Economics of Water in Developing Countries
P.B. Anand

Technological Change and Environmental Policy
A Study of Depletion in the Oil and Gas Industry
Shunsuke Managi

Environmental Governance and Decentralisation
Edited by Albert Breton, Giorgio Brosio, Silvana Dalmazzone and Giovanna Garrone

Choice Experiments Informing Environmental Policy
A European Perspective
Edited by Ekin Birol and Phoebe Koundouri

Markets for Carbon and Power Pricing in Europe
Theoretical Issues and Empirical Analyses
Edited by Francesco Gullì

Markets for Carbon and Power Pricing in Europe

Theoretical Issues and Empirical Analyses

Edited by

Francesco Gullì

Università Bocconi, Milan, Italy

NEW HORIZONS IN ENVIRONMENTAL ECONOMICS

Edward Elgar

Cheltenham, UK • Northampton, MA, USA

© Francesco Gulli 2008
© OECD/IEA 2008 for Chapter 4 by Julia Reinaud

All rights reserved. No part of this publication may be reproduced, stored in a retrieval system or transmitted in any form or by any means, electronic, mechanical or photocopying, recording, or otherwise without the prior permission of the publisher.

Published by
Edward Elgar Publishing Limited
The Lypiatts
15 Lansdown Road
Cheltenham
Glos GL50 2JA
UK

Edward Elgar Publishing, Inc.
William Pratt House
9 Dewey Court
Northampton
Massachusetts 01060
USA

A catalogue record for this book
is available from the British Library

Library of Congress Control Number: 2008927677

Mixed Sources
Product group from well-managed
forests and other controlled sources
www.fsc.org Cert no. SA-COC-1565
© 1996 Forest Stewardship Council

ISBN 978 1 84720 809 5

Printed and bound in Great Britain by MPG Books Ltd, Bodmin, Cornwall

Contents

Contributors

Derek W. Bunn London Business School, UK.

Liliya Chernyavs'ka IEFE (Instituto di Economia e Politica dell'Energia e dell'Ambiente), Bocconi University, Milan and DIEM (Departimento di Economia e Metodi Quantitativi), Università di Genova, Italy.

Carlo Fezzi CSERGE (Centre for Social and Economic Research on the Global Environment), School of Environmental Science, University of East Anglia, Norwich, UK.

Francesco Gullì Bocconi University, Milan, Italy.

Sebastiaan Hers ECN, Energy Research Centre of the Netherlands.

Juha Honkatukia VATT, Government Institute for Economic Research, Finland.

Pedro Linares Instituto de Investigación Tecnológica, Universidad Pontificia Comillas, Spain.

Ville Mälkönen VATT, Government Institute for Economic Research, Finland.

Adriaan Perrels VATT, Government Institute for Economic Research, Finland.

Julia Reinaud IEA (International Energy Agency), Paris, France.

Francisco J. Santos Instituto de Investigación Tecnológica, Universidad Pontificia Comillas, Spain.

Jos Sijm ECN, Energy Research Centre of the Netherlands.

Bas Wetzelaer ECN, Energy Research Centre of the Netherlands.

1. Introduction

Francesco Gullì

The European Emissions Trading Scheme (EU ETS) is the first international trading scheme for carbon dioxide (CO_2) emissions in the world. Its aim is to reduce the cost of meeting the Kyoto Protocol requirements by creating an explicit and common price for carbon.

The EU ETS covers several industry sectors of which power generation is the largest. Therefore, on the one hand, the performance of the trading scheme largely depends on the efficacy in inducing the power industry to reduce CO_2 emissions significantly in the short and long runs. On the other hand, it might have a considerable impact on consumer surplus and firms' profits and competitiveness. Either the performance of the EU ETS or its impact on social welfare depends on how and to what extent the CO_2 price is passed through into power prices.

Given this premise, it is easy to understand why researchers, operators and regulators are so interested in the interaction between carbon and power prices. Nevertheless, the current literature on this topic is quite controversial, from both the theoretical and the empirical points of view.

On the theoretical side, an open question is how the CO_2 cost pass-through is correlated with the structural features of the output market, namely the power market. In fact, while it is quite clear what can occur under perfectly competitive scenarios, opinions diverge when the assumption of perfect competition is abandoned. Some authors state that under imperfect competition electricity prices increase more than in a competitive scenario, while others argue in favour of the opposite result (electricity prices increase less under market power). This controversial framework emerges because each contribution is based on specific and different hypotheses on the strategic behaviour of the firms, the technology mix and the regulation of both power and allowance markets. Consequently the results of each study cannot be generalized as they offer only a partial view of the problem.

The empirical literature is even more controversial. Some authors estimate full or almost full pass-through rates (PTRs). Others find that power prices do not internalize carbon costs or that there is limited evidence that CO_2 is factored into wholesale price. Indeed, most empirical analyses are simply trying to check whether there is a full pass-through and generically attribute the 'deviation' from this 'rule' to various structural factors (among which the exercise of market power in the output market) without attempting to measure their specific effects.

In addition, these studies differ significantly in their methodological approaches. Some rely on forward markets whereas others analyse spot prices. Some are based on the econometric elaboration of time series, whereas others examine the change in the price and/or spread duration curves (the 'load duration curve approach') and so on. Thus, no one empirical study, if considered separately, is useful to check the robustness of the theoretical models and, once again, is able to provide results which can be generalized.

The question of how the ETS can affect emissions is no less disputed. All authors agree that emissions are highest under the most-competitive scenarios. Nevertheless some contributions show that emission reductions are lowest under perfect competition, while others state that generally higher emission reductions are achieved in the case without market power.

Moreover policy makers', regulators' and operators' declarations and position papers do not help to clarify the overall framework, proving that opinions are not convergent even outside the scientific community. For instance, in Germany throughout 2005, the energy-intensive industries debated with power firms the question of responsibility for the carbon price pass-through into product prices. In other countries, such as Italy, the power industry ensured that there was no CO_2 cost pass-through in the wholesale power prices and, consequently, no windfall profit (mostly due to the pass-through of the opportunity costs of freely allocated CO_2 emission allowances).

These positions, however, became very difficult to defend when the carbon price collapsed at the end of April 2006. Since this fall was immediately followed by a drop in wholesale power prices in some European markets, it appeared unequivocally clear that there was an interaction between carbon and power prices. In other words, the empirical evidence confirmed what the theoretical analysis suggested, and thereafter the debate moved from the question of whether power companies gain windfall profits or not to more interesting arguments which can be summed up by means of the following questions.

Why do power prices seem to be correlated with the carbon price in some markets and not in others? Why do power firms pass through into power prices in some cases more and in others less than the carbon opportunity cost? What is the relationship between the pass-through and the structure of the power market? What is the influence of the technology mix and of the available generation capacity? How can market power in the power market affect the pass-through and vice versa? Can 'carbon trading' determine a rise rather than a decline in carbon emissions of the power system, at least in the short and medium runs? Should efforts be focused on bringing the electricity price down? Should regulators change the method of allocating the CO_2 emission allowances in order to improve the efficiency and effectiveness of the ETS and eliminate the windfall profits? Should policy makers and regulators care about the redistribution of the cost of the EU ETS among industry and consumers?

It is difficult to answer these questions without addressing first to what extent and under which conditions the CO_2 price is passed through into power prices. This requires carrying out a robust simulation model, on the theoretical side, and going beyond the results of a (country and methodological) specific study, on the empirical side. In other words, it is necessary to provide a comprehensive analysis that would be useful to understand how the pass-through depends on market structural features, on the one hand, and how methodological approaches affect the empirical results, on the other.

This book attempts to set out such an analysis and to answer these questions by bringing together and interpreting the contributions by the leading experts of each EU country or regional market. The volume is divided into two parts and has the following structure.

Part I includes an overview of the EU ETS, including its early results, and two chapters on the theoretical issues. These contributions are useful to interpret the empirical analyses in accordance with the statements of economic theory.

In particular, Chapter 2, by Chernyavs'ka, is organized as follows. First, the author describes the EU directive on emissions trading, discussing the CO_2 allowance market regulation (industrial sector covered, methods of allocation, regulatory periods and so on.). Then the allocation plans and the early results of the EU ETS are presented and discussed. Comments about the allowance price dynamic are proposed as well as considerations about the organization of the European CO_2 markets. Finally, the author explores the possibility of learning some lessons for the future, mainly by looking at the post-Kyoto and at the new EU targets (reducing emissions of greenhouse gases by 20 per cent by 2020).

In Chapter 3, Gullì examines the impact of trading of CO_2 emission allowances on electricity pricing in the short run. The author is mainly interested in exploring the role of electricity market structures. He uses a simple analytical model to verify whether (and under what conditions) the impact of the ETS under market power could be lower (or higher) than that under perfect competition. Furthermore, the author examines how emissions trading impacts on carbon emissions in the short run, that is, whether the environmental regulation can determine an increase (rather than a decrease) in pollution.

In Chapter 4, Reinaud focuses on the situation of energy-intensive industries going beyond the analysis of the spot electricity prices. She examines the way carbon price is passed through into end-user prices under different electricity pricing mechanisms such as short- and long-term contracts, regulated tariffs and so on.

Part II includes the empirical analyses of the main European markets. These studies are based on different methodological approaches and are collected and ordered so as to offer a comprehensive and thorough view of the topic.

In particular, Chapter 5, by Sijm, Hers and Wetzelaer, explores a variety of options to address EU ETS- induced increases in power prices and windfall profits, notably whether these options are effective and whether they also have other (adverse) effects. The study starts with the estimates of the average PTRs in Germany and the Netherlands. The authors find that empirical estimates of carbon cost PTRs on forward wholesale power markets varied from 0.4 to more than 1.0 in 2005–06.

Bunn and Fezzi (Chapter 6) address the economic impact of the EU ETS for carbon on wholesale electricity and gas prices. Specifically, the authors analyse the mutual relationship between electricity, gas and carbon prices in the daily spot markets in the United Kingdom and Germany. Using a structural co-integrated VAR (Vector Autoregression) model, they show how the prices of carbon and gas jointly influence the equilibrium price of electricity. Furthermore, the analysis derives the dynamic pass-through of carbon into electricity price and the response of electricity and carbon prices to shocks in the gas price.

Honkatukia, Mälkönen and Perrels (Chapter 7) examine the extent to which the costs of the EU ETS are reflected in the electricity prices in the Finnish power market. The study involves a simple theoretical illustration and an empirical exercise of electricity price formation. The authors use two econometric methods (the vector error correction model and the autoregressive conditional hederoskedasticity model) and find that about 50–100 per cent of a price change in the EU ETS is passed on to the Finnish NordPool spot price.

In Chapter 8, Chernyavs'ka and Gullì carry out an empirical analysis in the Italian context (an emblematic case of an imperfectly competitive market), which can be split in four sub-markets (North, macro-South, macro-Sicily and Sardinia) with different structural features. The authors use the 'load duration curve approach', which allows them to investigate how the pass-through depends on the degree of market power in power markets, other than on other structural features.

Finally, the contribution by Linares and Santos (Chapter 9) deals with the interaction between carbon markets and the policies supporting renewable energies. The authors look at how the EU ETS and a tradable green certificate system for the promotion of renewable energies may affect the Spanish electricity sector in the long term. The analysis was carried out using a generation-expansion model, which accounts for the possible oligopolistic behaviour of generation firms.

It is clearly beyond the scope of this introduction to enter into the details of each study, since the reader can find a full description of the methodologies and results in the corresponding chapters. The following provides a summary of the book's findings with regard to the theoretical and methodological issues as well as the empirical results and their policy implications.

The theoretical analysis shows that under imperfect competition the extent to which the carbon cost is passed through into power prices depends on several structural factors of the power market, namely: (i) the degree of market concentration; (ii) the technology mix; (iii) the available capacity; and (iv) the allowance prices. Depending on these factors, the marginal pass-through rate (MPTR) can be either above or below 1, that is, the increase in price under market power can be either higher or lower than that under perfect competition. Also, under certain conditions, the impact on power prices can even be slightly negative (at least, in principle), that is, the ETS can involve a decrease rather than an increase in prices. Market power, therefore, determines a significant deviation from the 'full pass-through' rule but we cannot know the sign of this deviation, a priori, that is, without first taking into account the structural features of the power market.

Another interesting result emerges from the theoretical analysis. The ETS causes a change in the degree of market power in the sense that, after the introduction of the trading scheme, the time (the number of hours in the year) over which power firms prefer to bid the maximum price (for example, the price cap) increases or decreases depending (again) on the structural factors of the power market. This means not only that the ETS can amplify or lessen the existing distortions in the output market but also that it might determine a rise rather than a decrease in carbon emissions, namely when the change in market power significantly expands the production share of the most-polluting plants. However, this does not necessarily imply that perfect competition is preferable to market power from the environmental point of view, but simply that under imperfect competition, and provided that certain conditions are satisfied, it might be more difficult to achieve the environmental targets.

With regard to the empirical results, Table 1.1 presents a summary of the estimated PTRs on the power markets analysed in this book. As can be noted, these values are significant in all cases and suggest that the

Table 1.1 Summary of the carbon cost pass-through rates

	Methodology	Price	Period	Average	Peak	Off-peak	
						Mid-merit	Very off-peak
Finland (Chapter 7)	Econometric VECM and AR-GARCH	Wholesale spot	2005–06	0.5–1.0			
Germany (Chapter 6)	Econometric VECM	Wholesale spot	2005–06	0.52			
Germany (Chapter 5)	Econometric OLS	Wholesale forward	2005		0.60	0.41	
			2006		0.57	0.64	
Italy–North (Chapter 8)	Load duration curve approach	Wholesale spot	2006		1.5–2.1	0.8–1.3	0.9–1.1
Italy–South (Chapter 8)	Load duration curve approach	Wholesale spot	2006		0.0–0.5	1.7–2.1	0.9–1.1
Italy–whole (Chapter 8)	Load duration curve approach	Wholesale spot	2006		1.1–1.5	1.2–1.5	0.9–1.1
Netherlands (Chapter 5)	Econometric OLS	Wholesale forward	2005		1.34	0.40	
			2006		1.10	0.38	
UK (Chapter 6)	Econometric VECM	Wholesale spot	2005–06	0.30			

Note: VECM = vector error correction model; AR-GARCH = autoregressive conditional heteroskedasticity model; OLS = ordinary least squares.

6

bandwidth for pass-through can be quite large, varying between countries and periods. The estimates range from 30 to 100 per cent if we refer to the average value, from 57 to 134 per cent in the peak hours and from 40 to 123 per cent in the off-peak hours. Furthermore, the analysis of how the PTR is distributed over time (between peak and off-peak periods) would seem to suggest that there is not the same behaviour everywhere (that is, no general rule). The PTR is higher in the peak than in the off-peak hours in Germany (2005), the Netherlands and Italy–South, and vice versa in Germany (2006) and Italy–North. The overall picture, therefore, would seem to support the conclusions of the theoretical analysis, that is, we cannot know how the ETS impacts on power prices (whether the PTR is low or high, more or less than 1) without first accounting for the structural features of the power markets under analysis.

Furthermore, the estimates have to be interpreted with due care as, to some extent, they depend on (shortcomings of) the data and the methodologies used or the assumptions made. With regard to the methodological issues, the contributors use many empirical methods to estimate carbon price PTRs. Each method has its own strengths and weaknesses, so that one approach cannot be considered as definitively preferable to another. Nevertheless, there are some important differences between the econometric and non-econometric techniques.

The econometric approach uses sophisticated statistical tools in order to measure carbon price PTRs. It is based on the statistical elaboration of time-series of either forward or spot prices (of both electricity and carbon) and estimates the impact of the ETS on the average price, eventually distinguishing between the peak and off-peak hours. The specifications of these models are generally quite simple. The set of drivers commonly includes the fuel costs and the temperature (Sijm et al., Chapter 5; Bunn and Fezzi, Chapter 6). Only one model (Honkatukia et al., Chapter 7) uses additional variables (namely, the production capacity and the utilization of the transmission capacity). Furthermore, models neither consider the real marginal technology hour by hour nor are suited to capture (by using appropriate drivers) the effect of market power. They assume that during the observation period power prices are set by a single (marginal) technology with a fixed, generic fuel efficiency. In other words, the econometric models are very useful for providing a precise (statistically significant) value of the carbon pass-through but they are not able to justify this value, that is to explain why a PTR is high, low or zero.

The non-econometric approach consists of two steps: (i) estimate the PTR by means of an analytical model; and (ii) compare the estimates with the observed data. It does not elaborate time series but carry out the pass-through distribution over time (the pass-through curve) starting from the load duration curve. This allows us to obtain the PTR hour by hour. The non-econometric approach has several advantages compared with the econometric one. First, as pointed out before, it provides a detailed analysis of the pass-through over time, on an hour-by-hour basis. As a result, it seems to be well suited to describe the impact of market power whose extent depends on the level of power demand (and hence on the time of consumption). Moreover, by using this approach, market power can be effectively simulated by means of a theoretical model assuming oligopolistic competition or (as in Chapter 3) a dominant firm framework. Second, the non-econometric approach allows us to take into account other important structural factors which cannot be included in econometric models, for example, the technological mix and the available capacity in the market. However, unlike the statistical approach, it does not provide a precise value of the pass-through but only a range of its variability. In this sense, the two approaches are complementary. The non-econometric one is useful to improve the specification of the statistical models and to interpret their results.

Finally, concerning the policy implications, this work can help to shed light on two issues: (i) the effectiveness and efficiency of the ETS itself (regardless of its specific design); and (ii) how the current design of the EU ETS should be changed in order to improve its performance.

With regard to the ETS itself, the theoretical and empirical analyses highlight that under imperfect competition power prices may increase less than under perfectly competitive scenarios. Thus, provided that certain conditions are satisfied, imperfect competition can partly lessen the ETS effectiveness in terms of emission abatement. Also, under certain conditions, the ETS can determine a rise rather than a decrease in carbon emissions, at least in principle. At the same time, the change in emissions becomes high only when the carbon price is above the 'switching price', that is, when the carbon cost internalization determines a switch in the merit order of power plants, for example between coal and gas-fired plants. Thus, in designing the ETS, regulators should mainly ensure that the allocation will create an adequate scarcity of tradable permits. Furthermore, policy makers should also take into account the interaction of the scheme with other energy and environmental policies. For instance, a combination of both carbon reduction and renewable promotion policies may result in lower costs than carbon reduction policies alone, with the additional benefit of increased deployment of the renewable technologies.

Looking at the design of the scheme, we have to be aware that the increase in power prices due to the pass-through of the (opportunity) costs of (freely allocated) CO_2 emission allowances is a rational and intended effect from an efficient carbon abatement policy perspective. Nevertheless, the supposed ETS-induced increases in power prices and generators' profits (windfall) have raised several concerns about its impact on the international competitiveness of some power-intensive industries, the purchasing power of electricity end-users such as small households or, more generally, the distribution of social welfare among power producers and consumers. As a result, in several countries, a variety of options have been suggested in order to address these concerns, such as changing the ETS allocation system, taxing windfall profits or controlling the market prices of EU carbon allowances, electricity or both. Some contributions of this book, and especially Chapter 5, examine these options in order to address their performance and suggest the best way of improving the design of the scheme.

Overall, this volume attempts to offer a comprehensive analysis of the relationship between carbon and power markets. As such we hope it will provide a useful contribution to the debate on the perspective of the EU ETS and to the literature on the interaction between environmental policy and the structure of the environmentally regulated markets.

PART I

Overview and theoretical issues

2. The European Emissions Trading Scheme: overview, lessons and perspectives

Liliya Chernyavs'ka

2.1 INTRODUCTION

The increasing risk that radical/dramatic events caused by climate change could occur, having a negative impact on all aspects of human activity, raises the question concerning reduction of greenhouse gas (GHG) emissions.

Now, in fact, most of the scientific community admits that there is a relationship between the increase in concentration of GHGs in the atmosphere and the rise in the average temperature of the planet, even though we are still far from explaining the exact mechanism of such a relationship. However, it is clear that the anthropogenic emissions have a strong negative role in the persisting increase in the concentration of GHGs and thus in climate change.

The Kyoto Protocol is the first step towards the international commitment to mitigate the process of climate alteration. This agreement, signed in 1997, sets the overall amount of the reduction (–5.2 per cent, with respect to the level of emissions registered in 1990) to be achieved by the parties. This commitment is shared out in different proportions among groups of countries and among countries within each group on the basis of their economic development and contribution to global emissions. For example, the target for the European Union (EU) was fixed at –8 per cent. The reductions are to be achieved in five years, namely from 2008 to 2012.

The Protocol also provides the rules and mechanisms (the so-called Kyoto 'flexible' mechanisms) to reach this goal most cost-effectively and equitably without precluding the economic development of all the parties.

In December 2002, after lengthy discussions, the EU opted for a cap-and-trade scheme as one of the main instruments to ensure the success in attaining the Kyoto target.[1] Such a decision had both an economic and a political basis. First, the European Commission (hereafter Commission) was looking for an efficient tool to reduce the costs of compliance that was also able to capture the structural differences among countries and sectors, creating as few distortions as possible. Second, on the political side, it was necessary to guarantee a univocal decision, taking into account the interests of each member state. Finally, at the international level, the EU aims to have a leadership position in the fight against global warming.

As a result, in October 2003 the European Council and Parliament approved Directive 2003/87/CE establishing a scheme for GHG emission allowances within the EU.

2.2   EMISSIONS TRADING DIRECTIVE 2003/87/CE

Directive 2003/87/CE (European Commission, 2003a) establishes a cap-and-trade scheme for CO_2 emission allowances in order to promote the reduction of carbon emissions in cost-effective and economically efficient ways. It has a pan-European coverage, including all new member states. This latter provision is necessary to guarantee lower costs of compliance, reflecting relatively low abatement costs in the Eastern European countries.

The European Emissions Trading Scheme (EU ETS) took effect on 1 January 2005. It foresees mandatory participation for the sectors mentioned in Annex I of the directive, and is planned to take place in two phases: Phase I, from 2005 to 2007, is a pilot period, necessary to try out the design of the trading framework and to provide the opportunity to accumulate necessary experience for the second phase; Phase II starts in 2008 and coincides with the Kyoto commitment period (2008–12). According to the directive, the tradable allowances are allocated directly to industrial emitters, which can exchange/trade them freely. The volumes of permits are fixed and determined before the starting date of trading. This ensures that, at least in principle, major predictability and thus stability of the system should be guaranteed. The participants are obliged to surrender the amount of allowances equal to their annual emissions after each calendar year. The eventual deficit has to be covered by purchasing the permits. If the operator does not surrender the emitted quantities, penalties are applied. Legislation stipulates two different penalties for the first and second periods: 40 €/ton and 100 €/ton, respectively. Moreover, payment of the penalty does not release the operator from the obligation to surrender the allowances. Such a framework further underlines the mandatory character of the participation and, from the theoretical point of view, it could lead to a situation in which the carbon price could exceed the penalties. We could also suppose that the increase in the sanction from one period to the next reflects in some way the expectations of the higher costs of abatement during the second period (Kyoto commitment).

Table 2.1 summarizes the key features of the EU ETS. With regard to sectoral coverage, participants in the scheme include energy activities (electricity generators, oil refineries and coke ovens) and some manufacturing sectors (such as production and processing of ferrous metals, cement clinker, glass and ceramics, and pulp and paper). The scheme includes more than 10,500 installations accounting for about 40 per cent of total GHG emissions of the EU. The directive also foresees the possibility for future expansion of the activities. The intention was to include the chemical and transportation sectors, but the problems with monitoring as well as high transaction costs meant that they had to be excluded from the actual coverage. For the same reason, only CO_2 was chosen to start with. Other gases could be included later on.

One of the main critical points of the entire system is the initial allocation of allowances, as this may generate distortions among countries, sectors and single installations.[2] The directive states that most of the allowances (95 per cent in Phase I and 90 per cent in Phase II) have to be allocated free of charge. This provision creates two problems: first, it may lessen firms' incentives to reduce carbon emissions; and second, since firms may pass through the carbon opportunity cost into product prices, free allocation may determine significant windfall profits.

Furthermore, the directive does not indicate the technical mechanism for the allocation (grandfathering, benchmarking, future emissions and so on). Almost all countries opted for grandfathering which, however, has certain weaknesses. First, it is necessary to evaluate the choice of the base period in order not to penalize those industries/sectors that could suffer a drop in production due to conjectural, atmospheric or other conditions and in order to reward possible early actions. Second, grandfathering tends to be more advantageous to the large emitters in comparison with less-polluting firms, undermining the 'polluters pay' rule. Thus the exploitation of clean technologies may not receive adequate incentives.

As a result of all this, the efficiency and effectiveness of the trading scheme could be undermined, as it could not ensure the abatement of emissions according to the least-cost principle. Moreover, we should take into consideration that the directive did not stipulate the exact amount of reduction to be achieved by each member state, leaving this decision to the national governments. This involved a real risk that further distortions could derive from the different choices of the different countries in terms of relative allocation, that is, the ratio between the amount of allowance allocated and the expected emissions at country, sector and participant levels.

Overall, the text of the directive seems to be a compromise between the urgency to reach the Kyoto target and the interests of the different

Table 2.1   Framework of the EU ETS

Feature	Description
Type of system	Cap-and-trade system based on direct emissions
Timing	Phase I: 2005–07, preliminary or try-out period
	Phase II: 2008–12, coincides with Kyoto commitment
Geographical coverage	EU25, with possibility of expanding to new member states
Coverage of activities	*Energy activities*: all combustion installations with more then 20 MW thermal input, including power sector; oil refineries; coke ovens
	Production and processing of ferrous metals
	Mineral industry: cement clinker, glass and ceramics
	Other activities: pulp and paper from timber
	Opt-out provisions: member states may apply to the Commission for installations to be temporarily excluded until 31 December 2007
	Opt-in provisions: member states may voluntarily extend the scheme to other installations, starting from Phase II
Coverage of GHG	Only CO_2 in Phase I
	Other gases may be included in Phase II, provided that adequate monitoring and reporting systems are available, and there is no damage to the environmental integrity of the ETS or distortions to competition
Size of the market[1]	Nearly 10,500 installations
	About 41% of total EU GHG emissions
Allocation	Free allocation within national allocation plans (NAPs) based on Annex III criteria and Commission Guidelines
	Member states can auction up to 5% in Phase I and up to 10% in Phase II
	NAPs have to be presented to the Commission to be evaluated and approved. The Commission may demand any change in order to make NAP comply with criteria of Annex III
Operational rules	On 30 April of each year, participants have to surrender a quantity of allowances equal to their emissions in the preceding calendar year
	Participants are allowed to trade the permits among themselves
	Participants are allowed to form an emissions pool by nominating a trustee who takes on the responsibility for surrender and trading allowances on behalf of all members of the pool
Banking	Implicit banking across years within each compliance period
	Member states can determine their own banking from Phase I (2005–07) to Phase II (2008–12)

Table 2.1 (continued)

Feature	Description
Penalties	Non-complying participants must pay a penalty of 40 €/ton of CO_2 during Phase I and 100 €/ton in Phase II Payment of the emission penalties does not release the operator from the obligation to surrender the allowances
Use/links with other Kyoto mechanisms[2]	Participants may convert emission credits from joint implementation (JI) and clean development mechanism (CDM) projects into EU allowances in order to fulfil their obligations under EU ETS All types of credits are allowed for conversion, except those from nuclear facilities and carbon sink enhancement projects The amount of credits allowed for conversion must be indicated in NAPs for each installation (% of total allowances allocated to the installation) The main efforts, however, have to come from domestic actions
Links with other schemes	Agreement with third parties may provide mutual recognition of allowances between the EU ETS and other schemes
Monitoring and reporting	Common monitoring, verification and reporting obligations were elaborated and delivered[3]
Verification	Verification through third-party or government authority
Registers	Linked and harmonized national registries with independent transaction log can track all the allowances

Notes:
1. On the basis of 2005 data provided by the European Commission (2008).
2. These Provisions are mentioned in the so-called 'Linking Directive' (European Commission, 2004a).
3. For further details, see European Commission (2004b, 2007).

Sources: European Commission (2003a, 2004a, 2004b, 2007, 2008a); Sijm (2004).

member states. Such compromise probably would not be possible if the document were more precise in indicating the methods and rules of allocation, caps to set and so on. At the same time, a broad outline would inevitably lead to a multiplicity of interpretations and thus to a lack of homogeneity.

As a result, the Phase I NAPs of each country differed in almost every respect.

2.3   PHASE I: FIRST PROBLEMS

The NAP is an instrument to accomplish Directive 2003/87/CE, which fixes the quantity of allowances that member states allocate to installations covered by the ETS (for each phase). This amount has to be determined before the beginning of the trading period and cannot be changed once it has been approved by the Commission. The first draft of the NAP had to be presented by 31 March 2004 for EU15 countries and by 1 May 2004 for newcomers. Once received, the Commission had to evaluate it within three months.

Each NAP is evaluated against a set of 11 criteria listed in Annex III of the directive. In order to assist the member states in the preparation of the NAPs, in January 2004, the Commission published guidelines for the application of the criteria, describing their scope and meaning, and highlighting whether they are compulsory or optional (European Commission, 2004c). These guidelines together with the Commission's 'The EU Emissions Trading Scheme: How to Develop a National Allocation Plan' (2003b) established the base for the NAPs. Particular attention was paid to the problems of allocation and the treatment of new entrants as these are the major critical points that could undermine the competitiveness of the European industry.

As specified earlier, the deadlines for the presentation of the NAPs were 31 March and 1 May 2004, for the core European countries and for new entrants, respectively. However only half of the countries had presented the required document by the deadline. The process of evaluation was concluded in June 2005, six months after the beginning of trading. This increased uncertainty during the first year of Phase I, penalizing participants with late allocation plans.

With regard to the evaluation process, the most frequent violations notified by the Commission were overallocation, possible introduction of *ex post* adjustments, discrimination/unequal treatment of new entrants and an incomplete list of installations.

Thirteen countries were required to reduce the amount of their allocated allowances (up to a total of 292,04 Mt of CO_2). This intervention can be interpreted as a signal of the tendency for some countries to overallocate their allowance.

The opposition to *ex post* adjustments derived from several sources: the need to create a market based on simple and clear rules, at the same time reducing the uncertainty regarding the quantities that could be traded and the intra-sector distortions; ensuring that the EU ETS would have a significant impact on product prices (mainly on power prices) and consequently on emissions by means of the impact on (decrease in) output demand. The *ex post* adjustment (updating), in fact, determines a reduction in the carbon opportunity cost (see Sijm et al., this volume, Chapter 5).

In line with earlier predictions, the NAPs were highly disparate. They were also too complex, especially those sections describing the allocation rules, and showed lack of transparency. Thus it is quite difficult to compare them. Moreover, the allocation methodologies were extremely complex and somewhat confusing. Most of the member states opted for grandfathering based on historical emissions. Only a few used the possibility to auction a part of the permits.

One of the most controversial and complex problems was the allocation to new entrants. About a hundred different rules and benchmarks were proposed, resulting in confusion and possible distortions. The need for a unique methodology that is able to provide incentives for the adoption of the cleanest and most efficient technologies became a clear issue for the future.

The analysis of the content of the allocation plans highlights another question to be answered as soon as possible. The definition of the combustion installation was generic and suitable for multiple interpretations, introducing relativity into the coverage of the ETS. Roughly speaking there were three main groups of interpretations: narrow (only the energy production sector), medium (production of electricity, heat or steam for the purpose of energy production) and broad (production of electricity, heat or steam). Not one member state adopted the narrow interpretation. Austria, Belgium, Cyprus, Denmark, Hungary, Ireland, Latvia, Malta, the Netherlands, Portugal, Slovenia and Sweden chose the broad interpretation, while the rest opted for the medium one. As a consequence of the adoption of the medium definition, some installations with high emissions remained outside the ETS. Some sectors, such as production and processing of ferrous metals, ceramics and so on, had, therefore, different coverage in the different countries with possible significant consequences in terms of distortions of competition (for further details, see Ecofys, 2006).

As pointed out earlier, the EU ETS is the largest international scheme; it includes more than 10,000 facilities of which about 16 per cent are installations that together hold less then 0.2 per cent of allocated allowances (Ecofys, 2007). They are small and medium installations with a rated thermal input exceeding 20 MW and a very low emission rate (less then 5,000 tCO_2/year). These have a marginal importance in terms of emissions, but they increase the administrative and transaction costs of the scheme.

The results of the first years of the EU ETS are summarized in Table 2.2. Note that only six countries closed the first year with a deficit of allowances with respect to the average annual allocation. The UK is the leader with a shortfall of 33 Mt, followed by Spain with 19.5 Mt and Italy with 18.4 Mt.

Table 2.2 Overview of allocated and surrendered/verified allowances, 2005–2007

Member state	Total emission CO_2 1990 (t)	Kyoto target (t)	Total emissions CO_2 2005 (t)	ETS emissions CO_2 2005 (t)	ETS emissions CO_2 2006 (t)
Austria	78,900,000	68,700,000	93,300,000	33,372,841	32,382,819
Belgium	146,800,000	135,900,000	143,800,000	55,354,096	54,784,462
Cyprus	6,000,000	n.t.	9,900,000	5,078,877	5,259,273
Czech Republic	196,300,000	180,600,000	145,600,000	82,453,727	83,625,869
Denmark	69,300,000	54,800,000	63,900,000	26,090,910	34,584,396
Estonia	43,500,000	39,600,000	20,700,000	12,621,824	12,109,281
Finland	71,100,000	71,100,000	69,300,000	33,072,638	44,648,475
France	564,000,000	563,900,000	553,400,000	126,430,451	128,132,861
Germany	1,231,500,000	973,700,000	1,001,500,000	473,715,872	478,448,314
Greece	111,700,000	138,800,000	139,200,000	71,033,294	70,199,609
Hungary	122,200,000	114,900,000	83,100,000	25,714,574	26,159,149
Ireland	55,800,000	63,000,000	69,900,000	22,397,678	21,746,117
Italy	519,500,000	485,700,000	582,200,000	225,875,412	227,074,462
Latvia	25,300,000	23,800,000	10,900,000	2,854,424	2,940,753
Lithuania	48,000,000	44,300,000	22,600,000	6,603,869	6,516,911
Luxemburg	12,700,000	9,100,000	12,700,000	2,603,349	2,712,972
Malta	2,200,000	n.t.	3,400,000	1,971,258	1,985,765
Netherlands	214,600,000	201,700,000	212,100,000	80,351,292	76,701,187
Poland	586,900,000	551,700,000	399,000,000	202,588,891	208,314,950
Portugal	60,900,000	77,400,000	85,500,000	36,413,004	33,096,808
Slovakia	73,400,000	67,500,000	48,700,000	25,237,739	25,537,273
Slovenia	20,200,000	18,600,000	20,300,000	8,720,550	8,842,182
Spain	289,400,000	332,800,000	440,600,000	181,574,302	180,649,540
Sweden	72,300,000	75,200,000	67,000,000	19,306,761	19,955,632
United Kingdom	779,900,000	682,400,000	657,400,000	242,396,039	251,215,421
Total	5,402,400,000	4,975,200,000	4,956,000,000	2,003,833,672	2,037,624,481

Member state	Total ETS emissions CO$_2$ 2005–06 (t)	Difference in ETS emissions 2006 vs. 2005 (t)	Number of installation covered	Average year's allocation 2005–07 (t)	Average allocation vs. ETS emissions CO$_2$ 2005 (t)	Average annual allocation at reserve (t)
Austria	65,755,660	−3.0	203	32,674,905	−697,936	330,050
Belgium	110,138,558	−1.0	327	59,853,575	4,499,479	2,545,876
Cyprus	10,338,150	3.6	13	n.a.	n.a.	n.a.
Czech Republic	166,079,596	1.4	405	96,907,832	14,454,105	348,020
Denmark	60,675,306	32.6	390	31,039,618	4,948,708	2,460,382
Estonia	24,731,105	−4.1	50	18,763,471	6,141,647	189,529
Finland	77,721,113	35.0	602	44,587,032	11,514,394	862,952
France	254,563,312	1.3	1,131	150,500,685	24,070,234	4,871,317
Germany	952,164,186	1.0	1,875	495,073,574	21,357,702	3,926,426
Greece	141,232,903	−1.2	168	71,135,034	101,740	3,286,839
Hungary	51,873,723	1.7	241	30,236,166	4,521,592	1,424,738
Ireland	44,143,795	−2.9	117	19,238,190	−3,159,488	3,081,180
Italy	452,949,874	0.5	1,002	207,518,860	−18,356,552	15,551,575
Latvia	5,795,177	3.0	103	4,054,431	1,200,007	505,760
Lithuania	13,120,780	−1.3	101	11,468,181	4,864,312	797,213
Luxemburg	5,316,321	4.2	15	3,356,667	753,318	387,006
Malta	3,957,023	0.7	2	2,942,314	971,056	2,288,466
Netherlands	157,052,479	−4.5	212	86,439,031	6,087,739	2,503,805
Poland	410,903,841	2.8	843	239,100,000	36,511,109	2,472,405
Portugal	69,509,812	−9.1	254	36,898,516	485,512	1,262,898
Slovakia	50,775,012	1.2	178	30,364,848	5,127,109	7,180
Slovenia	17,562,732	1.4	98	8,691,990	−28,560	66,667
Spain	362,223,842	−0.5	1,056	162,111,391	−19,462,911	13,162,130
Sweden	39,262,393	3.4	753	22,530,831	3,224,070	678,149
United Kingdom	493,611,460	3.6	793	209,387,854	−33,008,185	15,527,484
Total	4,041,458,153	1.7	10,834	2,074,874,995	76,120,200	78,537,547

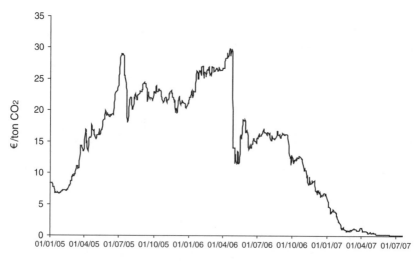

Source: EEX (2008).

Figure 2.1   Evolution of CO_2 prices, 2005–2007

All other member states have a net surplus of permits resulting in more then 76 Mt of overallocation. There was no substantial change in the surrendered emissions from 2005 to 2006.

Following this brief description of the main problems raised during the presentation and evaluation of NAPs, we shall now discus price dynamics and organization of the European market for tradable permits. Some important marketplaces (such as ECX: European Climate Exchange; EEX: European Energy Exchange; EXAA: Energy Exchange Austria; NordPool and Powernext) were created during the first year of the ETS. Most of these already specialized in energy trading, while others (for example, ECX) had a particular focus on environmental goods. The difference in the price of permits is negligible as the number of traders is very large and the good is always 1 tonne of CO_2. The price of carbon has been very volatile and its dynamic reflects all the uncertainties and rumours surrounding this market.

Figure 2.1, which shows the carbon price dynamic, highlights the fact that the market was heavily influenced by the process of revision and approval of the NAPs. The official statements (and rumours) from the Commission constituted one of the main price drivers. The interpretation of the NAPs (whether involving stringent allocation or not) caused the market to fluctuate, until the results of the first year were announced. Later, when clear overallocations were confirmed, the price collapsed and reached values close to zero by the middle of 2007.

By the end of the first year of the emissions trading it was clear that the directive had too many gaps and there was need for revision. The main open questions could be divided into three groups: (i) key elements of the EU ETS; (ii) expansion of the coverage of the system (unilateral inclusion of sectors and gases); and (iii) the process of preparation, presentation and evaluation of NAPs.

With regard to the first group, it is necessary:

- to choose a clear and univocal definition of combustion installation in order to have uniform coverage of the scheme;
- to identify clearly the entity/dimension (in terms of both power and emissions) of the installation covered by the system and to allow small and medium installations to opt out;
- to define specific reduction caps at national and sectoral levels (bearing in mind the efforts to assign reduction targets to the non-trading sectors); and
- to indicate the method of allocation, defining allocation mechanism, applicable sectors, technological benchmarks, treatment of closures and new entrants as well as combined heat and power plant (CHP) provisions.

The unilateral inclusion would be feasible only if the appropriate measures regarding monitoring and verifications could be implemented.

The first experience of the NAPs was not totally positive. However, problems with delays as well as lack of transparency in the evaluation process should be solved in Phase II.

The reviewing process, undertaken by the European Commission in 2005, provided an opportunity not only to discuss the problems but also to set up some feasible solutions for the short (Phase II) and medium (from 2013 and beyond) terms. Such timing was unavoidable because for major changes it was necessary to modify the existing directive, a task that was not feasible in the short term. However, efforts to improve the functioning of the EU ETS within Phase II had been made.

Moreover, it is necessary to underline the importance of Phase I. Despite all the problems, the first international emissions trading scheme had been started. Unique information had been gathered and experience had been gained, contributing to a better knowledge of the sectors covered by the scheme and an understanding of the functioning of important instruments of environmental policy. The price of atmospheric pollution had finally been set.

2.4   PHASE II

Before discussing the changes made in Phase II, and the results of the presentation of the second tranche of NAPs, we shall recall the new provisions concerning the 2008–12 period that had already been included in Directive 2003/87/CE.

In October 2004, the so-called Linking Directive 2004/101/CE was discussed and approved. It was necessary to create the link between the EU ETS and the flexible mechanisms of the Kyoto Protocol such as JI and CDM. The proposed mechanism allows the use of credits from JI and CDM for compliance. In the current version of the directive there are no restrictions on the deployment of these credits at national and European levels. The quantities to be used should be indicated in the NAPs at the single installation level.

Moreover, the NAPs had to be presented well before the start of the new period of trading, namely 18 months before (in June 2006). And, as mentioned earlier, the Commission had to start the process of the revision of Directive 2003/87/CE by changing some of the key elements in order to increase its efficiency in reaching the new and more pressing target by 2020.

Phase II coincides with the Kyoto commitment (2008–12), thus member states should increase their efforts to reach the targets fixed for both the EU (–8 per cent) by the Kyoto Protocol and for individual countries by the Burden Sharing Agreement. Temporary exclusion of an installation is no longer permitted, but the member states could include new activities/sectors and new gases, thus expanding the coverage of the scheme. Finally, as mentioned earlier, penalties were increased from 40 €/t CO_2 to 100 €/t CO_2.

In order to overcome the shortcomings of the existing directive and consolidate positive experience, in December 2005 the Commission published its *Further guidance on allocation plans for the 2008 to 2012 trading period of the EU Emissions Trading Scheme* (European Commission, 2005). In fact, the Commission recognized that the emissions trading directive was rather broad and is subject to multiple interpretations, increasing the complexity of the system and making the process of evaluation extremely difficult and unclear.

This document is an attempt to provide a clear and univocal interpretation of all the provisions of Directive 2003/87/CE, and also introduces a unique and compulsory format for the presentation of the relevant information within the NAPs. This requires a large amount of detailed information in order to assess all aspects of the present and future trends in GHG emissions. Once again, the legislator underlines the importance of the domestic actions, drawing up a list of criteria to be used to evaluate the consistency of the national caps and their targets. Domestic measures aimed at reducing the emissions have to be applicable to both trading and non-trading sectors and would be integrated with credits from JI and CDM.

The guidelines did not stipulate specific national caps. However, they mentioned the reduction (of 6 per cent) to be made with respect of the first period of trading. It is clear that this reduction would be distributed among the countries, taking into account how far they were from the Kyoto target and the efficiency of the domestic measures already in place.

The possibility of using the credits from the flexible Kyoto mechanisms is of strategic importance, as it enables the Kyoto obligations to be fulfilled, thus minimizing the cost of compliance. In order to evaluate the correct usage of the mechanisms, detailed information on timing, entity of the project and the expected volume of permits to be acquired have to be indicated.

All of the problems raised during Phase I are rather difficult to tackle. The treatment of new entrants, closures and small and medium installations was not resolved to the satisfaction of all parties. The decision regarding the possibility of setting up a unique common reserve for new entrants, as well as creating common rules on closures was postponed until June 2006, but even after that date no major changes took place. As for the allocation, the Commission encourages the deployment of allocation methods other than grandfathering. In order to widen the coverage of the directive, the broad interpretation of the definition of the combustion installation was chosen. The problem of windfall profits was not addressed in the guidelines.

Thus we could say that the problems revealed in Phase I of trading were solved only partially. However, the unique definition of the combustion installation as well as other provisions will all help to increase the homogeneity of the coverage, allocation rules and, consequently, the NAPs. The additional measures aimed at decreasing emissions are becoming highly relevant, as they will have a direct influence on absolute caps of member states.

Moving from the first to the second phase, the Commission is gradually reducing the degrees of freedom of national governments in making their decisions (for example, on the entity of caps or limits of JI and CDM). Also in this phase, the problem of windfall profits has remained unsolved.

With regard to the current situation, all the NAPs have been presented and evaluated, without significant delays, and their main features are described in Table 2.3. The homogeneity of the plans increased remarkably. At the same time the coverage of the EU ETS increased, including many of the installations of the sectors not covered directly by Directive

Table 2.3 *Main features related to the allocation of Phase II*

Member state	Total emissions CO$_2$ 1990 (t)	Kyoto target (t)	Total projected emissions 2010 (t) BAU	Total emissions CO$_2$ 2005 (t)	Average emissions ETS 2005–06 (t)
Austria	78,900,000	68,700,000	92,500,000	93,300,000	32,877,830
Belgium	146,800,000	135,900,000	141,600,000	143,800,000	55,069,279
Cyprus	6,000,000	n.t.	12,200,000	9,900,000	5,169,075
Czech Republic	196,300,000	180,600,000	145,700,000	145,600,000	83,039,798
Denmark	69,300,000	54,800,000	67,800,000	63,900,000	30,337,653
Estonia	43,500,000	39,600,000	18,900,000	20,700,000	12,365,553
Finland	71,100,000	71,100,000	85,000,000	69,300,000	38,860,557
France	564,000,000	563,900,000	569,000,000	553,400,000	127,281,656
Germany	1,231,500,000	973,700,000	955,400,000	1,001,500,000	476,082,093
Greece	111,700,000	138,800,000	150,400,000	139,200,000	70,616,452
Hungary	122,200,000	114,900,000	87,400,000	83,100,000	25,936,862
Ireland	55,800,000	63,000,000	68,400,000	69,900,000	22,071,898
Italy	519,500,000	485,700,000	587,300,000	582,200,000	226,474,937
Latvia	25,300,000	23,800,000	13,600,000	10,900,000	2,897,589
Lithuania	48,000,000	44,300,000	33,500,000	22,600,000	6,560,390
Luxemburg	12,700,000	9,100,000	14,200,000	12,700,000	2,658,161
Malta	2,200,000	n.t.	2,200,000	3,400,000	1,978,512
Netherlands	214,600,000	201,700,000	218,000,000	212,100,000	78,526,240
Poland	586,900,000	551,700,000	420,000,000	399,000,000	205,451,921
Portugal	60,900,000	77,400,000	88,000,000	85,500,000	34,754,906
Slovakia	73,400,000	67,500,000	58,300,000	48,700,000	25,387,506
Slovenia	20,200,000	18,600,000	21,600,000	20,300,000	8,781,366
Spain	289,400,000	332,800,000	332,800,000	440,600,000	181,111,921
Sweden	72,300,000	75,200,000	70,300,000	67,000,000	19,631,197
United Kingdom	779,900,000	682,400,000	624,900,000	657,400,000	246,805,730
Total	5,402,400,000	4,975,200,000	4,879,000,000	4,956,000,000	2,020,729,077

Member state	Average year's allocation 2008–12 (t)	Average annual allocation at reserve (t)	Reduction required by EU (t)	Violated criteria	JI & CDM (%)	Kyoto mechanisms (t)
Austria	30,729,906	330,000	2,070,094	1,5,12	10.00	9,000,000
Belgium	58,507,703	5,000,000	4,820,532	1,2,3,6,10	n.a.	7,000,000
Cyprus	5,479,780	960,000	1,641,718	1,2,3,6,10	n.a.	n.a.
Czech Republic	86,836,264	n.a.	15,064,736	–	n.a.	n.a.–
Denmark	24,500,000	500,000	–	12	17.01	4,200,000
Estonia	12,717,058	1,840,000	11,657,987	1,2,3,5,6	n.a.	n.a.
Finland	37,557,891	1,400,000	2,042,109	1,2,3,10,12	10.00	2,400,000
France	132,800,000	3,940,000	–	6 (1,2,3)	n.a.	n.a.
Germany	453,070,175	n.a.	28,929,825	1,2,3,5,10	n.a.	n.a.
Greece	69,087,549	6,156,092	6,414,060	1,2,3,6,10	n.a.	n.a.
Hungary	26,908,852	n.a.	3,824,461	1,2,3,10	n.a.	n.a.
Ireland	21,151,244	1,138,800	1,486,756	1,5,6,10,12	21.91	3,600,000
Italy	201,572,000	15,650,000	13,253,514	1,6,10,12	14.99	19,000,000
Latvia	3,283,303	3,492,000	4,480,580	1,2,3	n.a.	n.a.
Lithuania	8,851,304	n.a.	7,738,696	1,2,3,6,10	n.a.	n.a.
Luxemburg	497,661	n.a.	1,259,094	1,2,3	n.a.	4,700,000
Malta	2,143,061	780,531	812,539	1,2,3,10,12	n.a.	n.a.
Netherlands	85,813,458	6,200,000	3,902,654	1,2,3,5,10,12	10.00	20,000,000
Poland	208,515,395	n.a.	76,132,937	1,2,3,5,6,10,12	10.00	n.a.
Portugal	34,810,329	5,080,000	1,089,671	1,6,12	10.00	5,800,000
Slovakia	30,912,261	1,804,222	10,387,739	1,2,3,5,6	10.00	n.a.
Slovenia	8,298,937	n.a.	–	6,12	15.76	600,000
Spain	152,250,729	7,825,000	422,271	1,6,10,12	n.a.	31,800,000
Sweden	22,802,439	n.a.	2,397,561	1,2,3,10,12	10.00	1,200,000
United Kingdom	246,200,000	16,320,250	–	10	n.a.	n.a.
Total	1,965,269,299	72,126,895	199,829,534	–	n.a.	109,300,000

2003/87/CE, such as chemicals and petrochemicals. Almost all the countries, except the UK, Slovenia, France and Denmark, were asked to reduce their amounts, altogether totalling 199.8 Mt of CO_2. These reductions are aimed at ensuring the consistency of the price of the permit and to bring the member states on track towards the Kyoto commitment.

Before dealing with future prospects, we shall discuss the costs of the EU ETS. Unfortunately exact figures are extremely difficult, if not impossible, to obtain. However in its working document (2008a), the European Commission estimate that administrative costs for operators vary from €2,000 to €15,000 per year and for authorities from €3,000 to €10,000 per site per year.

As stated earlier, there are still a number of issues that have to be resolved in order to improve the EU ETS and make it more efficient after 2012. The experience that will be gained during the 2008–12 period should provide clearer and more convincing answers to the following questions: the relation of the EU ETS with other similar initiatives and with the global carbon market for JI and CDM credits; the possibility of expanding the coverage to other sectors; the permit's price formation mechanisms and so on.

2.5   2013 AND BEYOND

In March 2007, the European Council approved an EU objective of 30 per cent reduction of GHG emissions by 2020 provided that developed countries would commit themselves to comparable emission reductions and that economically advanced developing countries should contribute appropriately. In a stand-alone action, the EU's commitment will decrease to 20 per cent by 2020. In the longer term, by 2050, the European Council has reaffirmed that developed countries should reduce their emissions by 60 to 80 per cent compared to 1990.

Bearing in mind these objectives, the Commission published its proposal for a new emissions trading directive, amending Directive 2003/87/EC in order to improve and extend the GHG allowance trading system (European Commission, 2008b).

In this section we shall present the most important elements of this proposal, to discover whether the persisting problems of the first emissions trading directive will be solved by this new draft.

Addressing one of the critical points, namely the scope of the directive, the proposal gives an explicit definition of the 'combustion installation' and a clear list of activities and gases covered by the scheme. Thus the following activities were added in order to expand the coverage:

- production and processing of ferrous metals (CO_2);
- production of aluminium (CO_2 and polychlorinated fluorocarbons PFCs);
- production and processing of non-ferrous metals (CO_2);
- installation for manufacture of rock wool or stone wool (CO_2);
- installations for the drying or calcination of gypsum or for the production of plaster board and other gypsum products (CO_2);
- Chemical industry:
   production of carbon black (CO_2);
   production of nitric acid (CO_2 and N_2O);
   production of adipic acid (CO_2 and N_2O);
   production of glyoxal and glyoxylic acid (CO_2 and N_2O);
   production of ammonia (CO_2);
   production of basic organic chemicals (CO_2);
   production of H_2 and synthesis gas (CO_2);
   production of soda ash and sodium bicarbonate (CO_2);
- capture, transport and geological storage of GHG emissions:
   installations to capture GHGs for the purpose of transport and geological storage in storage site (all GHGs listed in Annex II);
   pipelines for transport of GHG for geological storage in a storage site (all GHGs listed in Annex II);
   storage sites for the geological storage of GHGs (all GHGs listed in Annex II).

The emissions from all these industries can be measured and verified with sufficient accuracy and their inclusion would increase the volume covered by the EU ETS by an additional 100 Mt of CO_2. Such an expansion should lead to a rise in the efficiency of trading. However, the road transport and shipping are not included in the proposal.

Another unresolved problem was the treatment of small installations. It seems that in the current draft the solution has been found. The combustion installations with a rated thermal input below 25 MW and annual emissions less than 10,000 tons of CO_2 in each of the three years preceding the year of application may be excluded. The Commission expects that about 4,200 (0.70 per cent) installations would opt out. This provision is necessary to reduce the administrative costs of the system.

The penalties remain the same, but should be indexed to the annual inflation rate of the Eurozone.

Moreover, the auction will become the basic method of allocation after 2012. In the case of the power sector, all the allowances will be auctioned. For the other sectors, a period of transition is foreseen. This period will start in 2013, beginning with the allocation of 80 per cent for free, subsequently achieving zero free allocation in 2020. The Commission foresees that in 2013 about two-thirds of the total quantity will be auctioned. Ninety per cent of this amount will be distributed among the member states according to their relative share of 2005 emissions in the EU ETS. The remaining 10 per cent should be redistributed, taking into account fairness and the common interest. Some of the revenues from the auctioning should be used to support environmental policies within the EU.

Some firms that are particularly exposed to international competition and thus to carbon leakage, as well as heat and steam delivered to district heating, will continue to receive the allowances for free. However, the free allocation will be subject to Community-wide rules.

A pan-European reserve should be created for new entrants. Allocation from this reserve will follow the general rules for existing installations.

The total amount of allowances should continue to decrease by a linear factor of 1.74 per cent.

Also, further harmonization of use of credits from the Kyoto flexible mechanisms is necessary. The EU ETS should be able to link to other national and international emissions trading schemes.

This analysis of the proposal of the new 'emissions trading' directive indicates that several problems which emerged during the first two phases have been successfully addressed (among them, the problem of windfall profits). Some important aspects (for example, free allocation rules) are still to be defined, but there is clear progress towards harmonization. The EU ETS is also becoming more centralized, that is, national governments are gradually losing their autonomy. However, the common gain is clear – there is greater efficiency and fewer distortions.

2.6   SOME FINAL REMARKS AND CONSIDERATIONS

The EU ETS was launched on 1 January 2005. This event, which only a few years ago seemed a remote possibility, heralded the EU as a leader in the climate change mitigation process. But, even more important, it opened a new era, highlighting the change in priorities of energy and environmental policies. Climate change has become a focal/hot point of the economic and political agendas, both at national and international levels.

Much positive and negative experience has been gained by all actors taking part in the EU ETS (industry, the Commission, financial institutions and so on) since 2005 and many steps/challenges should be undertaken in the future, the most important of which we shall outline here.

First, the first largest international emissions trading system has been launched and has completed its first period of trading. This fact proves that it is feasible. Despite many misgivings, such global trading pollutant systems can be put in place and can potentially bring desirable results.

Initial problems relating to the installation of national and international authorities involved in this complex trading scheme were overcome. There have been problems in coordination and the sharing of responsibilities. The continual delays with respect to the Phase I timetable (especially within the first year of trading) are a reflection of this. However, the system is now established and the process is continuing without major problems (at least on the administrative side).

At first, there was a serious lack of precise and reliable information on many important aspects for the future and overall design of the scheme. For example, there was no recent information on emissions at the installation level and sometimes at the sector/activity level. Together with a high degree of information asymmetry, this led to significant distortions in the initial allocation – the overallocation experienced in Phase I is a clear consequence of this. During this phase, this problem was largely solved, and a reliable system of information, collection, monitoring and verification was created. Future allocations will be based on these new data, reducing the risk of distortions.

It was immediately clear that the initial allocation is of fundamental importance for the success of the ETS. Many studies have assessed allocation methodologies in order to determine the weak and strong points and, consequently, to indicate the most appropriate of them (see Harrison and Radov, 2002; Hepburn et al., 2006; Ellerman et al., 2007 and Harrison et al., 2007).

Directive 2003/87/CE left the choice of allocation method to national states. Thus a number of different methodologies/approaches have been proposed. The preferred methods was free allocation based on grandfathering which, together with other factors, resulted in significant problems of equity (for example, windfall profits) and distortions in competitiveness (McKinsey and Ecofys, 2006; Neuhoff et al., 2006; Reinaud, 2005; Sijm et al., 2006).

Thanks to the experience gained and to the theoretical and empirical evidence demonstrated by different studies, auctioning now seems to be the most suitable method of allocation. It will allow the resolution of many important problems (which were still unsolved under Phase II), such as windfall profits, overallocations (possibility of), creation/application of complex allocation formulae and so on. It is robust, simple and decreases the complexity of the system. Of course it has its negative aspects, such as the possibility of so-called 'carbon leakage', (due to the decrease in competitiveness of EU industries) and it raises a huge redistribution problem (as auctions will generate considerable revenues).

Particular attention should be paid to the design of auctions in order not to create distortions due to, for example, information asymmetry (regarding abatement and other costs) or the different financial situations of participants. And, once again, economic theory could make an important contribution, indicating the most feasible solutions.

The rise in consumer prices due to ETS is one of the most debated topics of recent years. There was and still continues to be a debate among industries, stakeholders (institutional) and consumers regarding their responsibilities and to find out what should or should not be done to reduce these effects. We should emphasize that this increase is a normal and desired consequence of emissions trading. Product prices have to change (increase) with the price of environmental commodities (CO2), because it is the right way to send signals to consumers in order to change their preferences and consequently their level of consumption.

Unfortunately it has been extremely difficult to verify the extent of this effect, as well as the effect on emissions abatement, in the early years of the EU ETS. In fact in Phase I, the carbon price was generally too low. The fact that surrendered emissions are substantially the same in 2005 and 2006 (see Table 2.2) confirms this statement. In any case, we should not underestimate the fact that a price was put on CO_2, even if it fell to very low values due to overallocation (after April 2006).

Furthermore, the trading system was put in place and has been tested. Markets, trading rules and different financial products related to this specific market were established, enabling the installations to exchange allowances. We are witnessing the creation of an environmental market with a complete set of actors. Further development of this market is desirable and is of vital importance, in particular greater articulation of services and products to hedge the different risks related to emissions trading. This will help to overcome the problems of price volatility, market liquidity and price formation, and consequently could have a positive impact on investment patterns.

Links to other systems, for example, the inflow of JI and CDM, are of vital importance. This is one of the main challenges of the 2008–12 period, although it is still quite unclear how the system will work. It is no secret that most operators still have no experience in this field. The possibility of introducing credits into the ETS system could potentially have a significant impact on the liquidity of the market and thus on the carbon price, also reducing the cost of compliance. We have yet to see what effect these measures will have.

As discussed in previous sections, the proposed new emissions trading directive foresees further expansion of the sectors and activities covered by the EU ETS. The increased scope might permit reductions to be realized most cost effectively, but at the same time it is clear that the inclusion of some sectors will lead to a dramatic increase in the complexity of the system and in transaction costs – for example, the transport sector, which is one of the largest and fastest growing emitters. This gives rise to the problem of the relationship between trading and non-trading sectors. This could be seen as a more general question of the efficiency and interaction between different instruments of environmental policy (for example, environmental taxation versus emissions trading or interaction/overlapping of these two instruments). In this case, economic theory could make an important contribution in supporting policy makers' decisions.

In conclusion, this brief overview of the EU ETS highlights that each phase of the trading scheme has its specific problems and challenges.

In the 2005–07 period, the main problems were the allocation of the emission allowances and all issues related to it, including its scope/coverage.

In the 2008–12 period, the main question will probably concern the inflow of JI and CDM and its impact on carbon price formation. At the same time, great (further) attention will be paid to verifying how the ETS can affect industry competitiveness, on the one hand, and to understanding whether the EU will be able to fulfil its commitment to the Kyoto Protocol.

Concerning the future of the EU ETS, 2012 and beyond, we can expect two main challenges: the first relates to the auction design and its realization – robustness, simplicity and non-distortions are desirable; the second is the future expansion of the ETS which will entail not only considering a greater scope within sectors and activities but also investigating the relation between trading and non-trading sectors.

NOTES

1. The effectiveness of emissions trading against other instruments has been widely discussed and assessed at the EU and international levels. For detailed information, see European Commission (2000), http://ec.europa.eu/environment/climat/emission/history_en.htm.
2. There are several studies dealing with the analysis of the performance of the different allocation methods. In particular, see Harrison and Radov (2002) and Harrison et al. (2007).

REFERENCES

Ecofys (2006), *Harmonization of Allocation Methodologies*, Report under the project 'Review of EU the Emissions Trading Scheme', European Commission, Directorate General for Environment.

Ecofys (2007), *Small Installations within the EU Emissions Trading Scheme*, Report under the project 'Review of the EU Emissions Trading Scheme', European Commission, Directorate General for Environment, ECS 04079.

Ellerman, A.D., Buchner, B.K. and Carraro, K. (eds) (2007), *Allocation in the European Emissions Trading Scheme: Rights, Rents and Fairness*, Cambridge: Cambridge University Press.

European Commission (2000), *Green Paper on greenhouse gas emissions trading within the European Union*, COM 87.

European Commission (2003a), Directive 2003/87/CE: 'Establishing a scheme for greenhouse gas emission allowances within the Community and amending Council Directive 96/61/EC', *Official Journal of the European Union*.

European Commission (2003b), 'The EU Emissions Trading Scheme: How to develop a National Allocation Plan', 2nd meeting of Working 3, Monitoring Mechanism Committee.

European Commission (2004a), *Directive 2004/101/EC of the European Parliament and of the Council of 27 October 2004 amending Directive 2003/87/EC establishing a scheme for greenhouse gas emission allowance trading within the Community, in respect of the Kyoto Protocol's project mechanisms.*

European Commission (2004b), 2004/156/EC: *Commission Decision of 29 January 2004 establishing guidelines for the monitoring and reporting of greenhouse gas emissions pursuant to Directive 2003/87/EC of the European Parliament and of the Council*, C(2004) 130.

European Commission (2004c), *Communication from the Commission on guidance to assist Member States in the implementation of the criteria listed in Annex III to Directive 2003/87/EC establishing a scheme for greenhouse gas emission allowance trading within the Community and amending Council Directive 96/61/EC, and on the circumstances under which force majeure is demonstrated*, COM/2003/0830 final.

European Commission (2005), Communication from the Commission: *Further guidance on allocation plans for the 2008 to 2012 trading period of the EU Emissions Trading Scheme*, COM(2005) 703 final.

European Commission (2006), Press Release: 'EU Emissions Trading Scheme delivers first verified emissions data for installations', IP/06/612.

European Commission (2007), 2007/589/EC: *Commission Decision of 18 July 2007 establishing guidelines for the monitoring and reporting of greenhouse gas emissions pursuant to Directive 2003/87/EC of the European Parliament and of the Council*, C(2007) 3416.

European Commission (2008a), Commission Staff Working document: *Accompanying document to the proposal for a Directive of the European Parliament and of the Council amending Directive 2003/87/CE so as to improve and extend the EU greenhouse gas emission allowance trading system. Impact Assessment*, SEC 52.

European Commission (2008b), *Proposal for a Directive of the European Parliament and of the Council amending Directive 2003/87/CE so as to improve and extend the greenhouse gas emission allowance trading system of the Community*, COM 16 final.

Harrison, D., Klevnas, P., Radov, D. and Foss, A. (2007), *Complexities of Allocation Choices in a Greenhouse Gas Emissions Trading Program*, Report to the International Emissions Trading Association (IETA), NERA Economic Consulting, Boston, MA.

Harrison, D. and Radov, D. (2002), *Evaluation of Alternative Initial Allocation*

Mechanisms in a European Union Greenhouse Gases Emissions Allowance Trading Scheme, NERA Economic Consulting, Boston, MA, Prepared for DG Environment, European Union.

Hepburn, C., Grubb, M., Neuhoff, K., Matthes, F. and Tse, M. (2006), 'Auctioning of EU ETS Phase II allowances: how and why?', *Climate Policy*, **6** (1), 137–60.

McKinsey and Ecofys (2006), *EU ETS Review: Report on International Competitiveness*, Report prepared for European Commission, Directorate General for Environment, December.

Neuhoff, K., Keats Martinez, K. and Sato, M. (2006), 'Allocation, incentives and distortions: the impact of EU ETS emissions allowance allocations to electricity sector', Cambridge Working Papers in Economics (CWPE), no. 0642.

Reinaud J. (2005), 'Industrial competitiveness under the EU Emissions Trading Scheme', International Energy Agency Information Paper, Paris: IEA, February.

Sijm J. (2004), 'The Impact of the EU Emissions Trading Scheme on the price of electricity in the Netherlands', in A.P. Ros and H.R.J. Vollebergh (eds), *Ontwikkeling en Overheid*, Sdu Publishers, The Hague, Netherlands, pp. 263–76.

Sijm, J., Neuhoff, K. and Chen, Y. (2006), 'CO_2 cost pass-through and windfall profits in the power sector', *Climate Change Policy*, **6** (1), 49–72.

3. Modelling the short-run impact of 'carbon trading' on the electricity sector

Francesco Gullì

3.1 INTRODUCTION

This chapter studies the impact of 'carbon emissions trading' (trading of CO_2 emissions allowances) on the electricity sector, focusing on the European Emission Trading Scheme (EU ETS). Started in 2005, the EU ETS[1] covers several sectors of which power generation is the largest one. Therefore, on the one hand, the performance of the trading scheme largely depends on its ability to induce the power industry to reduce CO_2 emissions significantly in the short and long runs. On the other hand, it might have a considerable impact on consumers' surplus and firms' profits and competitiveness. Either the performance of the EU ETS or its impact on social welfare depends on how and to what extent the CO_2 price is passed through into power prices.

This study focuses on this latter issue, attempting to provide a better understanding of how a CO_2 price could impact on electricity pricing[2] and carbon emissions.

The economic literature on emissions trading is extensive and covers several fields.[3] However, existing studies have mainly been concerned with design issues rather than with the impact on correlated (product) markets. With regard to the electricity sector, only recently has a specific research effort been made to study the effects of the ETS on product prices, but studies generally assume purely competitive frameworks which are far from the reality of electricity markets. These, in fact, are more or less concentrated markets where one or more firms are able to exercise market power. Thus there is a need to extend the study to imperfect competition and in particular to answer three important questions:

1. How does the impact of the ETS on electricity pricing depend on electricity market structures?

2. What role does market power in electricity markets play, in this respect?[4]
3. How does the ETS impact on carbon emissions in the short run?

Studies aimed at answering these questions do exist but they provide a very controversial framework.

Wals and Rijkers (2003) and Sijm et al. (2005), by using a game theoretical simulation model based on the theory of Cournot competition and conjecture supply functions,[5] find that the electricity price in a competitive scenario increases more than under market power, on both a percentage and an absolute basis. They attribute this result to the assumption of the linear demand function that they adopt. Surprisingly, however, Lise (2005) achieves the opposite result (electricity prices increase more under market power) even though the author uses the same model. Reinaud (2003), relying on price competition, and Newbery (2005), by assuming constant price elasticity, state that electricity prices are likely to increase more under market power.

Moreover, the question of how the ETS can affect emissions is no less controversial. All authors agree that emissions are highest under the most competitive scenarios. Nevertheless some contributions (Lise, 2005 and Sijm et al., 2005) show that emission reductions are lowest under perfect competition while others (Lise et al., 2006) state that generally higher emission reductions are achieved in the case without market power.

This controversial framework also highlights that results significantly depend on the choice of competition models.[6] In the economic literature on the electricity sector several approaches are generally used for modelling competition and various classifications are proposed.[7] Examining recent developments in the literature on electricity spot markets, von der Fehr and Harbord (1998) distinguish three groups: standard oligopoly models;[8] the 'supply-function' approach;[9] and the 'auction' approach.[10]

In this chapter we shall follow those authors who argue in favour of the 'auction' approach. In fact, several electricity spot markets have characteristics which make standard models poorly suited to their analysis. In particular, in these markets the pricing mechanism is a uniform, first-price auction. Furthermore, since we have to isolate the effect of environmental regulation, in the form of a typical 'cap-and-trade' regulation (namely, a market of carbon emission allowances), we do not account for the problems of capacity withholding, grid congestion and contract markets which, in the opinion of some authors (Borenstein et al., 1999), can be better investigated by using the standard oligopoly models.

The chapter proceeds as follows. Section 3.2 summarizes the assumptions underlying the model and in particular those concerning power demand and supply, and electricity and allowance market regulations. Section 3.3 describes the impact of the ETS on power generation costs, a fundamental step for further evaluations. The competitive outcome is illustrated in Section 3.4, which provides a benchmark for the subsequent analysis. Section 3.5 simulates the impact of the ETS under market power in the electricity market,[11] by using a dominant firm facing a competitive fringe model. We shall present various scenarios by altering the following factors: (i) the leader's share of the total capacity in the market; (ii) the plant mix operated by either the dominant firm or the competitive fringe; (iii) the allowance price (above or below the so-called 'switching price'); and (iv) the available capacity in the market (whether there is excess capacity or not). In Section 3.6, a quantitative simulation is carried out by using plausible variable costs and emission rates. This simulation provides useful insights about the pass-through rate (PTR) under perfect and imperfect competition. Section 3.7 shows the analysis of how the ETS impacts on aggregate carbon emissions in the short and medium runs. Finally, Section 3.8 summarizes the main results of the analysis.

Consistently with major economic remarks, the model confirms that the ETS causes a rise in power prices due to the pass-through of the carbon opportunity cost. However, the main finding of the analysis is that the impact of the ETS significantly depends on electricity market structures (apart from the other factors). The carbon opportunity cost is fully included in energy prices when the electricity market is assumed to be perfectly competitive. Under imperfect competition, prices may increase more or less than under competition, depending on the structural features of power markets. Furthermore, the analysis highlights that under market power the ETS always determines a decrease in emissions except for the case in which there is excess capacity in the market and under specific technological conditions.

Before proceeding it is important to underline that, throughout the chapter, we shall focus on short-term issues, that is, we shall analyse the ETS impact on electricity pricing in the short run, leaving the question of how the ETS can affect investment decisions for further research.

3.2   THE MODEL: BASIC ASSUMPTIONS

This section describes the structure of the model, detailing the main assumptions on the regulation of the electricity and carbon markets.

Consistently with most contributions on this topic, we assume that power demand is inelastic,[12] predictable with certainty and given by a typical load duration curve $D(H)$, where H is the number of hours (the reference time unit adopted here) in the reference time period (for example, the year) that demand is equal to or higher than D, where $0 \leq H \leq H_L$. $D_L = D(H_L)$ is the base-load demand (the minimum level) and $D_M = D(0)$ is the peak-load demand (the maximum level). Note that the assumption on the price elasticity of demand (inelastic demand) will be abandoned in Section 3.8 when we shall attempt to assess the impact of the ETS on carbon emissions.

With regard to power supply, we model technologies by means of two distinctive elements: variable costs (essentially, fuel costs) and CO_2 emission rates (emissions per unit of electricity generated).

In particular, the CO_2 emission rate is $e \geq 0$ and the variable cost of production is $v \geq 0$ for production levels less than capacity, while production above capacity is impossible (that is, infinitely costly).

Since we simulate a uniform, first-price auction, it is enough to focus on technologies which have a positive probability of becoming the marginal operating unit. This allows us to ignore, without loss of generality, those technologies suited to meet the base-load demand (that is, nuclear and large hydropower plants, renewable technologies, and so on) or which are supplied inelastically.

Given these premises, we restrict the analysis to two groups of plants, a and b, and assume that each group includes a very large number n of homogeneous generating units[13] such that:

$$K_j = \Sigma_{i=1,2,\dots,n} k_j^i = n k_j, \quad j = a,b \text{ and } v_j^i = v_j; \ e_j^i = e_j, \forall i,j,$$

where K_j is the total capacity of the group j, $v_j^i = v_j > 0$ and $k_j^i = k_j > 0$ are the variable cost and the capacity of the i-th unit belonging to the group j, respectively. Thus K_a and K_b are the installed capacity of groups a and b, respectively.

Furthermore, we assume $v_a < v_b$ and $K_a + K_b = K_T = D_M$, that is, the units of a and b are sufficient to meet the peak demand, and consider two scenarios: Scenario 1 in which there is trade-off between variable costs and emission rates (hereafter 'trade-off in the plant mix'), that is, the technology with lower variable cost is the worse polluter ($v_a < v_b$ and $e_a > e_b$, a typical relevant example is given by coal plants (a) versus CCGT (combined cycle gas turbine) technologies (b)); Scenario 2 in which there is no such trade-off, that is, the technology with lower variable cost is also the cleaner technology ($v_a < v_b$ but $e_a < e_b$, a typical relevant example is given by CCGT plants (a) versus gas-fired steam-cycle plants (b)).

Emission abatement is supposed to be impossible or, equivalently, abatement cost is infinitely costly. This hypothesis is consistent with the time horizon of the analysis (short-term analysis of the ETS impact).

With regard to the wholesale market, we assume a typical day-ahead market. Before the actual opening of the market (for example, the day ahead) the generators simultaneously submit bid prices for each of their units on an hourly basis. We ignore the existence of technical constraints such as start-up costs. The auctioneer (generally, the so-called 'market operator') collects and ranks the bids by applying the merit-order rule. The bids are ordered by increasing bid prices and form the basis upon which a market supply curve is derived.

If called upon to supply, generators are paid according to the market-clearing spot price (the system marginal price, equal to the highest bid price accepted). All players are assumed to be risk neutral and to act in order to maximize their expected payoff (profit). Production costs, emission rates as well as the installed capacity of the plants are common knowledge.

Given the regulatory framework described above, it is straightforward that price equilibria will depend on the power demand level. Since this latter varies continuously over time, a useful way of representing the price schedule is to derive the so-called 'price duration curve' $p(H)$, where H is the number of hours in the year that the power price is equal to or higher than p.

With regard to the allowance market, we suppose that this market is very large (consistently with the extent of the EU ETS) and that firms are price takers.[14] Therefore, the allowance price, p^{tp}, is given exogenously. Carbon emission allowances are allocated free of charge and on the basis of the amounts emitted in a base period (typical grandfathering) or on the basis of the expected emissions in the future.[15]

Finally, we assume that firms' offer prices are constrained below some threshold level, $\hat{p}$, which can be interpreted in several ways.

It may be a (regulated) maximum price, $\bar{p}$, as officially introduced by the regulator or we can suppose that it is not introduced officially, but simply perceived by the generators, that is, firms believe that the regulator will introduce (or change) price regulation if the price rises above the threshold. This latter interpretation is well-suited to the topic analysed here. In fact, firms might decide to bring bid prices down not only to avoid regulation in the wholesale electricity market but also to avoid change in allowance allocation (for example, underallocation) or change in taxation.[16] For these reasons we think that it is acceptable, assuming that the price cap is insensitive to the CO_2 price.

Alternatively, we can suppose that there is so much generation that the price is never above the marginal cost of a peaker. In order to simulate this situation, we introduce a third technology, c, such that $v_c > \max [v_a, v_b]$ and whose capacity is great enough, $K_c = \bar{K}_c$, that the dominant firm does not try to let it all run and drive the price up to the price cap. Instead, $K_c = 0$, is useful to simulate the situation in which there is no excess capacity in the market and prices can reach the price cap, $\bar{p}$. Finally, we assume that $e_a >$ $e_c > e_b$ in Scenario 1 and $e_c > e_b > e_a$ in Scenario 2. These latter assumptions are crucial for our analysis but not arbitrary. Technology c, in fact, can be interpreted as a typical peaking technology (old oil-fired or gas turbine plants) whose electrical efficiency is generally much lower than that of the CCGT plants. Furthermore, this technology is generally more polluting than CCGT (or gas-fired steam-cycle plants) but cleaner than coal plants.

In brief, we shall consider two scenarios (Scenario 1 and Scenario 2, with and without 'trade-off in the plant mix', respectively) and, for each of them, two cases of available capacity in the market, namely excess capacity ($K_c = \bar{K}_c$) and scarcity of generation capacity ($K_c = 0$).

3.3   THE IMPACT ON POWER GENERATION COSTS

The first step of the analysis is to evaluate how the carbon ETS can affect power generation costs.

Definition 3.1   The carbon opportunity cost of the i-th generating unit belonging to the group j of plants is equal to the price of the CO_2 allowance, p^{tp}, multiplied by its emission rate, e_j^i.

Given this definition and in line with economic theory, the marginal cost of production is expected to include the full carbon opportunity cost, regardless of whether allowances are allocated free of charge or not,

$$MC_j^i = v_j^i + p^{tp} e_j^i, \tag{3.1}$$

where MC_j^i is the marginal cost of the i-th unit belonging to the group j of plants.

This will be a central issue within the study and suggests the following definitions:

Definition 3.2   For the purpose of this analysis, the generating units belonging to the group j of plants are the most- (least-)efficient units if their marginal cost (including the carbon opportunity cost) is lower (higher) than that of the units belonging to the other group.

Definition 3.3   The 'switching price', p^{tp*}, is the allowance price such that the marginal cost of the plants of the group a, MC_a, is equal to that of the plants of the group b, MC_b, that is, $p^{tp*} = (v_b - v_a)(e_a - e_b)$.

Definition 3.4 For the purpose of this chapter and given Definition 3.3, the allowance price is low if $p^{tp} \leq p^{tp*}$, and high otherwise.

Obviously, these last two definitions are valid only for Scenario 1.

3.4   PERFECT COMPETITION

Although the case of perfect competition lacks realism, it is a good, paradigmatic, benchmark for evaluating the consequences of market power in the wholesale spot market.

The generation system includes $2n$ (where n is very large) independent generators belonging to the two categories of plants presented above.

Definition 3.5 The marginal carbon opportunity cost is the price of the CO_2 emission allowance multiplied by the emission rate of the marginal production unit.

Given equation (3.1) and Definition 3.3 we can characterize the perfectly competitive Nash equilibria. The results are illustrated in the following proposition:

Proposition 3.1 (i) Under perfect competition, electricity prices fully internalize the marginal carbon opportunity cost. (ii) Let $\overline{MC}$ and $\underline{MC}$ be the marginal costs of the least- and most-efficient plants, respectively, and let $\hat{p}$ be the price threshold. Then the price equilibria are as follows:

$$p = \begin{cases} \hat{p} & for \ D = D_M \\ \overline{MC} = \max \{MC_a; MC_b\} & \forall D \in]D_M; \underline{K}] \\ \underline{MC} = \min \{MC_a; MC_b\} & \forall D \in]\underline{K}; D_L] \end{cases}$$

$$where \ \hat{p} = \begin{cases} \overline{p} & for \ K_c = 0 \\ MC_c & for \ K_c = \overline{K}_c \end{cases} \quad and \ \underline{K} = \begin{cases} K_a & if \ p^{tp} \leq p^{tp*} \\ K_b & if \ p^{tp} > p^{tp*} \end{cases}$$

Proof The market-clearing price is the highest bid price accepted. Therefore, under perfect competition it equals the marginal cost of the marginal unit which fully includes the carbon opportunity cost. In Scenario 1, for a low (high) price of allowances, the marginal unit will belong to group b (a) whenever demand is above K_a (K_b) and to group a (b), otherwise.

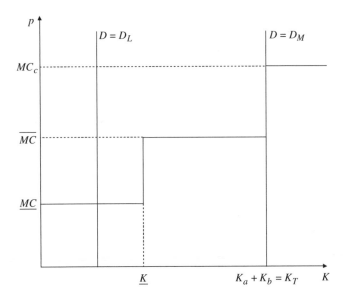

Figure 3.1   Perfectly competitive prices $(K_c = \overline{K_c})$

In Scenario 2, whatever p^{tp}, the marginal unit will belong to group b whenever demand is above K_a and to group a, otherwise. Figure 3.1 presents this result graphically (for the case of $K_c = \overline{K_c}$).

In Figure 3.2, the price duration curves, $p(H)$, are reported (before and after the ETS), for Scenario 1. We can observe that when $p^{tp} \leq p^{tp}*$ (low allowance prices) the impact of the ETS on the volume-weighted average electricity price, $\Delta p_{av} = \int_0^{H_L} \Delta p(H)D(H)dH \ / \int_0^{H_L} D(H)dH$ equals the volume-weighted average marginal opportunity cost. When $p^{tp} > p^{tp}*$ (high allowance prices), the volume-weighted marginal opportunity cost exceeds Δp_{av}.

These results suggest the following definition:

Definition 3.6   The marginal pass-through rate (MPTR) is the ETS impact on electricity prices, Δp, divided by the difference between the marginal production costs of the marginal unit (under perfect competition) after and before the ETS,[17]ΔMC, that is, $MPTR = \Delta p / \Delta MC$.

Applying Definition 3.6, we get a 100% MPTR under perfect competition.

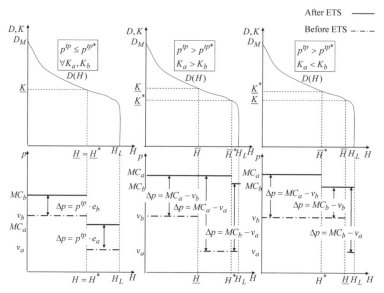

Figure 3.2   Impact of the ETS on electricity prices under perfect competition: Scenario 1

3.5   IMPERFECT COMPETITION

We are now able to simulate the impact of market power[18] on power pricing. For this purpose, we adopt a dominant firm facing a competitive fringe model rather than the usual dupolistic–oligopolistic framework. This choice is due to several reasons, either methodological or practical. On the methodological side, the attraction of this characterization is that it avoids the implausible extreme of perfect competition and pure monopoly, at the same time escaping the difficulties of characterizing an oligopolistic equilibrium (Newbery, 1981). This does not mean, however, that it is only a useful benchmark. It is also useful on the practical side, as long as it is suited to represent the reality of several electricity markets. We especially refer to those markets emerging from restructuring processes where the incumbent is obliged to sell a portion of its capacity to different firms and new independent producers meet the rise in power demand over time.

The general formulation of the model assumes that the dominant firm owns and operates $z \in [0;2n]$ units of both group a and group b while the remaining units are operated by $2n-z$ firms behaving as a competitive fringe. Obviously, $z=0$ corresponds to the case of pure competition while $z=2n$ corresponds to that of pure monopoly.

In order to derive the price schedule in the form of a price duration curve, we introduce the following parameters.

The first parameter is $\delta \in [0;1]$ representing the share of the total power capacity in the market operated by the dominant firm. Complementary to this, the competitive fringe operates share $(1 - \delta)$ of the total power capacity. Thus, δ can be interpreted as a measure of the degree of market concentration.

The other parameters are $\mu^d \in [0;1]$ and $\mu^f \in [0;1]$ representing the share of own-power capacity that the strategic operator and the competitive fringe get in the most-efficient plants, respectively. By complement, $\bar{\mu}^d = (1 - \mu^d)$ and $\bar{\mu}^f = (1 - \mu^f)$ are the shares in the least-efficient ones.

By facing the competitive fringe, the dominant firm has two alternative strategies: (i) bidding the price threshold $(\hat{p})$ and so accommodating the maximum production by the fringe or (ii) competing *à la* Bertrand with the rivals in order to maximize its market share.

Let K^f be the installed capacity in the most-efficient plants operated by the competitive fringe. Thus $K^f = \mu^f(1-\delta)K_T$, and $H^f = D^{-1}(K^f)$.

Similarly, let $\overline{K} = D_M - \overline{K}^d$ be the peak demand minus the dominant firm's capacity in the least efficient plants $(\overline{K}^d)$. Given that $D_M = K_T$, then we get that $\overline{K} = (1 - \delta\bar{\mu}^d)K_T$, and $\overline{H} = D^{-1}(\overline{K})$.

Finally, $\underline{K} = [\mu^d\delta + \mu^f(1-\delta)]K_T$ is the total capacity in the most-efficient plants, already introduced in the previous section.

It is important to note that δ determines not only the degree of market concentration but also the total share of the most-efficient plants in the market, $\underline{K}$. In particular, increasing δ implies increasing $\underline{K}$ if $\mu^d > \mu^f$, and vice versa if $\mu^d < \mu^f$.

Figure 3.3 shows a (generic) example of possible power supply configuration.

The following Lemma describes the shape of the price duration curve:

Lemma 3.1   *There exists $\hat{D} \in] \overline{K}; K^f]$ such that the system marginal prices equal the price threshold $\hat{p}$ when $D \geq \hat{D}$ and the marginal cost of the least-efficient plants $(\overline{MC})$ when $D < \hat{D}$. When $D < \underline{K}^f$, pure Bertrand equilibria (first marginal cost pricing) arise and prices equal the marginal cost of the most-efficient plants $(\underline{MC})$, where:*

$$
\hat{D} = \begin{cases} \tilde{D}(\delta, \underline{\mu}^d, \zeta) = [\mu^d\,\delta\zeta + (1 - \delta)]K_T & \text{for } \hat{D} \geq \underline{K} \text{ case } (i) \\[2em] \tilde{D}(\delta, \underline{\mu}^f, \zeta) = (1 - \delta)\left[\dfrac{1 - \mu^f}{1 - \zeta} + \mu^f\right]K_T & \text{for } \hat{D} < \underline{K} \text{ case } (ii) \end{cases}
$$

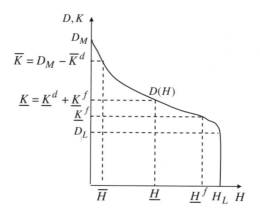

Figure 3.3   An example of supply configuration

$$\text{and } \zeta = \frac{\overline{MC} - \underline{MC}}{\hat{p} - \underline{MC}} \text{ with } \hat{p} = \begin{cases} \overline{p} & \text{for } K_c = 0 \\ MC_c & \text{for } K_c = \overline{K}_c. \end{cases}$$

Proof   See Appendix 3A. ∎

Therefore, two price duration curves are possible, depending on whether the discontinuity is at $\tilde{H} = D^{-1}(\tilde{D})$ or at $\tilde{\tilde{H}} = D^{-1}(\tilde{\tilde{D}})$. The following proposition identifies the critical value of δ that discriminates between these two cases:

Proposition 3.2   *Under market power, there exists* $\underline{\delta}$ ($\underline{\mu}^d$, $\underline{\mu}^f$, v_j, e_j, p^{tp}) *such that:*

$$\hat{p} = \begin{cases} \overline{p} & \forall D \in [0; \hat{D}] \\ \overline{MC} & \forall D \in]\hat{D}; \underline{K}^f] \\ \underline{MC} & \forall D \in]\underline{K}^f; D_L \end{cases}$$

where:

$$\hat{p} = \begin{cases} \overline{p} & \text{for } K_c = 0 \\ MC_c & \text{for } K_c = \overline{K}_c \end{cases}; \hat{D} = \begin{cases} \tilde{D} \text{ if } \underline{\delta} < \delta \text{ case}(i); \\ \tilde{\tilde{D}} \text{ if } \underline{\delta} \geq \text{ case } (ii) \end{cases}$$

$$\underline{\delta} = \frac{\underline{\mu}^f - 1}{\underline{\mu}^f - 1 + \underline{\mu}^d(\zeta - 1)}.$$

Proof   See Appendix 3A. ∎

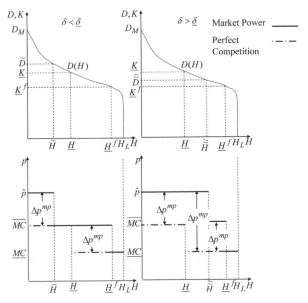

Figure 3.4   Impact of market power on electricity prices (symmetric plant mix: $\underline{\mu}^d = \underline{\mu}^f; \hat{p}$: price threshold)

By differentiating $\tilde{D}$ and $\tilde{\tilde{D}}$ with respect to $\underline{\mu}^d$ and $\underline{\mu}^f$, we find that the degree of market power (which decreases in $\hat{D}$) is an increasing function of $\underline{\mu}^f$, when $\delta > \underline{\delta}$, and a decreasing function of $\underline{\mu}^d$, when $\delta < \underline{\delta}$ (see Appendix 3A). In other words, by intuition, if the demand is high enough, the dominant firm maximizes its profit by bidding the price cap (thereby accommodating the maximum production by the fringe and behaving as a residual monopolist) rather than by bidding the marginal cost of the least-efficient plant (thereby maximizing its production). The level of demand above which this occurs ($\hat{D}$) increases in the share of the most-efficient plants operated by the dominant firm ($\underline{\mu}^d$) and in the marginal cost difference between the two kinds of technologies (the numerator of ζ). In contrast, the level decreases in the fringe's share of the most-efficient plants ($\underline{\mu}^f$).

Finally, we shall make some remarks on the impact of market power on electricity prices, Δp^{mp}, which results from the comparison of the price duration curves under market power and those under perfect competition.

Figure 3.4 presents the outcome graphically. Lemma 3.2 distinguishes two possible cases. When $\delta < \underline{\delta}$, the effect of market power on electricity prices is relatively slight and concentrated in the periods of high and medium–low demand, whereas there is no distortion in periods of medium and very low demand. When $\delta > \underline{\delta}$, the outcome is quite different. This time, the largest distortions occur in medium-load demand hours.

Lemma 3.1 highlighted that the degree of market power depends on ζ. Since this latter depends on the carbon price, the environmental regulation is able to modify the degree of market power in the output market. Indeed, according to the definition adopted in this analysis, the dominant firm exerts its market power not only when it bids the price threshold (first market power effect) but also when it is able to set prices just below the marginal cost of the least-efficient plants, whereas under perfect competition, prices would converge to the marginal cost of the most-efficient plants. In what follows we ignore this 'second effect' and consider $\hat{D}$ as a proxy of market power. Note that this choice is reasonable since the second market power effect depends on $\underline{K}^f$, which does not depend on the allowance price.

Given this assumption, the following lemma describes how and under what conditions the environmental regulation can affect the degree of market power:

Lemma 3.2 $\hat{D}$ *is non-increasing in* p^{tp} *if* $(e_b - e_a)(\hat{v} - v_a) < (\hat{e} - e_a)$ $(v_b - v_a)$, *under low allowance prices, and if* $(e_a - e_b) < (\hat{e} - e_b)$ $(v_a - v_b)$, *under high allowance prices, where: (i).* $\hat{e} = e_c$ *and* $\hat{v} = v_c$, *with excess capacity, and (ii)* $\hat{e} = 0$ *and* $\hat{v} = \bar{p}$, *without excess capacity.*

Proof For the formal proof, see Appendix 3A. Intuitively, the environmental regulation can increase market power when the change in the cost structure between the technologies makes more profitable bidding the price threshold rather than the marginal cost of the least-efficient plants, that is, when the proportional increase (decrease) in the difference between the price threshold and the marginal cost of the most efficient plants is higher (lower) than the proportional increase (decrease) in the difference between the marginal cost of the least efficient and the most efficient plants. Namely, this occurs when $(e_b - e_a)(\hat{v} - v_a) < (\hat{e} - e_a)(v_b - v_a)$, if $p^{tp} \leq p^{tp*}$, and when $(e_a - e_b)(\hat{v} - v_b) < (\hat{e} - e_b)(v_a - v_b)$, if $p^{tp} > p^{tp*}$. Under 'trade-off in the plant mix' and excess capacity, this condition always (never) is satisfied if $p^{tp} \leq p^{tp*}$ (if $p^{tp} > p^{tp*}$). Without 'trade-off in the plant mix' it is never satisfied if there is a scarcity of capacity. Otherwise, it is satisfied only under certain values of v_j and e_j ∎

Corollary 3.1 *The sensitivity of market power to the carbon price increases (decreases) in* $\mu_a^d (\mu_a^f)$, *if* $p^{tp} \leq p^{tp*}$. *Vice versa, if* $p^{tp} > p^{tp*}$, *under 'trade-off in the plant mix'.*

Proof See Appendix 3A. ∎

Figure 3.5 shows graphically the results described by Lemma 3.2 and Corollary 3.1. It can be noted that the level of demand over which the

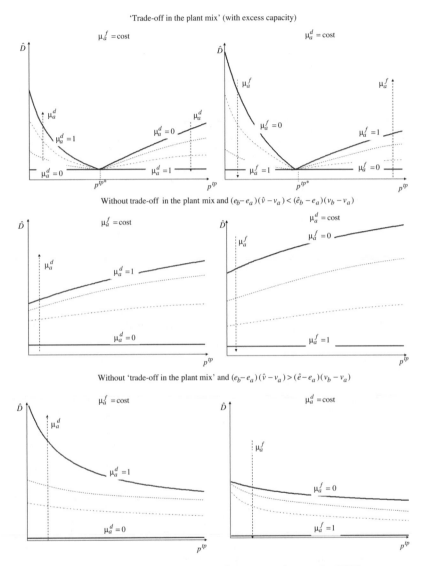

Figure 3.5   Examples of change in market power due to the ETS

dominant firm prefers to bid the threshold can either decrease or increase in the allowance price depending on three factors: (i) the plant mix operated by either the dominant firm or the competitive fringe; (ii) the allowance price (whether above or below the switching price); and (iii) the power capacity in the market (whether there is excess capacity or not).

Table 3.1 $\hat{D}/D_M$ *as a function of the allowance price (change in market power)*

	Allowance price (€/tCO$_2$)					
	0	20	40	60	80	100
With trade-off (excess capacity)						
$\hat{p}=MC_c, \delta=0.7$						
$\mu_a^d=1, \mu_a^f=0$	0.640	0.398	0.300	0.300	0.300	0.300
$\mu_a^d=\mu_a^f=0.5$	0.442	0.349	0.303	0.341	0.384	0.430
$\mu_a^d=0, \mu_a^f=1$	0.300	0.300	0.300	0.383	0.468	0.560
With trade-off (without excess capacity)						
$\hat{p}=\bar{p}, \delta=0.7$						
$\mu_a^d=1, \mu_a^f=0$	0.347	0.325	0.300	0.300	0.300	0.300
$\mu_a^d=\mu_a^f=0.5$	0.325	0.313	0.301	0.317	0.343	0.387
$\mu_a^d=0, \mu_a^f=01$	0.300	0.300	0.300	0.334	0.386	0.473
Without trade-off (excess capacity)						
$\hat{p}=MC_c, \delta=0.7$						
$\mu_a^d=1, \mu_a^f=0$	0.806	0.727	0.664	0.612	0.581	0.560
$\mu_a^d=\mu_a^f=0.5$	0.553	0.513	0.482	0.456	0.440	0.430
$\mu_a^d=0, \mu_a^f=1$	0.300	0.300	0.300	0.300	0.300	0.300
Without trade-off (without excess capacity)						
$\hat{p}=\bar{p}, \delta=0.7$						
$\mu_a^d=1, \mu_a^f=0$	0.360	0.402	0.466	0.572	0.732	0.852
$\mu_a^d=\mu_a^f=0.5$	0.330	0.351	0.383	0.436	0.516	0.576
$\mu_a^d=0, \mu_a^f=1$	0.300	0.300	0.300	0.300	0.300	0.300

Finally, some numerical examples help us to appreciate the extent of this effect.

Table 3.1 reports the results corresponding to the situations with and without 'trade-off in the plant mix' under either excess or scarcity of generation capacity. These results are obtained by using emission rates and variable costs reported in Table 3A.1. Three combinations of μ_a^d and μ_a^f are simulated: the two extreme situations and the case of perfect symmetry ($\mu_a^d=\mu_a^f=0.5$). As can be noted, the time (the number of hours) over which the dominant firm prefers to bid the price threshold ($\hat{H}$, the inverse of $\hat{D}$) changes only slightly if the share of the most-efficient plants operated by the dominant firm (μ_a^d) is low or, under high allowance prices, if μ_a^d is high. Otherwise, the change in market power is significant especially when there is excess capacity in the market.

From this outcome the following implications arise. First, when we try to estimate to what extent the carbon price is passed through into power prices, we have to take into account also that change in price may be amplified or lessened by change in market power. Second (and most important), the change in market power due to the ETS might significantly affect the amount of emissions as it can modify the share of production by the different kinds of plants (favouring the most- or least-polluting plants). This effect may be able to influence greatly the cost of achieving the emission target, that is, the effort to pursue the reduction in carbon emissions.

3.6   THE IMPACT ON POWER PRICES: MARKET POWER VERSUS PERFECT COMPETITION

As pointed out before, under perfect competition the MPTR is always equal to 1 (see Definition 3.6). Thus, by estimating the MPTR we are able to know whether the impact of the ETS on power prices under imperfect competition is higher (*MPTR>1*) or lower (*MPTR<1*) than that under perfectly competitive scenarios.

In order to carry out the MPTR curve (that is, how the MPTR is distributed over time), we have to depict the price and marginal cost (of the marginal unit) duration curves before and after the ETS, distinguishing between low ($0 < p^{tp} \leq p^{tp*}$) and high ($p^{tp} > p^{tp*}$) allowance prices (only for Scenario 1). Table 3.2 shows different expressions of MC_c, $\overline{MC}$, $\underline{MC}$, μ^d, μ^f corresponding to the situations after and before the ETS. We shall use the superscript star (*) in order to address the critical threshold of D, H and δ when $p^{tp} \neq 0$ (that is, the situation after the ETS).

In what follows, we shall present some relevant examples of MPTR curves corresponding to different scenarios in terms of available capacity, market concentration and plant mix. For the sake of simplicity, we shall illustrate only the outcome under low allowance prices while that under high allowance prices is reported in Appendix 3A.

Scenario 1 (Trade-off in the Plant Mix): Low Allowance Prices

In this case, $\hat{D}$ always decreases in p^{tp} under excess capacity, whereas it may either decrease or increase under scarcity of generation capacity (see proof of Lemma 3.2). In both situations (excess and scarcity of generation capacity), we analyse only the case in which $\hat{D}$ decreases in p^{tp} (increasing market power) because this is the most likely situation given a plausible plant mix in the market: coal plants (*a*), CCGT (*b*) and oil-fired plants (*c*). In fact, by using the emission rates and variable costs of these technologies (Table 3A.1), we get $(e_b - e_a)(\hat{v} - v_a) < (\hat{e} - e_a)(v_b - v_a)$, regardless of the available capacity in the market (that is, regardless of whether there is excess capacity or not).

Table 3.2   Parameter expressions before and after the ETS

	Before ETS	Scenario 1		Scenario 2
	$p^{tp}=0$	$p^{tp} \leq p^{tp}*$	$p^{tp} > p^{tp}*$	$\forall p^{tp}$
MC_c	v_c	MC_c	MC_c	MC_c
$\overline{MC}$	v_b	MC_b	MC_a	MC_b
$\underline{MC}$	v_a	MC_a	MC_b	MC_a
μ^d	μ_a^d	μ_a^d	μ_b^d	μ_a^d
μ^f	μ_a^f	μ_a^f	μ_b^f	μ_a^f

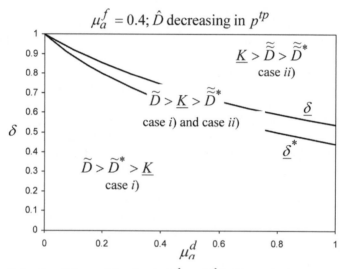

Figure 3.6   Possible combinations of $\hat{D}$ and $\hat{D}*$: Scenario 1

Decreasing $\hat{D}$ implies that we may face three combinations of $\hat{D}$ and $\hat{D}*$ depending on whether the degree of market concentration is above or below the critical values identified in Proposition 3.2, that is, $\underline{\delta}$ (before the ETS) and $\underline{\delta}*$ (after the ETS). In Figure 3.6, by using the expression of $\underline{\delta}$ (Proposition 3.2), we have depicted $\underline{\delta}$ and $\underline{\delta}*$ as a function of μ_a^d (assuming that $\mu_a^f=0.4$, without loss of generality). As can be noted, the critical value after the ETS ($\underline{\delta}*$) is always lower than that before the ETS ($\underline{\delta}$). Thus, from Lemma 3.1 and Proposition 3.2, the possible combinations of $\hat{D}$ and $\hat{D}*$ are: 1) $\tilde{D} > \tilde{D}* > \underline{K}$ if $\delta < \underline{\delta}*$ (case *i* for both $p^{tp}=0$ and $p^{tp} \neq 0$); 2) $\tilde{D} > \underline{K} > \tilde{\tilde{D}}*$ if $\underline{\delta}* < \delta < \underline{\delta}$ (case *i*) for $p^{tp}=0$ and case *ii*) for $p^{tp} \neq 0$); 3) $\underline{K} > \hat{\tilde{D}} > \tilde{\tilde{D}}*$ if $\underline{\delta}* < \underline{\delta} < \delta$ (case *ii* for both $p^{tp}=0$ and $p^{tp} \neq 0$).

Figures 3.7 and 3.8 illustrate the MPTR curves obtained by dividing the

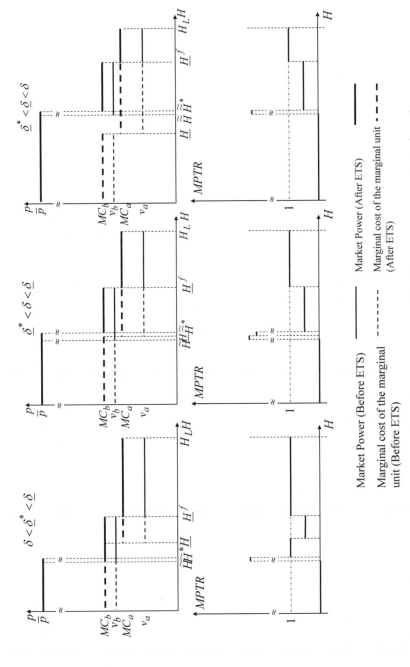

Figure 3.7   MPTR curve (Scenario 1): low allowance prices and without excess capacity ($\underline{\mu}^d = \underline{\mu}^f$)

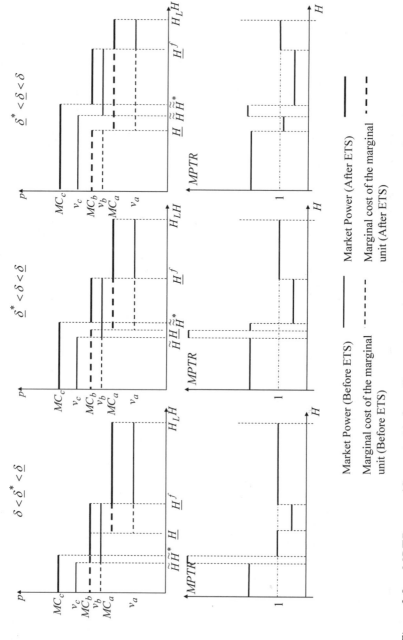

Figure 3.8   MPTR curve (Scenario 1): low allowance prices and with excess capacity ($\underline{\mu}^d = \underline{\mu}^f$)

change in prices by the change in marginal production cost of the marginal unit.[19] For the sake of simplicity and without loss of generality, we assume that the dominant firm and the competitive fringe operate the same share of the most-efficient plants $\mu^d = \mu^f$.[20]

Figures clearly show that results largely depend on the power demand level (peak versus off-peak hours) and on the available capacity in the market.

In the peak hours, there would not be any CO_2 cost pass-through under scarcity of generation capacity (provided that δ is high enough) whereas, under excess capacity, the MPTR would be more than 1.

In the off-peak hours power prices can include the full marginal carbon cost but this can be much less if the share of the most-polluting plant in the market is high enough. This is more likely to occur under excess capacity than under scarcity of generation capacity.

Note that the differences between competition and market power are due to the disparity in emission rates. In fact, there would be no difference if $e_a=e_b=e_c$, regardless of either the plant mix or the degree of market concentration.

Then, the impact of emission rate differences can be interpreted as the combination of two components. On the one hand, it determines a different degree of opportunity cost internalization (the pass-through component, which is the prevalent effect). On the other hand, it alters the degree of market power (the, market power component) because of the shift from $\tilde{H}$ to $\tilde{H}^*$ (or from $\tilde{\tilde{H}}$ to $\tilde{\tilde{H}}^*$).

Under low allowance prices the pass-through component is more than 1 only when there is excess capacity and in the peak hours (Figure 3.8). The market power component, instead, is always above 1 but moves from peak (high demand) towards off-peak hours (low demand) as long as the degree of market concentration increases. Therefore, under excess capacity, the probability that the volume-weighted average $MPTR$, $MPTR_{av}$, could be less than 1 increases in the degree of market concentration.

Similarly without excess capacity, but this time the time-period over which the rise in market power occurs is so short that the $MPTR_{av}$ might be below 1, even under a relatively low degree of market concentration (Figure 3.7).

In addition, when $\delta < \underline{\delta}$ the $MPTR$[21] decreases in μ^f and increases in μ^d. Inversely, when $\delta > \underline{\delta}$ it decreases in μ^d and is low sensitive to μ^f.

Finally, if we remove the assumption that $\mu^d = \mu^f$ we have the following outcome moving from a low to a high degree of market concentration. If $\mu^d > \mu^f$, the share of the most-polluting plants in the market increases by amplifying the impact of δ. Inversely, if $\mu^d < \mu^f$. In this latter case, the share of the most-polluting plants in the market declines, offsetting the effect of δ.

When allowance prices are high (higher than the switching price), the interpretation is a little bit more complex (see Appendix 3A). This time in fact we have also to account for the switching effect (due to the switch of the power producers' position on the merit order). This effect is equal to the difference in variable costs of the technologies a and b, $|v_a - v_b|$, and, because of the trade-off between variable costs and emission rates (in the technology set), it counterbalances the pass-through component.

Figures 3A.1 and 3A.2 show how the switching component influences the MPTR curve. Under both relatively low and high degrees of market concentration there is a higher probability (higher than in the case of low allowance prices) that the average MPTR is below 1. These effects seem to be even more evident when the hypothesis of excess capacity is removed.

Scenario 2 (Without Trade-off in the Plant Mix)

In this scenario, as pointed out before (proof of Lemma 3.2), under excess capacity both cases, $\hat{D} < \hat{D}^*$ and $\hat{D} > \hat{D}^*$, are possible, whereas under scarcity of generation capacity market power always decreases in p^{tp} ($\hat{D} > \hat{D}$), regardless of v_j and e_j. This time a, b and c may be CCGT, gas-fired steam-cycle plants and oil-fired steam-cycle plants, respectively (plausible plant mix).

By using the emission rates and variable costs of these technologies (Table 3A.1), we get $(e_b - e_a)(\hat{v} - v_a) < (\hat{e} - e_a)(v_b - b_a)$, under excess capacity (that is, increasing market power, decreasing $\hat{D}$), and $(e_b - e_a)(\hat{v} - v_a) > (\hat{e} - e_a)(v_b - v_a)$, without excess capacity (that is, decreasing market power, increasing $\hat{D}$).

Increasing $\hat{D}$ (scarcity of generation capacity) implies that we may face three possible combinations of $\hat{D}$ and $\hat{D}^*$ depending on whether the degree of market concentration is above or below the critical values identified in Proposition 3.2, that is, $\underline{\delta}$ (before the ETS) and $\underline{\delta}^*$ (after the ETS). As above we have depicted $\underline{\delta}$ and $\underline{\delta}^*$ as a function of μ_a^d (assuming $\mu_a^f = 0.4$, without loss of generality). As can be noted (Figure 3.9), this time the critical value after the ETS ($\underline{\delta}^*$) is always higher than that before the ETS ($\underline{\delta}$). Thus, from Lemma 3.1 and Proposition 3.2, the possible combinations of $\hat{D}$ and $\hat{D}^*$ are: 1) $\tilde{D}^* > \tilde{D} > \underline{K}$ if $\delta < \underline{\delta} < \underline{\delta}^*$ (case *i* for both $p^{tp} = 0$ and $p^{tp} \neq 0$); 2) $\tilde{D}^* > \underline{K} > \tilde{D}$ if $\underline{\delta} < \delta < \underline{\delta}^*$ (case *ii* for $p^{tp}=0$ and case *i* for $p^{tp} \neq 0$); 3) $\underline{K} > \tilde{D}^* > \tilde{D}$ if $\underline{\delta} < \underline{\delta}^* < \delta$ (case *ii* for both $p^{tp} = 0$ and $p^{tp} \neq 0$).

Decreasing $\hat{D}$ (excess capacity) implies that we face the same combinations already described for Scenario 1: (i) $\tilde{D} > \tilde{D}^* > \underline{K}$ if $\delta < \underline{\delta}^* < \underline{\delta}$; (ii) $\tilde{D} > \underline{K} > \tilde{D}^*$ if $\underline{\delta}^* < \delta < \underline{\delta}$; (iii) $\underline{K} > \tilde{D} > \tilde{D}^*$ if $\underline{\delta}^* < \underline{\delta} < \delta$.

In the peak hours (Figures 3.10 and 3.11), the results are similar to those emerging from Scenario 1 (MPTR more than 1, under excess capacity, and less than 1, under scarcity of generation capacity).

In the off-peak hours, instead, the outcome is substantially different. This time, power prices fully include the marginal carbon opportunity cost

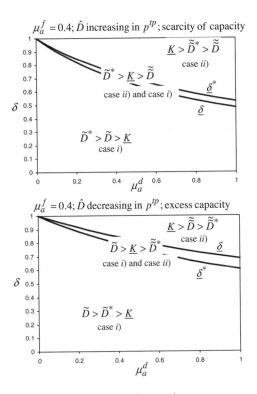

Figure 3.9 Possible combinations of $\hat{D}$ and $\hat{D}^*$: Scenario 2

(and much more in the mid-merit hours), regardless of the share of the most- (least-) polluting plants in the market.

Consequently, under excess of generation capacity the $MPTR_{av}$ will always be more than 1. Furthermore, it is important to highlight that the ETS may determine a decrease in the degree of market power, implying that the $MPTR_{av}$ may even be negative if the degree of market concentration is high and there is scarcity of generation capacity.

3.7 QUANTITATIVE SIMULATIONS

In this section the impact of emissions trading on the average electricity price is assessed. In particular, we calculate the volume-weighted average MPTR (hereafter $MPTR_{av}$) which is given by $MPTR_{av} = \int_0^{H_L} MPTR(H)D(H)dH \Big/ \int_0^{H_L} D(H)dH$.

For this purpose we adopt (Table 3A.1) plausible values (typical of the

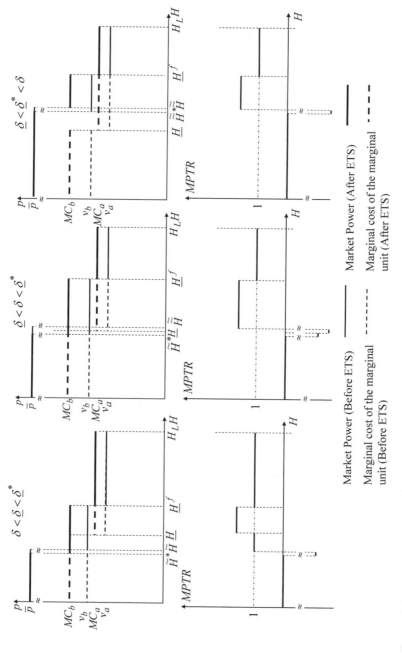

Figure 3.10 *MPTR curve (Scenario 2): without excess capacity* ($\underline{\mu}^d = \underline{\mu}^f$)

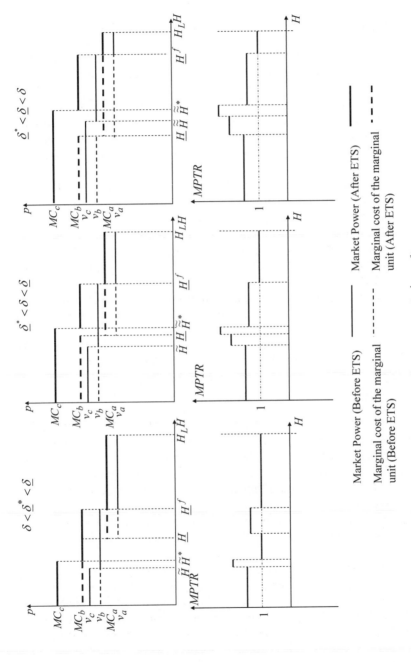

Figure 3.11 MPTR curve (Scenario 2): with excess capacity ($\underline{\mu}^d = \underline{\mu}^f$)

Italian electricity market) of variable costs, emission rates and price cap.[22] Note that, within such a setting, the switching price, as labelled in Definition 3.3, stays at about 40 €/tonCO$_2$. With regard to the allowance price, 20 €/tonCO$_2$ and 60 €/tonCO$_2$ are chosen to characterize the cases of the low and high allowance prices, respectively.[23] Finally, without any loss of generality, we assume that the load duration curve is a linear function of *H*.[24]

Although either the low or the high allowance price scenarios yield interesting results, for analytical purposes we illustrate the former context exclusively and let the appendix guide the reader through the other. Linkages (that is, similarities and differences) between the two cases are discussed here.

The outcomes are presented in Figures 3.12 and 3.13, from which we can make the following comments.

First, without excess capacity (Figure 3.12), market power can always lessen the impact of the ETS on electricity prices whatever the underlying technological structure (the plant mix) of the industry. Furthermore, what is important to underline is that, if there is no trade-off in the plant mix, the $MPTR_{av}$ can even be slightly negative, that is, the ETS can determine a decrease rather than an increase in average power prices. This effect is due to the fact that the ETS, under certain conditions, can cause a decrease in market power.

This pattern does not extend to the case of excess capacity (Figure 3.13). Here $MPTR_{av} < 1$ only with a trade-off in the plant mix and for a certain range of parameter values. In particular, market power can lessen the impact of the ETS on electricity prices only when the share of the most-polluting plants in the market is large enough[25] (high μ_a^d combined with high δ or high μ_a^f combined with low δ). Instead, when μ_a^d is sufficiently low, $MPTR_{av}$ is never below 1 whatever δ and μ_a^f.[26] Without a trade-off in the plant mix, the impact under market power is always more than that under perfect competition and an increase in μ_a^d (except when μ_a^f and δ are low enough).

Therefore, quantitative simulations confirm the visual interpretation proposed in the previous section.

Second, the simulation highlights that the relative impact of market power may be relevant. The average MPTR ranges from 0.5 to 2.0 under excess capacity and from –0.1 to 1 without excess capacity.

Similar results arise in the case of high allowance prices (Figure 3A.3). This time, however, if there is a trade-off in the plant mix and μ_a^f is sufficiently large, $MPTR_{av}$ can be less than 1 even if δ and μ_a^d are low.[27]

Overall, the ETS impact under imperfect competition is always less than that under perfect competition when there is a scarcity of generation capacity in the market. Instead, when there is excess capacity the $MPTR_{av}$

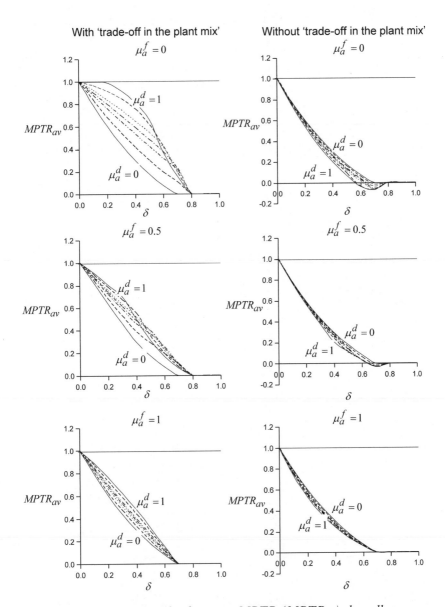

Figure 3.12   *Volume-weighted average MPTR (MPTR$_{av}$): low allowance prices and without excess capacity*

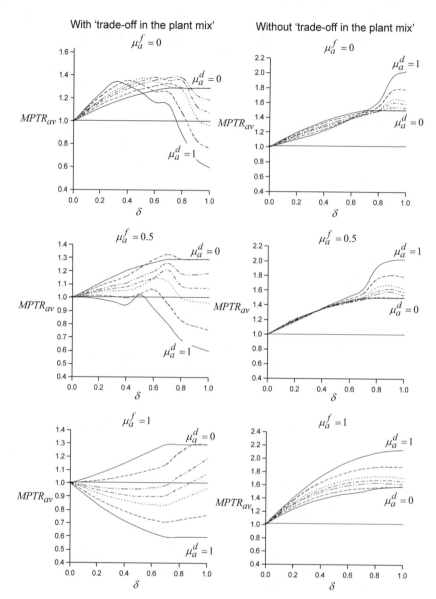

*Figure 3.13   Volume-weighted average MPTR (MPTR$_{av}$): low allowance
              prices and with excess capacity*

is always more than 1, except when there is a certain technological mix in the power system.

3.8   THE IMPACT ON EMISSIONS

In order to estimate the impact of the ETS on emissions, we abandon the assumption of price inelasticity of demand and suppose, without loss of generality, that $D(p,H)=\alpha(H)-\beta p$, that is, a downward-sloping linear demand whose slope does not depend on the period of consumption.[28]

In the short run, the environmental regulation can modify the amount of pollutant emissions through two ways. On the one hand, it may determine a rise in power prices and consequently a decrease in power demand (and production). On the other hand, if the allowance price is above the switching price, it may determine a switch in the merit order of the generation plants, drastically modifying the production by the different groups of plants (and consequently, total emissions).

In imperfectly competitive markets, apart from these two effects, we have to take into account an additional effect, that is, the impact of environmental regulation on the degree of market power.

To understand how a change in market power may affect emissions, it is helpful to start by showing the simplified case in which the dominant firm operates only one group of generating plants and the fringe operates the other one. Figure 3.14 illustrates how the change in market power modifies the production by the two groups of plants and consequently the total emissions by the power system in the reference period. Note that in all cases we refer to power markets organized in the form of a uniform price auction.

Figure 3.14A highlights what occurs when the degree of market power decreases ($\Delta \hat{D} > 0$) and there is no trade-off in the plant mix. We assume that the dominant firm operates only CCGT plants and the fringe only gas-fired steam-cycle plants (gas-SC). Before the ETS, the dominant firm accommodates maximum production by the fringe (in gas-SC plants) and bids the price threshold by restraining its production (CCGT plants). After the ETS, the dominant firm prefers to maximize its production (CCGT plants) by bidding prices below the marginal cost of the fringe's plants (gas-SC plants). Therefore, since CCGT plants are less polluting than gas-SC plants, the change in market power determines a decrease in carbon emissions and vice versa if the ETS causes a rise in market power (Figure 3.14B).

Under the trade-off in the plant mix and for allowance prices below the switching price, the outcome is exactly the opposite (Figure 3.14C), assuming that the dominant firm operates only coal plants and the fringe only CCGT plants. This time, the increase in market power determines a decrease in

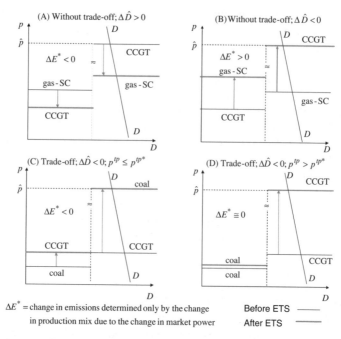

Figure 3.14   Change in market power and change in emissions: examples

emissions. If the allowance price is above the switching price, the change in pollutant emissions due to the change in market power is marginal (Figure 3.14D) assuming that the dominant firm operates only CCGT plants and the fringe only coal plants. However, this does not mean that there would not be any change in emissions. Instead, they fall markedly, but this would be due to the switch in the merit order and not to the change in market power.

Once again, some numerical examples are useful to appreciate the extent of these effects. As above, we assume that $D(p,H) = \alpha(H) - \beta p$ (with $\beta = 0.5$) and the extreme combinations of μ_a^d and μ_a^f together with the symmetric case ($\mu_a^d = \mu_a^f = 0.5$).

Tables 3.3 and 3.4 report the percentage change in emissions for both the perfectly and imperfectly competitive scenarios. From these tables, the following conclusions can be drawn.

First, under the trade-off in the plant mix and below the switching price, the ETS determines a decrease in emissions which is higher under imperfect than under perfect competition in most cases, and vice versa, if the allowance price is above the switching price.

Second, as expected, under the trade-off in the plant mix, total emissions fall strongly if the allowance price is above the switching price. This effect

Table 3.3   *Change in carbon emissions: numerical simulations (trade-off in the plant mix)*

	Perfect competition $p^{tp}(€/tCO_2)$				Imperfect competition $p^{tp}(€/tCO_2)$			
	0 IN²	20 %	40¹ %	60 %	0 IN²	20 %	40¹ %	60 %
$\delta=0.7, \beta=0.5$								
With excess capacity ($\hat{p}=MC_c$)								
$\mu_a^d=1, \mu_a^f=0$	100	−0.41	−12.38	−12.88	90.0	−9.70	−17.00	−17.19
$\mu_a^d=\mu_a^f=0.5$	90.0	−0.27	−29.18	−29.57	87.7	−2.20	−21.53	−22.53
$\mu_a^d=0, \mu_a^f=1$	75.0	−0.05	−28.05	−28.36	75.0	−0.50	−0.06	−7.89
Without excess capacity ($\hat{p}=\bar{p}$)								
$\mu_a^d=1, \mu_a^f=0$	100	−0.41	−12.38	−12.88	81.2	−1.10	−2.17	−2.17
$\mu_a^d=\mu_{a'}^f=0.5$	90.0	−0.27	−29.18	−29.57	85.3	−0.22	−18.44	−18.79
$\mu_a^d=0, \mu_a^f=1$	75.0	−0.05	−28.05	−28.36	75.0	0.00	0.00	−1.63

Notes:
1. Switching price.
2. IN: Index number.

Table 3.4   *Change in carbon emissions: numerical simulations (trade-off in the plant mix)*

	Perfect competition $p^{tp}(€/tCO_2)$				Imperfect competition $p^{tp}(€/tCO_2)$			
	0 IN²	20 %	40¹ %	60 %	0 IN²	20 %	40¹ %	60 %
$\delta=0.7, \beta=0.5$								
With excess capacity ($\hat{p}=MC_c$)								
$\mu_a^d=1, \mu_a^f=0$	100	−0.23	−0.46	−0.69	88.3	1.11	2.11	3.03
$\mu_a^d=\mu_a^f=0.5$	106.0	−0.27	−0.54	−0.81	92.5	−0.09	−0.10	−0.17
$\mu_a^d=0, \mu_a^f=1$	114.9	−0.28	−0.55	−0.82	100	−0.42	−0.84	−1.26
With excess capacity ($\hat{p}=\bar{p}$)								
$\mu_a^d=1, \mu_a^f=0$	100	−0.23	−0.46	−0.69	87.0	−0.28	−0.64	−1.14
$\mu_a^d=\mu_a^f=0.5$	106.0	−0.27	−0.54	−0.81	94.7	−0.08	−0.17	−0.29
$\mu_a^d=0\mu_{a'}^f=1$	114.9	−0.28	−0.55	−0.82	100	0.00	0.00	0.00

Notes:
1. Switching price.
2. IN: Index number.

is mostly due to the switch in the merit order and only partially to the decrease in demand and change in market power.

Third, in imperfectly competitive markets emissions may even increase if there is no trade-off in the plant mix and under excess of generation capacity, provided that the share of the least-polluting plants operated by the dominant firm is large enough.

Resuming, taking market structures into account is essential to evaluate how the ETS impacts on emissions in the short run. This analysis in fact demonstrates that under imperfect competition the ETS, by affecting the degree of market power, is able to influence total emissions significantly. In some cases, change in market power amplifies the decrease in emissions. In other cases, it can reduce or offset this effect, which may even involve a rise in pollution. Thus, under certain conditions imperfect competition might make it more difficult to achieve the environmental targets.

3.9 CONCLUSIONS

The analysis described in this chapter highlights that the impact of the ETS on power prices significantly depends on electricity market structures. Under perfect competition, power prices fully internalize the carbon opportunity cost. Under market power the extent to which the carbon cost is passed through into power prices depends on several factors: (i) the degree of market concentration, (ii) the plant mix operated by either the dominant firm or the competitive fringe, (iii) the price of the CO_2 emission and allowances; and (iv) the available capacity in the market (whether there is excess capacity or not).

In particular, the theoretical analysis points out that the pass-through under imperfect competition is always lower than under perfect competition if there is a scarcity of generation capacity in the market. Otherwise, the MPTR is always above one, except for the two cases with a trade-off in the plant mix: under low allowance prices (below the switching price), when a large share of the most-polluting plants operated by the dominant firm combines with a high degree of market concentration; and under high allowance prices, if the fringe's share of the least-polluting plants is large enough. Furthermore, the average pass-through under market power can even be slightly negative (decreasing rather than increasing prices) if the ETS determines a decrease in the degree of market power. This can occur if there is no trade-off in the plant mix and under a scarcity of generation capacity provided that the degree of market concentration is high enough.

Finally, the ETS can determine a change in short-run emissions through three effects: (i) a change in power demand due to a change in power prices; (ii) a possible switch in the merit order; and (iii) a change in the degree of market power. The analysis highlights that this last effect can cause an increase in carbon emissions only when there is no trade-off in the plant mix and under excess capacity, provided that the leader's share of least-polluting (most efficient) plants in the market is large enough. Otherwise, the ETS always determines a decrease in emissions, generally lower under market power than under perfectly competitive scenarios, however. Thus, under certain conditions imperfect competition might make it more difficult to achieve the environmental targets.

APPENDIX 3A

Proof of Lemma 3.1

It is immediately intuitive that when $D \geq \overline{K}$ the system marginal price equals $\overline{P}$ (for $K_c = 0$) or MC_c (for $K_c = \overline{K}_c$). When $D < \underline{K}^f$, pure Bertrand equilibria (first marginal cost pricing) arise and prices equal the marginal cost of the most-efficient plants ($\underline{MC}$). In fact, on the one hand, whenever the demand is so high that both the leader's and the fringe's least-efficient units can enter the market, the dominant firm would not gain any advantage by competing *à la* Bertrand, that is, by attempting to undercut the rivals. Therefore, it will maximize its profit by bidding the price threshold.[29] On the other hand, whenever the power demand is lower than the fringe's power capacity in the most-efficient plants, competing *à la* Bertrand is the leader's only available strategy in order to have a positive probability of being dispatched. As a consequence, prices will converge to the marginal cost of the most-efficient plants.

It remains to identify the leader's optimal choice on $D \in]\overline{K};\underline{K}^f]$.[30] Under the assumptions of the model, each generator in the competitive fringe has a unique dominant strategy whatever the market demand: bidding according to its own marginal cost of production (which, after the implementation of the ETS, includes the carbon opportunity cost). Conversely, the best choice of the dominant firm might consist in (i) bidding the price cap ($\overline{p}$, if there is no excess capacity, that is, $K_c = 0$) or the backstop price (MC_c, if there is excess capacity, that is, $K_c = \overline{K}_c$) or in (ii) bidding $\overline{MC}$.[31]

Let π_1^d and π_2^d be the profits corresponding to the first and second strategies above, respectively. Whenever the least-efficient units could enter the market (that is, $D(H) > \underline{K}^f$), the profit the dominant firm earns by choosing the first strategy (that is, $\forall H \in]\overline{H}; \underline{H}]$) is:

$$\pi_1^d = (\hat{p} - \underline{MC})[D(H) - K_T(1 - \delta)] - \sum_{i=1}^{z}\sum_{j=a,b}(k_j^i f_j^i - p^{tp}\overline{E}_j^i), \quad (3A.1)$$

where f_j^i is the capital cost per unit of installed capacity of the i-th unit belonging to group j of plants and $\overline{E}_j^i$ is the amount of allowance allocated (free of charge) to the generic plant i belonging to group j.

If the dominant firm chooses the second strategy, it earns:

$$\pi_2^d = (\overline{MC} - \underline{MC})\mu^d\delta K_T \sum_{i=1}^{z}\sum_{j=a,b}(k_j^i f_j^i - p^{tp}\overline{E}_j^i), \qquad (3A.2)$$

where $\hat{p} = \begin{cases} \overline{p} & \text{for } K_c = 0 \\ MC_c & \text{for } K_c = \overline{K}_c. \end{cases}$

Therefore the leader's optimal strategy is bidding $\hat{p}$ if and only if $\pi_1^d \geq \pi_2^d$, that is, if and only if:

$$D \geq [\mu^d\delta\zeta + (1-\delta)]K_T = \tilde{D}(\delta,\mu^d,\zeta), \qquad (3A.3)$$

where $\zeta = \dfrac{(\overline{MC} - \underline{MC})}{\hat{p} - \underline{MC}}.$

When $D \in]\underline{K}; \overline{K}^f]$ (that is, $H \in]\underline{H}; H^f]$) the profit the dominant firm earns by choosing the first strategy is:

$$\pi_3^d = (\text{p} - \underline{MC})[D(H) - K_T(1-\delta)] - \sum_{i=1}^{z}\sum_{j=a,b}(k_j^i f_j^i - p^{tp}\overline{E}_j^i), (3A.4)$$

and by choosing the second strategy, the profit is:

$$\pi_4^d = (\overline{MC} - \underline{MC})[D(H) - K_T\mu^f(1-\delta)] - \sum_{i=1}^{z}\sum_{j=a,b}(k_j^i f_j^i - p^{tp}\overline{E}_j^i). \qquad (3A.5)$$

Thus the dominant firm will choose the first strategy (bidding the price cap or the backstop price) if and only if $\pi_3^d \geq \pi_4^d$, that is, if and only if:

$$D \geq (1-\delta)\left[\frac{(1-\mu^f)}{(1-\zeta)} + \mu^f\right]K_T = \tilde{\tilde{D}}(\delta, \mu^f, \zeta). \qquad (3A.6)$$

Therefore the leader's best reply is a function of power demand. We still have to demonstrate that the two critical values $\tilde{D}$ and $\tilde{\tilde{D}}$ never work together, that is, if $\tilde{D} \in] \overline{K}; \underline{K}]$ then $\tilde{\tilde{D}} \notin [\underline{K}; \overline{K}^f]$ and vice versa.

Given that $\overline{K}^f = (1-\mu^f)(1-\delta)K_T$, $\underline{K}^d = \mu^d\delta K_T$, $K^f = (1-\delta)K_T$ and $\underline{K} = [\mu^d\delta + \mu^f(1-\delta)]K_T$ with equation (3A.3) can be rewritten as:

$$D(H) \geq \tilde{D}(\delta, \mu^d, \zeta) = \zeta\underline{K}^d + K^f \qquad (3A.7)$$

and equation (3A.6) as:

$$D(H) \geqslant \widetilde{\widetilde{D}}(\delta, \mu^f, \zeta) = \frac{\overline{K}^f}{1-\zeta} + \underline{K}^f. \tag{3A.8}$$

Let us assume, for instance, that $\tilde{D} > \underline{K}$. From (3A.7) $\overline{K}^f/(1-\zeta) > \underline{K}^d$ and from (3A.8) $\widetilde{\widetilde{D}} > \underline{K}$. Thus, $\widetilde{\widetilde{D}} \notin]\underline{K}; \underline{K}^f[$

Let us similarly suppose that $\widetilde{\widetilde{D}} < \underline{K}$. From (3A.8) $\underline{K}^d > \overline{K}^f/(1-\zeta)$ and from (3A.7) $\tilde{D} < \underline{K}$. Thus, $\tilde{D} \notin]\bar{K}; \underline{K}[$

In addition, from (3A.7) and (3A.8), if $\tilde{D} = \underline{K}$ then $\widetilde{\widetilde{D}} = \underline{K}$ and vice versa. Also, note that $\tilde{D} < \bar{K}$ and $\widetilde{\widetilde{D}} > \underline{K}^f$

Finally let us present some comparative statics:

$$\frac{\partial \tilde{D}}{\partial \mu^d} = \delta \zeta K_T > 0; \frac{\partial \widetilde{\widetilde{D}}}{\partial \mu^f} = -(1-\delta)\frac{\zeta}{1-\zeta} \delta K_T < 0.$$

In fact, when $\delta > \underline{\delta}$, increasing the fringe's share of the most-efficient plants implies that bidding the marginal cost of the least-efficient plants becomes less profitable for the dominant firm compared to bidding the price cap, or the backstop price (π_4^d in equation (3A.5) decreases, whereas π_3^d in equation (3A.4) does not depend on μ^f), and inversely when we look at the case of $\delta < \underline{\delta}$ and at the rise of μ^d. In the latter case, increasing the leader's share of the most-efficient plants implies that bidding the marginal cost of the least-efficient plants becomes more convenient for the dominant firm (π_2^d in equation (3A.2) increases whereas π_1^d in equation (3A.1) does not depend on μ^d). Furthermore,

$$\frac{\partial \tilde{D}}{\partial \zeta} = \mu^d \delta K_T > 0; \frac{\partial \widetilde{\widetilde{D}}}{\partial \zeta} = \frac{(1-\delta)(1-\mu^f)}{(1-\zeta)^2} K_T > 0.$$

Thus, market power is a decreasing function of ζ.

Proof of Proposition 3.2

This proposition follows directly from Lemma 3.1. Since $\tilde{D}$ and $\widetilde{\widetilde{D}}$ never work together and provided that when $\tilde{D} = \underline{K}$ then $\widetilde{\widetilde{D}} = \underline{K}$ (see the proof of Lemma 3.1 above), in order to identify the critical value of δ it is sufficient to carry out the locus of points $(\tilde{\delta})$ that $\tilde{D} = \underline{K}$ which is equal to the locus of points δ $(\widetilde{\widetilde{\delta}})$ that $\widetilde{\widetilde{D}} = \underline{K}$:

$$\tilde{\delta} = \widetilde{\widetilde{\delta}} = \underline{\delta} = \frac{\mu^f - 1}{\mu^f - 1 + \mu^d(\zeta - 1)}.$$

Furthermore, note that $\tilde{D} < \overline{K}$ and $\tilde{\tilde{D}} > \underline{K^f}$.

Proof of Lemma 3.2

The derivative of $\hat{D}$ with respect to p^{tp} can be written as:

$$\frac{\partial \hat{D}}{\partial p^{tp}} = \frac{\partial \hat{D}}{\partial \zeta} \frac{\partial \zeta}{\partial p^{tp}}. \tag{3A.9}$$

Since (from (3A.3) and (3A.6)):

$$\frac{\partial \tilde{D}}{\partial \zeta} = \mu^d \delta K_T > 0 \text{ and } \frac{\partial \tilde{\tilde{D}}}{\partial \zeta} = \frac{(1-\delta)(1-\mu^f)}{(1-\zeta)^2} K_T > 0, \tag{3A.10}$$

then, market power is a decreasing function of ζ.

By differentiating ζ with respect to p^{tp} we get:

$$\frac{\partial \zeta}{\partial p^{tp}} = \begin{cases} \dfrac{(e_b - e_a)(v_e - v_a) - (e_c - e_a)(v_b - v_a)}{[(v_c - v_a) - p^{tp}(e_c - e_a)^2]} & \text{under excess capacity} \\[2ex] \dfrac{(e_b - e_a)(\bar{p} - v_a) + e_a(v_b - v_a)}{(\bar{p} - v_a - p^{tp} e_a)^2} & \text{without excess capacity} \end{cases}$$

if $p^{tp} \leq p^{tp*}$, and:

$$\frac{\partial \zeta}{\partial p^{tp}} = \begin{cases} \dfrac{(e_a - e_b)(v_c - v_b) - (e_c - e_b)(v_a - v_b)}{[(v_c - v_b) - p^{tp}(e_c - e_b)^2]} & \text{under excess capacity} \\[2ex] \dfrac{(e_a - e_b)(\bar{p} - v_b) + e_b(v_a - v_b)}{(\bar{p} - v_b - p^{tp} e_b)^2} & \text{without excess capacity} \end{cases}$$

if $p^{tp} > p^{tp*}$.

Consequently:

- if $e_a > e_c > e_b$ and $p^{tp} \leq p^{tp*} \Rightarrow \frac{\partial \zeta}{\partial p^{tp}} < 0$ and $\frac{\partial \hat{D}}{\partial p^{tp}} < 0 \;\; \forall v_j, e_j$ under excess capacity whereas under a scarcity of capacity $\frac{\partial \hat{D}}{\partial p^{tp}} < 0$ only when $(e_b - e_a)(\bar{p} - v_a) < -e_a(v_b - v_a)$;

- if $e_a > e_c > e_b$ and $p^{tp} > p^{tp*} \Rightarrow \frac{\partial \zeta}{\partial p^{tp}} > 0$ and $\frac{\partial \hat{D}}{\partial p^{tp}} > 0 \; \forall v_j, e_j$ under excess capacity whereas under a scarcity of capacity $\frac{\partial \hat{D}}{\partial p^{tp}} > 0$ only when $(e_a - e_b)(\bar{p}_b - v_b) < -e_b(v_a - v_b)$;

- if $e_c > e_b > e_a \Rightarrow \frac{\partial \zeta}{\partial p^{tp}} < 0$ and $\frac{\partial \hat{D}}{\partial p^{tp}} < 0$

only when $\begin{cases} (e_b - e_a)(v_c - v_a) < (e_c - e_a)(v_b - v_a) & \text{under excess capacity} \\ (e_b - e_a)(\bar{p} - v_a) < -e_a(v_b - v_a) & \text{without excess capacity.} \end{cases}$

From comparative statics above, $\tilde{D}$ and $\tilde{\tilde{D}}$ are increasing functions of ζ. Thus, if there is excess capacity and 'trade off in the plants mix' market power always increases (decreases) in p^{tp} if $p^{tp} \leq p^{tp*}$ (if $p^{tp} > p^{tp*}$). Without 'trade-off in the plant mix' market power always decreases in p^{tp} if there is a scarcity of capacity. Otherwise the change in market power depends on the relative values of variable costs and emission rates of the different kinds of technologies.

Proof of Corollary 3.1

By differentiating $\frac{\partial \hat{D}}{\partial p^{tp}}$ with respect to μ_a^d and μ_a^f we get (from (3A.9) and (3A.10))

if $p^{tp} \leq p^{tp*} \Rightarrow \dfrac{\partial^2 \tilde{D}}{\partial p^{tp} \partial \mu_a^d} = \dfrac{\partial \zeta}{\partial p^{tp}} K_T$ and $\dfrac{\partial^2 \tilde{\tilde{D}}}{\partial p^{tp} \partial \mu_a^f} = -\dfrac{1}{(1-\zeta)^2} \dfrac{\partial \zeta}{\partial p^{tp}} K_T$

if $p^{tp} > p^{tp*} \Rightarrow \dfrac{\partial^2 \tilde{D}}{\partial p^{tp} \partial \mu_a^d} = -\delta\dfrac{\partial \zeta}{\partial p^{tp}} K_T$ and $\dfrac{\partial^2 \tilde{\tilde{D}}}{\partial p^{tp} \partial \mu_a^f} = \dfrac{1}{(1-\zeta)^2} \dfrac{\partial \zeta}{\partial p^{tp}} K_T$

Thus from comparative statics above (Proofs of Lemma 2) we get:

i) if $e_a > e_c > e_b$ and $p^{tp} \leq p^{tp*} \Rightarrow \dfrac{\partial^2 \tilde{D}}{\partial p^{tp} \partial \mu_a^d} < 0$ and $\dfrac{\partial^2 \tilde{\tilde{D}}}{\partial p^{tp} \partial \mu_a^f} > 0 \ \forall v_j, e_j$ under excess capacity whereas

under a scarcity of capacity whereas $\dfrac{\partial^2 \tilde{D}}{\partial p^{tp} \partial \mu_a^d} < 0$ and $\dfrac{\partial^2 \tilde{\tilde{D}}}{\partial p^{tp} \partial \mu_a^f} > 0$ only when $(e_b - e_a)(\bar{p} - v_a) < -e_a(v_b - v_a)$;

ii) if $e_a > e_c > e_b$ and $p^{tp} > p^{tp*} \Rightarrow \dfrac{\partial^2 \tilde{D}}{\partial p^{tp} \partial \mu_a^d} < 0$ and $\dfrac{\partial^2 \tilde{\tilde{D}}}{\partial p^{tp} \partial \mu_a^f} > 0 \ \forall v_j, e_j$ under excess capacity whereas

under a scarcity of capacity whereas $\dfrac{\partial^2 \tilde{D}}{\partial p^{tp} d\mu_a^d} > 0$ and $\dfrac{\partial^2 \tilde{\tilde{D}}}{\partial p^{tp} \partial \mu_a^f} < 0$ only when $(e_a - e_b)(\bar{p} - v_b) < -e_b(v_a - v_b)$;

iii) if $e_c > e_b > e_a$ and $(e_b - e_a)(\hat{v} - v_a) > (\hat{e} - e_a)(v_b - v_a) \Rightarrow \dfrac{\partial^2 \widetilde{D}}{\partial p^{tp} \partial \mu_a^d} > 0$

and $\dfrac{\partial^2 \widetilde{D}}{\partial p^{tp} \partial \mu_a^f} < 0$;

iv) if $e_c > e_b > e_a$ and $(e_b - e_a)(\hat{v} - v_a) < (\hat{e} - e_a)(v_b - v_a) \Rightarrow \dfrac{\partial^2 \widetilde{D}}{\partial p^{tp} \partial \mu_a^d} < 0$

and $\dfrac{\partial^2 \widetilde{D}}{\partial p^{tp} \partial \mu_a^f} > 0$.

High Allowance Prices

In this subsection, we report the figures referring to the high allowance price scenario. Figures 3A.1 and 3A.2 illustrate the MPTR curves and Figure 3A.3 shows the results of quantitative simulations (the volume-weighted average MPTR). Comments on these figures are reported in the text of this chapter.

For the sake of simplicity, we report only examples referring to Scenario 1. Figures 3A.1 and 3A.2 refer to an allowance price around 60 €/tonCO$_2$, just above the switching price between coal and CCGT plants. As can be noted, the outcome is very similar to that under low allowance prices.[32] This time, however, it is more likely that the MPTR could be less than 1 in the off-peak hours.

Technical Parameters of Power Plants

Table 3A.1 reports variable costs, emission rates and energy efficiencies of power generating technologies adopted throughout the chapter.

Table 3A.1   Technical parameters of the power generating plants

	Oil-fired steam cycle	Gas-fired steam cycle	CCGT	Coal	CHP-CCGT
Variable cost (v), €/MWh	60	56	42	25	33
CO$_2$ emission rate (e), kg/MWh	790	500	400	840	550
Efficiency (η)	0.35	0.40	0.50	0.40	0.70*

Note: * Including heat (that is, useful heat plus power divided by fuel consumption).

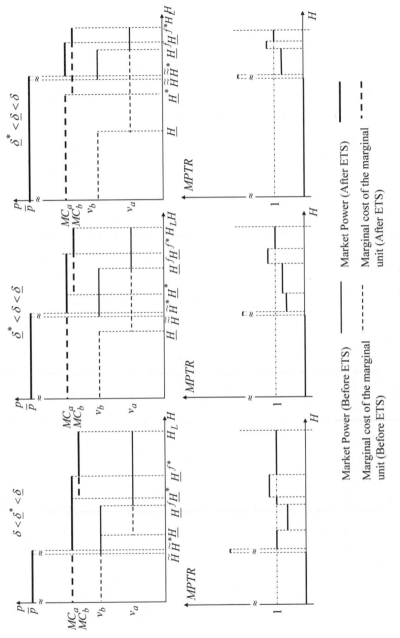

Figure 3A.1   MPTR curves ($\underline{\mu}^d = \underline{\mu}l$): high allowance prices and with excess capacity

73

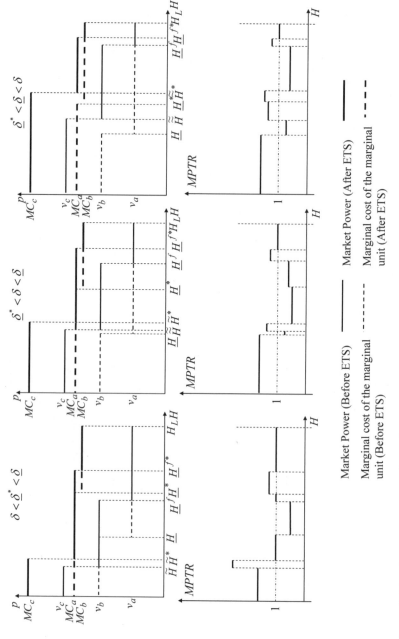

Figure 3A.2   *MPTR curves* ($\underline{\mu}^d = \underline{\mu}^f$): *high allowance prices and with excess capacity*

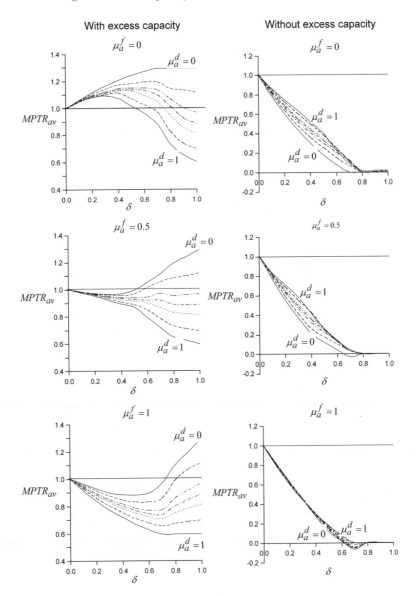

Figure 3A.3 MPTR$_{av}$ *with trade-off in the plant mix and high allowance prices*

NOTES

1. For a detailed decription of the EU ETS and its implications, see Chernyavs'ka (this volume, Chapter 2).
2. Indeed, this is a very recent question. Currently, in Europe there is a controversial debate on whether (and to what extent) the rise in power prices is due to the pass-through of the carbon opportunity cost.
3. Main contributions deal with (i) comparative studies of alternative policy tools (Bohm and Russell, 1985), (ii) analysis of static and dynamic efficiency, (iii) studies of the effects of uncertainty and risk (Montero, 2004) as well as (iv) market power (Hahn, 1984; Malueg, 1990; Eshel, 2005) and (v) transaction costs (Stavins, 1995).
4. This question is also important for another reason. The impact of the ETS on electricity prices influences power demand and consequently the environmental performance of the market. Many authors deal with the link between market structure and environmental issues. For a survey, see Requate (2005).
5. The COMPETES model. For details of this model, see Day et al. (2002) and Hobbs and Rijkers (2004a, 2004b).
6. In particular price elasticity choice is very important in simulating the impact of the ETS and can undermine the effectiveness of a model. For example, the existence of Nash equilibria within the Cournot model requires substantial negative price elasticity. This is the case, for example, of the COMPETES model cited above, whereas completely inelastic demand seems to be more appropriate for the power industry, at least in the short run. Moreover, Bolle (1992) proves that in this latter case no equilibrium exists in the supply-function model.
7. See Smeers (1997, 2005), von der Fehr and Harbord (1998) and Borenstein et al. (1999).
8. Among these models the authors include the 'capacity-constrained, Bertrand competition' approach and the 'repeated interaction, price collusion' approach. Other authors (Borenstein et al., 1999) emphasize the usefulness of the flexible Cournot–Nash approach, in order to incorporate other institutional aspects of the electricity markets (bilateral trading, startup costs, ramping rate, transmission constraints and so on) and to study the capacity withholding problem.
9. This group is based on competition with supply functions, which means that producers can select their strategies from a space with an infinite number of dimensions. One of the main advantages of a supply-function equilibrium model is that it seems to be suited to the characteristics of the actual electricity markets. The general formulation of this model was introduced by Klemperer and Meyer (1989). Bolle (1992) and Green and Newbery (1992) provide applications to the UK electricity market. For an interesting comment about the results of this latter contribution, see von der Fehr and Harbord (1993, 1998). Recent works using the supply-function approach have extended the previous analyses in order to include contract markets and contestable entry (Newbery, 1998).
10. Many contributions use the 'auction' approach in order to model competition in electricity markets. Among them, the contribution by von der Fehr and Harbord (1993). This approach has recently been extended in order to study the discriminatory or 'pay your bid' electricity auctions (von der Fehr et al., 2006).
11. The model presented in this section is an extension of that used by Bonacina and Gullì (2007).
12. Most contributions using auction models assume inelastic demand (for example, von der Fehr and Harbord, 1993; Crampes and Creti, 2005; von der Fehr et al., 2006). In this chapter this hypothesis mainly reflects the fact that hourly demand forecasts announced by the market operator are fixed quantities. Indeed, the aggregate demand should exhibit some elasticity, to the extent that eligible customers are allowed to announce demand bids. Nevertheless, observation highlights that the price elasticity of demand is very low (Crampes and Creti, 2005). Furthermore, a reasonable way (even if not optimal) to justify this assumption is to consider the short term. However, it is important to under-

line that focusing on the short term implies not considering medium- and long-term strategies of utilities in managing their fuel and hydro reserves, and therefore may not represent correctly their bidding strategies. This may explain to a certain extent the difference between empirical and simulated results.

13. Assuming that each group includes the same number n of units implies that k_j depends on K_j. This is an arbitrary assumption, however, which does not undermine the significance of the analysis.

14. The electricity sector accounts for basically 50 per cent of the EU ETS. Therefore, in principle it has a certain power to influence prices in the carbon market. However, in our analysis, what is important is the ability to do this in the single electricity firm. This ability is relatively low if we consider the entire European carbon market. Moreover, most studies on carbon emissions trading schemes assume the firms behave as price takers in the carbon market. This assumption is acceptable when there are other firms outside the oligopolistic industry (other output industries or other power industries) that operate on the same permit market (Requate, 2005). This is the case for the European carbon market which is the largest multi-country and multi-sector ETS.

15. For a comparative analysis of the different allocation methods, see Burtraw et al. (2001) and Harrison and Radov (2002).

16. Underallocation and change in firms' taxation are some of the options taken into consideration for the second phase of the EU ETS in some countries in order to reduce the so-called (and supposed) 'windfall profits'.

17. This way of defining the MPTR seems to be more appropriate from a theoretical point of view as long as one intends to consider the overall change in marginal prices due to the ETS. See Sijm et al. (2005).

18. Throughout this chapter, we consider that there is market power when firms are able to set prices above the level that would arise under perfect competition.

19. Without any loss of generality, curves are carried out by assuming 20 € /tonCO$_2$, which is consistent with the average values in 2005 and 2006.

20. The reason for this latter choice is that we intend to separate the effect of market concentration and that of plant mix. In fact, as pointed out previously, increasing degree of market concentration implies increasing total capacity in the most-efficient plants if $\mu^d > \mu^f$, and inversely if $\mu^d < \mu^f$. Instead, if $\mu^d = \mu^f$ the overall plant mix does not depend on δ, so simplifying the economic interpretation.

21. In fact, a rise in μ^f determines decreasing $\underline{H}$ and $\underline{H}^f$ while $\tilde{H}$ and $\tilde{H}^*$ do not vary. At the same time, to the extent that μ^d decreases, $\underline{H}$ moves slowly towards the low load together with $\tilde{H}$ and $\tilde{H}^*$. The range of negative differential impact will therefore tend to disappear.

22. We assume $\bar{p} = 500$ €/MWh which is the value currently adopted for the Italian wholesale spot market.

23. Indeed, 20 € /tonCO$_2$ is widely considered as the most likely price in the long run for the European market whereas 60 €/tonCO$_2$ is low plausible but not impossible. The EU ETS, in fact, introduces two levels of excess emissions penalty in the case in which operators do not deliver sufficient allowances by 30 April each year to cover their emissions during the preceding year: 40 € /tonCO$_2$ in the first period and 60 € /tonCO$_2$ in the second period. Nevertheless these values must not be considered as possible maximum allowance prices (in the respective periods) because firms must deliver the allowances corresponding to the exceeding emissions in any case.

24. In particular we set $D(H) = D_M + \theta H$, where $\theta = (D_L - D_M)/H_L < 0$ and $D_L = 0.3D_M$.

25. Intuitively, under perfect competition, prices include the carbon opportunity cost of the most-polluting plants (a) at most hours whereas, under market power, firms pass through into prices the carbon cost of both the peaking technology (c) and the least-polluting plants (b) in a certain number of hours (increasing in δ).

26. Intuitively, when δ is high (and regardless of μ^f_a) or both δ and μ^f_a are low, prices include the carbon cost of the least-polluting plants (b) at most hours, under perfect competition. Under market power, instead, prices include the carbon cost of the peaking technology (c) in a certain number of hours. When low δ are combined with high μ^f_a, firms pass through

into prices the carbon cost of the most-polluting plants (*a*) at most hours, under both perfect competition and market power. Nevertheless, there is a small period of (peak) hours in which prices converge to the marginal cost of the least-polluting plants (*b*), in the former case, and to the marginal cost of the peaking technology (*c*), in the latter case.

27. In this case, in fact, the increase in prices equals the carbon cost of the most-polluting plants (*a*) at most times, under perfect competition. Under market power, instead, the increase in prices is significantly less than the carbon cost of the most-polluting plants at most times, because of the switching effect.
28. Indeed, this assumption does not reflect what occurs in the real power market where price elasticity changes during the period of consumption.
29. Strictly speaking, only offer prices of units that may become marginal units (that is, units belonging to group *b*) need to equal the price cap or the backstop price.
30. Note that assuming a dominant firm with a competitive fringe model, rather than an oligopolistic framework, ensures that equilibria in pure strategies do exist. For an explanation of why equilibria in pure strategies do not exist in the case of oligopolistic competition, see von der Fehr and Harbord (1993).
31. Strictly speaking, bidding $\overline{MC}$ for units of kind *b* and $p \leq \overline{MC} - \epsilon$ (where $\epsilon \simeq 0^+$) for units of kind *a*.
32. As pointed out before, explaining how the ETS can impact on market power under high allowance prices is beyond the scope of this chapter. However, it is possible to demonstrate that $\hat{D} > \hat{D}^*$ if the allowance price is not very high (even if it is above the switching price). This is the case simulated in Figures 3A.1 and 3A.2.

REFERENCES

Bohm, P. and Russell, C. (1985), *Comparative Analysis of Alternative Policy Instruments*, Handbook of Natural Resource and Energy Economics, Amsterdam: North-Holland.

Bolle, F. (1992), 'Supply function equilibria and the danger of tacit collusion: the case of spot markets for electricity', *Energy Economics*, **14**, 94–102.

Bonacina, M. and Gulli, F. (2007), 'Electricity pricing under "carbon emission trading": a dominant firm with competitive fringe model', *Energy Policy*, **35**, 4200–220.

Borenstein, S., Bushnell, J. and Knitell, C.R. (1999), 'Market power in electricity markets: beyond concentrations measures', *Energy Journal*, **20** (4), 65–88.

Burtraw, D., Palmer, K., Bharvirkar, R. and Paul, A. (2001), 'The Effect of Allowance Allocation on the Cost of Carbon Emission Trading', Resources for the Future, Discussion Paper, 01–30, August.

Crampes, C. and Creti, A. (2005), 'Capacity competition in electricity markets', *Economia Delle Fonti di Energia e dell'Ambiente*, **2**, 59–83.

Day, C., Hobbs, B. and Pang, J.S. (2002), 'Oligopolistic competition in power networks: a conjectured supply function approach', *IEEE Transactions on Power Systems*, **27** (3), 597–607.

Eshel, D.M.D. (2005), 'Optimal allocation of tradable pollution rights and market structures', *Journal of Regulatory Economics*, **28** (2), 205–23.

Green, R.J. and Newbery, D.M. (1992), 'Competition in the British electricity spot market', *Journal of Political Economy*, **100** (5), 929–53.

Hahn, R.W. (1984), 'Market power and transferable property rights', *Quarterly Journal of Economics*, **99** (4), 753–65.

Harrison, D. and Radov, D. (2002), *Evaluation of Alternative Initial Allocation*

Mechanisms in a European Union Greenhouse Gases Emissions Allowance Trading Scheme, NERA Economic Consulting, Boston, MA, Prepared for DG Environment, European Union, March.

Hobbs, B. and Rijkers, F. (2004a), 'Strategic generation with conjectured transmission price responses in a mixed transmission system I: Formulation', *IEEE Transactions on Power Systems*, **19** (2), 707–17.

Hobbs, B. and Rijkers, F. (2004b), 'Strategic generation with conjectured transmission price responses in a mixed transmission system I: Application', *IEEE Transactions on Power Systems*, **19** (2), 872–8.

Klemperer, P.D. and Meyer, M.A. (1989), 'Supply function equilibria in oligopoly under uncertainty', *Econometrica*, **57** (6), 1243–77.

Lise, W. (2005), '*The European electricity market – what are the effects of market power on prices and the environment?*', Paper presented at the EcoMod2005 International Conference, Istanbul ECN-RX-05-190, 29 June–2 July.

Lise, W., Linderhof, V., Kulk, O., Kemfert, C., Ostling, R. and Heinzow, T. (2006), 'A game theoretical model of the Northwestern European electricity market – market power and the environment', *Energy Policy*, **35** (15), 2123–36.

Malueg, D.A. (1990), 'Welfare consequences of emission credit trading programs', *Journal of Environmental Economics and Management*, **18** (1), 66–77.

Montero, J.P. (2004), 'Market for environmental protection: design and performance', *Estudios de Economía*, **31**, 79–99.

Newbery, D. (1981), 'Oil prices, cartels, and the problem of dynamic inconsistency', *Economic Journal*, **91** (363), 617–46.

Newbery, D. (1998), 'Competition contracts and entry in the electricity spot market', *RAND Journal of Economics*, **29** (4), 726–49.

Newbery, D. (2005), 'Emission trading and the impact on electricity prices', mimeo, Department of Applied Economics, University of Cambridge, 14 December.

Reinaud, J. (2003), 'Emissions Trading and its Possible Impacts on Investment Decisions in the Power Sector', IEA Information Paper, International Energy Agency, Paris.

Requate, T. (2005), 'Environmental Policy under Imperfect Competition – A Survey', CAU, Kiel, Economics Working Papers, 2005–12.

Sijm, J., Bakker, S., Chen, Y. and Harmsen, H. (2005), CO_2 *Price Dynamics: The Implications of EU Emissions Trading for the Price of Electricity*, ECN Report, Petter, *ECN*-C-05-081, September.

Smeers, Y. (1997), 'Computable equilibrium models and the restructuring of the European electricity and gas markets', *Energy Journal*, **18** (4), 1–32.

Smeers, Y. (2005), 'How Well Can One Measure Market Power in Restructured Electricity Systems?', SESSA Working Paper 8, Brussels.

Stavins, R.N. (1995), 'Transaction costs and tradable permits', *Journal of Environmental Economics and Management*, **29** (2), 133–48.

von der Fehr, N., Fabra, N. and Harbord, D. (2006), 'Designing electricity auctions', *RAND Journal of Economics*, **37**, 23–46.

von der Fehr, N. and Harbord, D. (1993), 'Spot market competition in the UK electricity industry', *Economic Journal*, **103** (418), 531–46.

von der Fehr, N. and Harbord, D. (1998), 'Competition in electricity spot markets – economic theory and international experience', Memorandum, no. 5, Department of Economics, University of Oslo.

Wals, A. and Rijkers, F. (2003), *How will a CO_2 price affect the playing field in the Northwest European Power Sector?*, ECN Report, September.

4. From electricity prices to electricity costs: impact of emissions trading on industry's electricity purchasing strategies[1]

Julia Reinaud

4.1 INTRODUCTION

The European Union introduced the European Emissions Trading Scheme (EUETS) on 1 January 2005, which sets caps for the CO_2 emissions of some 11,500 plants across the EU25. Installations have the flexibility to increase emissions above their caps provided that they acquire emission allowances to cover emissions above that level. Installations with emissions below caps are allowed to sell unused allowances. The EU ETS has sparked a vibrant EU allowance (EUA) market, with transactions totalling €28 billion in 2007 (PointCarbon, 2008), and created a visible price of CO_2. This price is now another cost component of covered installations, including power generators, by far the largest emitter in the scheme. Other local or regional governments are at various stages of discussion or implementation of emissions trading schemes (Reinaud and Philibert, 2007).

With the introduction of CO_2 emission constraints on power generators in the EU, climate policy is starting to have notable effects on energy markets. The rise in electricity prices over the last few years has taken place in a context of high fossil-fuel prices, with an upward trend in oil and gas prices. Since 2005, electricity prices have been affected by two major fundamental changes: an increase in fossil-fuel prices and natural gas in particular, and the introduction of a CO_2 price, itself boosted by gas prices.[2] The two factors have been compounded into higher market prices – and costs – for energy-intensive users (see Figure 4.1).

This chapter sheds light on the links between CO_2 prices, electricity prices and electricity costs to industry. Beyond a theoretical approach to the CO_2 and electricity pricing interactions, it describes:

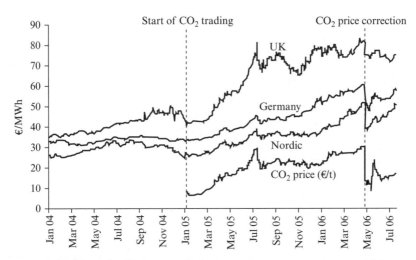

Source: Cartal (2006) sourcing Morgan Stanley.

Figure 4.1   Electricity and CO$_2$ prices between January 2004 and July 2006

- how industrial users purchase their electricity in Europe;
- how such a practice may affect the CO$_2$ price signal; and
- how increases in electricity prices may translate into increases in electricity costs for energy-intensive industries (EIIs).

4.2   CO$_2$ PRICES IN ELECTRICITY PRICES: A CONDITION FOR COST-EFFECTIVE CO$_2$ REDUCTIONS

Economic theory explains why, under a cap-and-trade system, the price of emissions ought to be treated as an opportunity cost – that is, as if each installation under compliance had to pay for every tonne of CO$_2$ emitted. As a generator holds allowances, the production of CO$_2$-emitting electricity competes with the possibility of selling the unused allowances. This so-called 'opportunity cost' of CO$_2$ allowances, equal to the CO$_2$ market price, is therefore incorporated into operators' decisions to generate electricity and is independent of whether allowances are given for free or paid for. Hence, when generators or market players price electricity, it is economically rational to include the CO$_2$ opportunity cost. This opportunity cost should also, in theory, be applicable to both spot and future power prices, and independent of the allocation mode.

In the first EU ETS trading period (2005–07), most EUAs have been distributed for free to installations. Whether or not the full opportunity cost of such free allowances finds its way to end-user electricity prices depends on several elements including: contractual agreements between suppliers and end-users, regulatory frameworks, but also the elasticity of demand and the rules used by governments to allocate EUAs. The possibility that future allowances could be distributed on the basis of current emissions creates an incentive not to pass through the full opportunity cost, as this may result in lower demand, lower emissions and a lower 'windfall profit' allocation for both fossil-fuel and carbon-free technologies. The economic rationale behind a 'cap-and-trade' system is none the less that the price of emissions should be reflected in final prices, to encourage lower consumption, and to encourage cleaner generation through higher expected revenues. Only then can such a scheme trigger an overall cost-effective response to the emission constraint.

There is no universal answer to how the EU ETS has affected electricity prices. First, there is no single EU electricity market, but several markets and regulatory frameworks across the EU (EASAC, 2006). Second, many other factors affect generation prices, such as high natural gas prices in 2005 or the potential use of market power by electric utilities. Third, in the cases where no data can be gathered on bidding strategies or the marginal supplier to the market, determining the precise level of pass-through of CO_2 prices in electricity prices is not possible. Without adequate information on the price-setting technologies across markets, countries and load periods, and without explaining away other volatility factors in the price, empirical estimates of pass-through rates remain tentative.

None the less, if any evidence is needed of the CO_2 pass-through into electricity prices, it was provided by the abrupt fall of the CO_2 price in May 2006, as market players were made aware of the excess quantity of EUAs for the year 2005. The fall by €10/tCO_2 was immediately followed by a drop in wholesale electricity prices of €5–10/MWh (PointCarbon).[3] This electricity price adjustment can be directly attributable to the CO_2 price fall, itself not connected to other energy market movements that could also affect electricity prices.

4.3 ENERGY-INTENSIVE INDUSTRIES

EIIs are defined as industries whose purchases of energy products and electricity exceed a certain threshold. These contain the iron and steel, aluminium, cement, paper and pulp and chemical sectors, among others. One

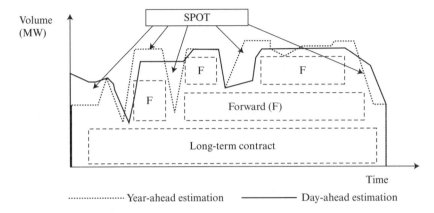

Note: The final cost for large electricity users should include a negotiated 'fee' to manage the load curve based on daily consumption and compensate for sales costs, and regulated grid charges.

Source: Boisseleau (2003).

Figure 4.2   *An example of an industrial facility's electricity purchasing strategy*

characteristic of energy-intensive users is that their profitability varies strongly according to energy prices. If such producers are unable to transfer their cost volatility onto their prices, it is in their interest to minimize the cost components' volatility. Volatility is inherent to the electricity market, and electricity prices are more volatile than other fuel commodities. CO_2 prices and their associated volatility may have participated in increasing the electricity price volatility.

Electricity consumption patterns of industrial facilities differ between and within sectors. Nevertheless, when purchasing electricity through the market, optimization of the production process leads a number of electric-intensive consumption profiles to mimic a 'ribbon' of base-load electricity.

Figure 4.2 gives an example of an energy-intensive facility's consumption load and the way electricity can be purchased to minimize price volatility. The consumption profile can be divided into several blocks. Where electricity can be purchased in advance (for example, through forward or futures contracts), the industrial facility may choose to do so. EIIs can purchase electricity by using a mix of instruments: long-term and forward contracts for the bulk of their consumption. Then, the quasi-instantaneous demand, here represented by the areas between the dashed lines and the solid line, can be met by spot transactions qualified as day-ahead. Intra-day or intra-hour adjustments are quoted differently.

As illustrated in Figure 4.2, end-user prices are a mix of various market prices and differ among end-user categories (for example, energy-intensive users, small enterprises and so on). Hence, the impact of CO_2 on end-user electricity prices is even less known than the impact on generation prices. How does the electricity cost faced by industrial energy users relate to the prices observed on electricity markets (whether they are organized through an exchange or not)? Obviously, the relationship hinges on industries' power-purchasing strategies. As a result, changes in electricity costs for energy-intensive industries may not simply be estimated from day-ahead or forward electricity price variations – although supply contracts are some-times indexed to exchange prices.[4] For example, as explained below, some industrial electricity users are still bound by long-term contracts. Others may have adopted purchasing strategies based on forward electricity prices, thus limiting their exposure to both electricity and CO_2 allowance price volatility.[5] This means that there may not be a direct correspondence between rising and falling electricity market prices and those being paid by customers.

4.4   FROM ELECTRICITY GENERATION PRICES TO INDUSTRIAL ELECTRICITY COSTS

The impact of CO_2 allowances on retail power prices requires, among other things, an analysis of contractual arrangements between industry and power suppliers in the different countries. However, precise data on the type of supply contracts are unavailable. Indeed, in liberalized energy markets, eligible customers are entitled to choose their energy supplier and contract among a range of possibilities.

In general, there are two categories of prices paid by eligible customers. In the first, the final price paid by the industry is based on the sum of several elements: the price for a block of electricity set by trading entities via electronic trading platforms (that is, of the electricity market), a nego-tiated 'fee' to manage the load curve based on daily consumption and compensate for sales costs, and regulated grid charges. Energy-intensive users mainly belong to this category. In the second category, many cus-tomers purchase at an 'all-inclusive price'. This practice is mainly exer-cised in the framework of regulated prices. There is also a third category, where prices can comprise different components. This is the case for industries that self-generate their electricity. In theory, unless dealt with differently, the price for electricity should be the sum of the variable cost components to produce electricity, and fixed costs associated with the plant.

There are many combinations of different underlying arrangements in the electricity market for industry in the EU25. To give an overall picture of industries' different electricity purchasing methods, this section distinguishes three main electricity purchasing strategies: (i) the installation purchases its electricity directly or indirectly through market mechanisms – both on a short- and a long-term basis; (ii) the installation adopts regulated tariffs, where such an option exists; and (iii) the installation produces the majority of its electricity consumption alone or with a third party.

4.5 ELECTRICITY PURCHASED THROUGH MARKET MECHANISMS

Electricity purchased through market mechanisms is defined differently from self-generation or electricity purchased at prices fixed by government authorities. Access to the market can be either direct if the industry buys electricity without an intermediary, or indirect if the industry uses a supplier or a broker to purchase electricity for its needs. Electricity can be bought on an organized market exchange (for example, Powernext, European Energy Exchange: EEX and so on) or a non-organized (that is, brokered) electronic trading platform (for example, Spectron, Platts and so on).

Contracts with suppliers or brokers can have fixed or flexible prices, indexed on specific elements such as fuel prices or the industry's product prices. The contracts can cover a customer's entire consumption, or only a share of the consumption. Contractual agreements can also be based on a specific technology or on a mix of technologies. If there is transparency in the price settlement, depending on the contract established with the supplier, industries' costs can be equal, depending on whether the installation purchases directly on the market or signs a purchase agreement with a supplier/generator for power contracts.[6] Price settlement is considered transparent when the price is indexed to a market indicator known by all parties or prices are fixed. In the case where the buyer decides to take the same price risk as that of the supplier, it could develop a similar price system as the one offered by the supplier.

Suppliers have a similar method to industries that purchase on the forward market in setting prices for fixed-term contracts (EC, 2005). The cost to serve the bulk consumption of industries is assessed with the help of forward price quotations prevailing at the time the offer is prepared. The result is the actual cost of covering forward the client's consumption on the market (ibid.). This practice applies irrespective of whether the consumer will in reality be supplied from the supplier's own generation portfolio or covered by electricity purchases from the market.

The volume of long-term contracts with electricity suppliers has undergone a cyclical movement. Before liberalization, and during its first years, long-term contracts were frequently concluded between EIIs and power producers – essentially the incumbent monopoly in each country – and many of these contracts are still running. The majority of the long-term contract prices were established on a cost-plus basis from the generator's perspective. However, a number of these long-term contracts are coming to an end in the EU15 countries. At present, given the current lack of confidence in short-term markets and the large increases in price over the past 10 years, long-term contracts have become attractive again because of the competitiveness of EIIs, in particular as they take into account major new investments.

At present, pre-liberalization-type long-term contracts are being replaced among others by shorter-term contracts (no longer than one to two years in the majority of European electricity markets), and a new form of long-term contract.

Shorter-term contracts

Supply contracts may be qualified as short term if they last for three years or less. In the UK, typical supply contracts run from April to March of the following year and are renegotiated each year. They are indexed to a large extent to market prices and often include a link to gas forward prices as well. As a result, industrial end-user prices are usually more volatile in the UK than in other countries in Europe.

In France, for industries which do not have long-term fixed prices, in most cases, the contractual prices may be the sum of several elements: the baseload curve price which depends on the market price (90 per cent or more based on future/forward prices or other indexes); a flexibility of the consumption curve which depends on the power consumption volatility; an adjustment cost in the case of very short-term changes in consumption (based on the balancing market prices); and the supplier's margin.[7]

The pricing formula may be the same in other European countries, and where no forward or future market exists, such as in Italy, the common practice may be for suppliers to develop annual supply contracts based on historical day-ahead prices if the market is mature enough, forward prices of the different price components (for example, fuel and CO_2), or the supplier's own generation portfolio if it owns one.

The preliminary question to ask regarding the influence of CO_2 allowance costs on contractual prices is whether they are all-inclusive prices or whether the contractual price makes reference to a market indicator. If the electricity price is indexed to an electricity market indicator, then it is probable that these include the opportunity cost of CO_2 allowances – unless regulatory intervention threatens to or has blocked any pass-through (for example, in Italy). If the breakdown of the contractual price is opaque, and the final customer pays all-inclusive prices, then the influence of the CO_2 cost component cannot be assessed.

A new form of long-term contract

Today, entering into long-term agreements without sharing part of the investment risk is not an attractive proposition from the viewpoint of a power generator. Two reasons may explain this: first, the electricity companies may not see the economic rationale of fixing prices for up to 20 years ahead in the current volatile market, when they may not even know from which source the electricity will be produced, and thus offer 'unacceptable' prices; second, there is a supposed fear that such long-term contracts will be deemed illegal due to competition law. This second reason remains a grey area, and further research needs to be carried out on the subject.

In some member states, agreements have been concluded, or are being planned, which promote long-term partnerships between customers and energy suppliers (EC, 2006).

Examples of new forms of long-term contracts   In France, in 2006, a consortium, Exeltium, was founded by seven energy-intensive companies. Membership requires purchasing shares in the independent company, at a price corresponding to an advance payment of long-term supplies. This is designed to provide funds to invest in generation. Exeltium launched a call for tender, addressing European electricity producers, with the aim of creating an electricity supply mechanism by mid-2007. The mechanism is based on the acquisition, by the industrial groups, of drawing rights with a duration of at least 15 years, which would reserve a stable energy supply for them, at prices linked to the most-competitive production costs.[8] Industry members would then pay for the variable costs of the purchased electricity. The members' aim is to secure blocks of electricity for a 15–20-year period. The price risk for each industry to manage is the adjustment between the contracted capacity and the facilities' real consumption. A French law was promulgated in order to define which energy-intensive users would be entitled to participate.The mechanism created by Exeltium is open to other industrial groups, within the limits of criteria set by the French authorities; it was established that some 50 companies are eligible, in addition to the seven founding members.

In the UK, Centrica, a gas and power supplier, announced a five-year coal-priced electricity supply contract with Drax Power Limited in 2006. Drax Power Limited is the owner and operator of Drax Power Station, the largest coal-fired power station in the UK. The agreement, which will provide Centrica with access to 600 MW of power, enables Centrica to further stabilize the cost of supplying electricity to its customers. The agreement will supply base-load power to Centrica under a contract linked to international coal prices, which will include seasonal fixed clean dark spreads.[9] (Whether or not Centrica will in reality be supplied by Drax is not the question, the idea behind this type of contract is that both parties have signed a contract based on a coal market risk.) This agreement provides the supplying company with greater coal and CO_2 exposure – the price of coal is less volatile than, for example, electricity or gas prices. Although this agreement is not between an industry and a supplier, it may very well be possible that similar contracts will be developed between these players.

The impact of the CO_2 constraint on contract prices is unclear and depends on the negotiated terms of the contract and whether the environmental constraint was regarded as probable at the time of negotiation. It is possible, for example, that fixed long-term contracts not indexed to market prices and concluded before market liberalization, do not take into account CO_2 prices and costs. In such a case, generators or suppliers cannot pass through the opportunity cost of allowances or the purchase of allowances for compliance. In our interviews, it was indicated that the new long-term contracts indexed to coal prices include an indexation to CO_2 prices.

Nevertheless, we should be careful when considering that long-term contracts can influence the pass-through. What matters in a well-functioning market is the reference price. Thus, although such contracts protect industries from increases in power prices (which can be due to CO_2 allowances), if the reference price includes a share of the CO_2 cost, long-term contracts which are indexed to market prices would in fact include a CO_2 cost.

The final electricity price

The final price quoted to the consumer (that is, the contractual price) will depend on whether the industrial consumer is able to negotiate with a supplier or whether it purchases its electricity directly through the market. On a centralized market exchange, the consumer may be a price taker, whereas on a brokered market, he/she may be able to discuss the price for bulk consumption with the electricity supplier or trader. In the scenario where industry contracts a power supplier, several elements may influence the final price paid by industry. These include the level of competition and regulatory involvement (for example, mandatory price indexes fixed by the regulator or the government, set limits on price variation, rebates based on special provisions and so on).

Further, the final price paid by EIIs can often be lower than the contractual price. This is because the EIIs may obtain several discounts by signing additional clauses to the supply contract (interruptible contracts, for example), or by diversifying the sources of electricity purchases.

Interruptible supply contracts In several European countries, some industrial facilities may have their power consumption reduced by a certain amount if market prices reach a certain level – specified in the contract. Interruptibility of power supply can be made with little or no prior announcement.

Often, EIIs which subscribe to interruptible contracts receive lower tariffs than those which do not, through paybacks. In Italy, for example, without any prior announcement of interruptibility, industries are paid €21/MWh; with a 24-hour warning, they receive €8/MWh. Likewise, Sweden has taken steps to sign up large industrial customers who are willing to have their supply interrupted. Those that choose to do so receive a discount on their electricity rate.

Readiness to accept part of the price volatility risk Where the industrial facility is not risk averse to price volatility or speculates that power prices will decrease, the contractual positions can be left open to renegotiation. For example, clauses can be introduced whereby prices are re-quoted every three months.

4.5 REGULATED ELECTRICITY PRICES

In Europe, not all countries have maintained regulated tariffs for EIIs – although the second electricity liberalization directive does not stipulate their removal. In several European countries (in Italy, for example), the government has planned tariffs to prevent EIIs from relocating in countries where the electricity is cheaper – 'delocalizable electricity-intensive companies'. Many large energy users have found themselves paying more since abandoning regulated tariffs for market prices. This is partly why several countries have allowed industries to re-enter regulated tariff schemes (for example, in Italy, Spain, and since November 2006, in France) (EASAC, 2006). These countries should be differentiated from those that do not allow non-captive customers to re-enter regulated price schemes (for example, in France before the adoption of a decree on 8 November 2006).

In the case of regulated tariffs, the decision to pass through the opportunity cost of CO_2 allowances depends on each government.

The retail market in Spain is characterized by the existence of the *tarifas integrals* to which all industrial consumers are allowed to return.[10] Furthermore, certain industrial facilities are entitled to so-called 'G4 tariffs'.[11] Spanish regulated tariffs are not connected to market prices: in June 2006, the latter reached approximately €24, while day-ahead power prices were around €55. The White Book (Ministerio de Economía y

Hacienda, 2005) that was published in 2005 nevertheless underlines the need to bring these tariffs in line with the actual cost incurred by companies. As a result, supply companies are anticipating that the regulated tariff will incorporate part of the cost associated with the CO_2 constraint. However, it is expected that only the cost of purchasing CO_2 will be included in the tariff, and not the opportunity cost of CO_2 allowances.

In Italy, industrial customers can, whenever they choose to do so, return to the captive market (whose customers are supplied by the single buyer). In this case they would pay a tariff linked to the weighted average portfolio cost of the single buyer (plus some cost components stipulated by the AEEG – the electricity regulator). Nevertheless, an *ad hoc* tariff for industries does not exist.

In Hungary, an eligible customer can move from the administratively priced captive to the free market segment and vice versa at almost no cost. The advantage of the free market lasts only until it is cheaper than public service. The size of the competitive free market segment is determined by the relative prices on the free market and of public supply.

In CENTREL markets, the electricity directive foresees the transition to full market eligibility somewhat vaguely.[12] While 'vulnerable' consumers might be supplied with electricity at an administratively set tariff, there seems to be no explicit constraint on who else might also be eligible for the status of a 'regulated' consumer after July 2007. Until eligible customers have the right to choose from the administrative and the competitive price – and this is a low-cost choice – some kind of competition between the two market segments may develop. A consequence might be that the free market price will converge to the administratively set price. It is, therefore, up to each regulator/government to decide whether regulated prices pass through the CO_2 cost.

Self-generation with or without a Third Party

The decision to auto-produce electricity is mostly available at the project design phase: afterwards, the choice is largely irreversible. Industry experts explain that the building of on-site cogeneration is economically justified only in the case of industrial processes using both electricity and heat. Generally, energy-intensive users decide to generate their own electricity in mainly three cases:

1. When the fuel price is low (that is, easy access to low-cost natural resources);
2. When the quality of the transmission or electricity is poor; and/or
3. When the cost savings from grid transportation are high.

An industrial facility can either invest heavily in a generation asset or invest in only a share (directly or indirectly through a consortium). By integrating vertically to ensure the supply of base-load electricity at low cost, industries are able to manage the supply of their base-load needs and the price volatility.

In Europe, several manufacturing sectors own power generators. Overall, out of 695 GW representing the total capacity in operation in EU16, 63 GW belong to industry. The self-generation capacity in the EU16 is for cement, chemicals and fertilizers, equipment manufacturers, metal mining and smelters, pulp paper and forest products, sugar mills and refinery plants.[13] These numbers include another category, 'autogenerators', which belong to another industry or commercial sector. The largest self-generating sector in EU19 is the chemical sector, with 8.25 GW of installed capacity, followed by the pulp and paper sector with 6.8 GW, refineries with 4.7 GW and metal mining with 4 GW.[14] The main fuel used in the case of self-generation is natural gas fired in a gas turbine, followed by oil and coal.

Ownership is a physical hedge against fluctuations in electricity prices (IEA, 2005). The role and significance of such a physical hedge must be analysed in the context of other contracting opportunities in the market. All electricity suppliers (including self-generators, since they can sell to the industrial facility or to the grid) can sell the electricity on the market rather than to identified end-users. Therefore the market price represents the opportunity cost of selling to end-users (that is, to the industrial facility) (Lewis et al., 2004).

Whether the industrial facility will pay an overall electricity price lower than the market one depends on an internal company decision (or a decision among plant shareholders if there is multiple ownership in the generation assets). For example, the electricity produced can be sold at production cost. This is the case for the Finnish electricity company Teollisuuden Voima Oy (TVO), a cooperative of large electricity consumers and municipal utility companies, which owns two nuclear power plants already in operation and a European pressurized reactor (EPR) to be commissioned in 2012.[15] TVO agreed to sell electricity 'at cost' during the life of the EPR plant (40 years) to its investors in proportion to their contribution to the investment. This is the so-called 'Mankala principle'.[16] This investment structure should ensure stable electricity prices and become a 'physical' hedge against fluctuations in electricity prices. Moreover, it reduces investment risks by securing the demand of energy generated through long-term commitments. However, the downside to these long-term contracts lies in the fuel-price volatility over the lifetime of the investment.

If the industrial facility fully owns the generation plant and pays the market price, the extent of the CO_2 pass-through to its cost will depend on the pass-through on the market. In reality, however, there will be a

Table 4.1   Summary of whether CO$_2$ price can be passed through following a selection of pricing mechanisms

	In theory could the CO$_2$ opportunity cost be passed through?
Annual power contracts for baseload for a single facility/company	Yes
Aggregation of purchasers	It depends on the negotiation power of the parties
Aggregation of purchasers – share in payment of upfront cost of capital	It depends on the negotiation power of the parties
Day-ahead price-indexed contracts	Yes
Fuel-indexed contracts	Indirectly, it could (e.g., if the coal price is influenced by the CO$_2$ price)
Floating price with a cap and a floor	Yes to up to the cap or floor levels
Regulated prices	It depends on the regulator
Investment in generation assets	It depends on the fuel source

lump-sum transfer within the company since allowances are allocated for free with the exception of CO$_2$ allowances purchased to cover excess emissions. Thus, although the benchmark price for the internal contracts may be the market price, overall, industrial facilities in such situations will pay less than their competitors who go through suppliers or purchase electricity directly on the market. There is a wealth transfer only between the electricity-producing and the electricity-purchasing divisions. It is also possible that although the reference price remains the market price, they may agree on a price between that estimated on a cost-plus basis and the market price.

To reach a conclusion on whether self-generation contracts make reference to CO$_2$ prices and include a pass-through rate is infeasible because each situation is specific and information on such contracts is confidential data. The answer depends on the tariff practice of the different generation plant shareholders, but reference to CO$_2$ prices and inclusion of a pass-through rate is possible.

4.6   RELEVANT PRICES FOR INDUSTRY IN EUROPE

Generic Purchasing Strategies

Several electricity purchasing strategies are theoretically available to EIIs in various regulatory environments (Table 4.1), although we note that not all European countries offer all options shown, and not all industrial facilities are in a position to negotiate with generators for supply contracts, in which case they accept the supply price offered on the bilateral market. For example, bilateral electricity supply contracts can be: indexed contracts (for example, indexed on fuel plus CO_2 prices, on other commodities' markets and so on); cross-market contracts (for example, the spark spread option – the buyer of such a contract has the option to switch one unit of gas for one unit of electricity at a specified price); floating contracts including cap-and-floor prices; fixed-price contracts; or contracts for differences (that is, compensation is paid for price differences over periods agreed in advance).

Table 4.2 assesses:

- whether there is a strong link between the electricity price paid by the EIIs and the day-ahead price and whether the different electricity purchasing strategies allow EIIs to hedge their electricity bills against power price variations;
- the extent to which each strategy involves a price risk from the industrial facility's viewpoint, or allows risk sharing between generators and consumers (when the EII does not self-generate electricity); and
- whether the EIIs' purchasing strategies allow them to have a choice of generation technologies from the supplier.

Dominant form of electricity contracts in Europe by region

While the European power market is gradually becoming integrated, it remains divided into national and to a degree, regional markets. Differences in regulatory regimes and power transmission bottlenecks between countries hinder increased integration. There are several electricity markets in Europe. For each market or region, some electricity prices are more-relevant indicators to most market transactions or contracts than others. Likewise, there are different prices depending on date of delivery of the electricity (for example, intra-day, day-, month-or year-ahead and so on).

In its medium-term strategy paper for Europe's internal electricity markets, the European Commission anticipates regionalizing European power markets between 2005 and 2009 into several transnational markets before integrating them into a single EU market by 2010 (EC, 2005). The regions are: west continental Europe, Iberia, Great Britain/Ireland, East Europe, South East Europe, the Nordic region and the Baltic states.

In Europe, since not all regions operate in the same markets, purchasing strategies differ by area the most representative price indicators paid by industrial facilities are discussed below, based on interviews with industry for the IEA 2007 report (Reinaud, 2007).

Table 4.2   Summary of different electricity purchasing strategies

	Relation to day-ahead price	Risk borne by EII	EII's role in generation technology
Annual power contracts for baseload for a single facility/company	Low	Low	None
Aggregation of purchasers	Low	Low	None
Aggregation of purchasers – share in payment of upfront cost of capital	Depends on the contract	Depends on the wholesale price level	Strong
Day-ahead price-indexed contracts	Strong	Low	None
Fixed prices and quantities	None	Low	None
Fuel-indexed contracts	None	Low	None
Cross-market contracts	None	Low	None
Floating price with a cap and a floor	Yes but in a limited manner	Low	None
Contract for difference	Low	Low	None
Regulated prices	Depends on the price setting body	Low	None
Investment in generation assets alone	Depends on the market-to-market intensity	Full	Strong
Investment in generation assets with several owners	Depends on the market-to-market intensity	High	Medium to strong

Source: Reinaud (2007).

Market exchange prices set by the marginal generator   In Scandinavia, prices established on the NordPool exchange, representing the hourly marginal cost of the marginal generation plant, are the dominant element of electricity supply contracts.

'Screen prices' with block trading for baseload needs   In the UK, prices paid by industrial facilities can be set on electronic platforms (that is, 'screen pricing') through block trading (daily, monthly, trimester), generally established by continuous trading. To obtain the final cost of supply, costs of

intra-day adjustment are included. The main exception to screen pricing is the long-term contract signed between Centrica and Drax, where the price is indexed to international coal and CO_2 prices.

In continental Europe, the main supply contracts are based on screen prices for annual blocks. The final cost of electricity includes the purchase of day-ahead needs with prices set on the market exchange as well as intra-day consumption adjustments.

Annual contracts In Italy, prices are based on annual contracts via tenders.

Regulated tariffs In Spain, 'regulated' tariffs may be a chosen option although since 2006, there has been negotiation between industry and generators for the supply through long-term contracts based on the generation costs of domestic coal-fired plants.

4.7 CONCLUSION

Changes in electricity costs for EIIs may not simply be estimated from day-ahead or forward electricity price variations. Whether or not industrial contract prices are below (or above) the market price, which includes the full opportunity cost of CO_2 allowances, depends on the contractual parties (that is, suppliers, generators, EIIs). To some extent, several electricity purchasing strategies may allow EIIs to bypass or lower the opportunity cost – although it is difficult to assess, in the final analysis, which of the mark-up or CO_2 opportunity costs are reduced through such strategies. Self-generation from either non-CO_2-emitting electricity plants (for example, TVO) or plants with lower production costs than the price-setting technology is one example. In this case, plant owners may even be able to collect the rent created by the opportunity cost if they sell their excess electricity on the market, while the market price is set by a fossil-fuel technology that includes the opportunity cost. Further, supply contracts for consumers with sufficient bargaining power to negotiate the electricity price (for example, through load-curve aggregation) is another illustration, as reflected in the growing pressure to allow such practices.

The main factor to bear in mind when stating that industry prices can be lower than market prices (which may include the opportunity cost) is when the industrial facility accepts risk sharing by investing directly or indirectly (for example, through shares in a company owning the power plant) in the cost of construction of a power plant and is, therefore, in a stronger position to negotiate the contractual price. However, in doing so, it is also exposed to the risk of a lower market price in the future.

There may be another reason why industry electricity prices are lower than market prices: are we comparing the same or relevant contracts? The market price that is comparable with a contractual price based on forward prices is, for example, the price of an annual forward contract entered into on the same day that the 'bilateral' annual contract was agreed upon between a supplier and a customer. This has not been a very easy comparison in the last couple of years, when forward and contract prices have been quite volatile.

Regardless of the price paid by EIIs, they continue to be exposed to electricity price volatility. CO_2 price volatility has also participated in the price increase. Managing this volatility is essential for industrial facilities, as it may damage the competitiveness of companies – mainly for those that cannot pass through an increase in costs to their prices. Along with the rise in prices driven by the new CO_2 cost component, electricity price uncertainty and CO_2 price volatility have encouraged industry to seek more predictable electricity prices. Not all electricity markets facilitate this objective.

NOTES

1. Based on Reinaud (2007).
2. For more information, see presentations given in Session 2 of the 5th annual IEA/IETA/ EPRI (International Energy Agency, International Emissions Trading Association, Electricity Power Research Institute) emissions trading workshop, www.iea. org/textbase/work/workshopdetail.asp?WS_ID=213.
3. EurActiv (2006).
4. In the European countries where exchange-based transactions represent only a fraction of total electricity supply, this index may appear questionable.
5. Contracts for future delivery of electricity also include a measure of CO_2 pass-through. Purchasers of electricity through such contracts ensure some protection against future volatility, including CO_2 price volatility.
6. This depends on the duration of each indicator (for example, monthly; quarterly; cal; cal +1; and so on) and the risk the supplier is willing to take.
7. According to the supplier we interviewed, this tends to represent 1–3 per cent of the price.
8. Details of the agreement were not disclosed, although it was mentioned that the final price paid by the consortium would be around €40/MWh (*La Tribune*, 16 January 2007).
9. There was no mention that Centrica would not pay the full opportunity cost of CO_2 allowances. Limits on the payment of all CO_2 allowances associated with the reserved electricity from coal-fired generation would probably have resulted in a different contract settlement according to internal sources. The agreement will run to the end of the EU ETS Phase II in December 2012.
10. Nevertheless, customers who change to regulated tariffs from market prices and vice versa must guarantee to not change schemes for at least one year (Decree 1435/2002, 27/12/2002, Article 4, subparagraphs 1 and 2).
11. Eligible customers must have a contracted load of 100 MW, and consume electricity more than 8,000 hours a year, or more than 800 GWh annually. Furthermore, on a

monthly average, the facility must consume electricity more than 22 hours a day and at a 145 kV voltage.
12. CENTREL is the regional group of four transmission system operator companies: ČEPS, a.s. (Czech Republic); MAVIR ZRt. (Hungary); PSE-Operator S.A. (Poland); and Slovenská elektrizačná prenosová sústava, a.s. (SEPS, a.s, Slovak Republic), www.centrel.org.
13. Included countries are Austria, Belgium, the Czech Republic, Germany, Greece, Finland, France, Ireland, Italy, Hungary, the Netherlands, Poland, Portugal, Spain, Sweden and the UK.
14. In this classification, 'autogenerators' was not considered as a homogeneous sector. If it was, it would be second with 7.7 GW of installed capacity.
15. TVO is part of the Pohjolan Voima Group, under the parent company Pohjolan Voima Oy (PVO), which owns some 60 per cent of TVO shares. PVO was established by large industrial electricity consumers, mainly from the Finnish pulp and paper industry. These large industrial electricity consumers still represent the largest share of the owners but today PVO is also partly owned by local municipalities – either directly or through municipality-owned utilities (IEA, 2005).
16. Among other power companies that operate on the same principle are Etelä-Pohjanmaan, Kemijoki and Teollisuuden Voima.

REFERENCES

Boisseleau, François (2003), '*the role of power exchanges for the creation of a single European electricity market: market design and market regulation*', thesis, University Paris Dauphine and Delft University.

Cartal, Aurélien (2006), '*EU ETS: Quel Impact pour la Compétitivité des Industries?*', Masters thesis, Université Paris Dauphine, Paris.

EurActiv (2006), 'Crashing carbon prices puts EU climate policy to the test', May, http://www.euractiv.com/en/sustainability/crashing-carbon-prices-puts-eu-climate-policy-test/article-154873.

European Academies Science Advisory Council (EASAC) (2006), '*Price-Setting in the Electricity Markets within the EU Single Market – Briefing Note*', London, IP/A/ITRE/NT/2006-5.

European Commission (EC) (2005), *Report on Progress in Creating the Internal Gas and Electricity Market*, Brussels, http://europa.eu.int/comm/energy/electricity/report_2005/index_en.htm.

European Commission (EC) (2006), *First Report of the High Level Group on Competitiveness, Energy and the Environment*, Brussels, http://ec.europa.eu/enterprise/environment/hlg/doc_06/first_report_02_06_06.pdf.

International Energy Agency (IEA) (2005), *Lessons from a Liberalised Electricity Market*, Paris: IEA.

Lewis, Philip E., Tor A. Johnsen, Teemu Närvä and Salman Wasti (2004), *Analysing the Relationship between Wholesale and End-User Prices in the Nordic Electricity Market*, Vasa: Finnish Ministry of Trade and Industry (Kauppa-ja teollisuus-ministeriö), http://www.vaasaemg.com/pdf/466696_Sahkonhintaselvitys KTM 2004ENG.pdf.

Ministerio de Economía y Hacienda (2005), *White Paper on the Reform of the Spanish Competition System*, www.minhac.es.

Point Carbon (2008), 'Carbon 2008 – Post-2012 is now'.

Reinaud, Julia (2007), 'CO_2 *Allowance* and *Electricity Price Interaction – Impact on*

Industry's Electricity Purchasing Strategies in Europe', OECD, IEA Information Paper, Paris.

Reinaud, Julia and Cédric Philibert (2007), 'Emissions Trading: Updates and Trends', IEA/OECD, OECD, Paris.

PART II

Empirical analyses

5. Options to address concerns regarding EU ETS-induced increases in power prices and generators' profits: the case of carbon cost pass-through in Germany and the Netherlands

Jos Sijm, Sebastiaan Hers and Bas Wetzelaer

5.1 INTRODUCTION

Power prices in EU countries have increased significantly since the European Emissions Trading Scheme (EU ETS) became effective on 1 January 2005. This suggests that these increases in power prices are due to this scheme, in particular the pass-through of the costs of EU allowances (EUAs) to cover the CO_2 emissions of eligible installations. In all sectors, however – including the power sector – eligible installations have usually received almost all of their needed allowances for free during the first phase of the EU ETS (2005–07).

In several EU countries, the coincidence of the increases in power prices and the implementation of the EU ETS has raised questions, and sometimes fierce political debate, on whether power producers have indeed passed through the costs of freely allocated CO_2 allowances to electricity prices, and to what extent the increase in these prices can be attributed to this pass-through or to other factors. In addition, it has raised discussions on whether – and to what extent – the supposed passing through of these costs has led to additional profits for power producers, that is, the so-called 'windfall profits' induced by the EU ETS. Finally, the supposed ETS-induced increases in power prices and generators' profits has raised concerns affecting the legitimacy of the present EU ETS, including concerns regarding its impact on the international competitiveness of some power-intensive industries, the purchasing power of electricity end-users such as small households or, more generally, the distribution of social welfare among power producers and consumers. As a result, in several countries policy makers and stakeholders have suggested a variety of options to address these concerns, including changing the emissions trading allocation system, taxing windfall profits or controlling market prices of EU carbon allowances, electricity or both.

Against this background, the objectives of this chapter include:[1]

- To analyse empirically the trends in power prices during the 2004–06 period for two specific EU countries, that is, Germany and the Netherlands, and to assess whether and to what extent changes in these prices can be attributed to the pass-through of the costs of freely allocated EU carbon allowances or to other factors.
- To discuss the issue of windfall profits, in particular to make some qualifications to the definition and empirical estimation of windfall profits, including some rough estimates of EU ETS-induced windfall profits in the power sector of Germany and the Netherlands.
- To evaluate some policy options to address concerns regarding supposed EU ETS-induced increases in power prices and generators' profits.

The structure of the chapter is as follows. First, Section 5.2 presents some empirical analyses of price trends, cost drivers and pass-through rates (PTRs) on electricity markets in Germany and the Netherlands from 2004 to 2006. Subsequently, Section 5.3 discusses the issue of ETS-induced windfall profits in general, while providing some rough estimates of such profits in Germany and the Netherlands in particular. Next, Section 5.4 evaluates some policy options to address concerns regarding supposed EU ETS-induced increases in power prices and generators' profits. Finally, Section 5.5 gives a brief summary of the major findings, conclusions and policy implications.

5.2 EMPIRICAL ANALYSES OF PRICE TRENDS, COST DRIVERS, POWER SPREADS AND PTRs ON ELECTRICITY MARKETS

Trends in Forward Power Prices and Cost Drivers

Figure 5.1 presents trends for 2004–06 in forward (that is, year-ahead) power prices versus fuel and CO_2 emission costs to generate one MWh of electricity during the off-peak period in Germany, while Figure 5.2 shows similar trends during the peak hours in the Netherlands. These figures, and

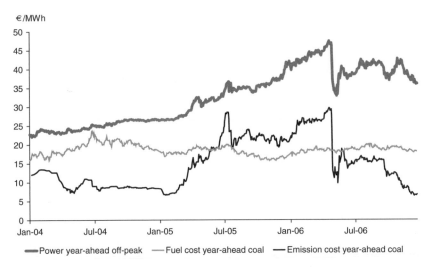

Figure 5.1 *Trends in power prices and cost drivers on forward markets in Germany during off-peak hours, 2004–2006*

the empirical analyses outlined below, are based on the following assumptions:

1. An average fuel efficiency of 35 per cent for a coal plant and 40 per cent for an open-cycle gas turbine.
2. A related emission factor of 0.97 versus 0.51 tCO_2/MWh for coal and gas, respectively.
3. CO_2 emission costs per fuel are equal to its emission factor versus the daily price of an EUA on the forward market.[2]

Figures 5.1 and 5.2 provide a first impression of the changes in power prices in 2004–06 and the potential link with underlying fuel and carbon costs, depending on the assumed price-setting technology in the countries and load periods considered as well as the emission factors and fuel efficiencies mentioned later in Tables 5.1 and 5.2, respectively. For instance, off-peak power prices in Germany are assumed to be set by a coal-fired installation. As can be observed from Figure 5.1, these prices increased substantially from less than 30 €/MWh in early 2005 to almost 50 €/MWh in April 2006. After a sudden collapse by some 15 €/MWh in late April–early May, off-peak prices in Germany started to rise again up to the summer of 2006 but, subsequently, stabilized at a level of 30–35 €/MWh in late 2006. These significant changes in power prices cannot be explained by changes

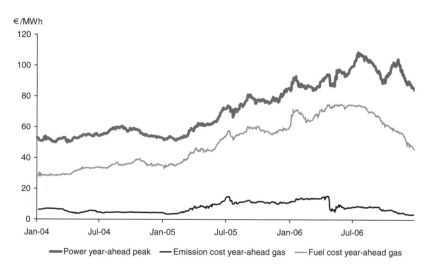

Figure 5.2   Trends in power prices and cost drivers on forward markets in the Netherlands during peak hours, 2004–2006

in coal prices, since the costs of this fuel have been rather stable at the level of 20 €/MWh over the period considered.

However, in the case of the forward off-peak power market in Germany there seems to be a close (causal) link between the prices of carbon and electricity as the changes in CO_2 emission allowance costs of coal-fired generation are more or less similar to the changes in power prices, notably during periods of major changes in the price of an EUA such as April–May 2006 (see Figure 5.1). Note, however, that the link between power prices and fuel/CO_2 cost drivers is less clear or even absent/contrary in the second half of 2006, suggesting that in this period changes in power prices have been largely affected by other factors than changes in fuel/CO_2 costs.

On the other hand, Figure 5.2 shows the trends in power prices and cost drivers on forward markets in the Netherlands during the peak period of 2004–06. For this case, power prices are assumed to be set by an open-cycle gas turbine with a fuel efficiency of 40 per cent. These prices were more or less stable during 2004, but increased rapidly from 50–55 €/MWh in early 2005 to 100–105 €/MWh in mid-2006. This increase in power prices can be largely related to rising gas prices (which, in turn, are usually related to oil-indexed prices), resulting in an increase in gas costs from 35–40 €/MWh in early 2005 to 70–75 €/MWh in mid-2006. The potential impact of gas-related CO_2 costs, however, is less substantial – rising from about 5 to 15 €/MWh between early 2005 and mid-2006 – partly due to the fact that the emission factor for gas is significantly lower than for coal.

Trends in Power Spreads on Forward Markets

In order to have a closer look and a better assessment of the potential impact of CO_2 emissions trading on forward power prices, fuel costs have been subtracted from these prices, resulting in the so-called 'power spreads'. For the present analysis, a *dark* spread is simply defined as the difference between the power price and the cost of *coal* to generate 1

BOX 5.1   DATA USED

For the empirical analyses over 2004–06, data of daily prices on forward (that is, year-ahead) markets have been used for the following commodities:

- *Power*   For Germany, power prices refer to the Phelix year-ahead contracts traded at the Leipzig-based European Energy Exchange (EEX), while for the Netherlands these prices refer to similar contracts traded at the Amsterdam-based European Energy Derivates Exchange (ENDEX). Both exchanges provide price data for base-load and peak periods, while off-peak prices have been derived from these data using country-specific definitions of peak versus off-peak periods.
- *Fuels*   Coal prices used for Germany and the Netherlands refer to the internationally traded commodity classified as coal ARA CIF API #2 (provided by McCloskey). Coal costs have been derived from the average of the daily bid and offer prices for yearly contracts (expressed in US$/tonne and converted to €/MWh by means of the daily dollar–euro exchange rate, the usual energy conversion factors and a fuel-efficiency rate of 35 per cent). Gas prices for Germany refer to the Bunde trading hub covering the whole period considered, that is, 2004–06 (as reported by Platts), while for the Netherlands gas prices refer to the Bunde hub during 2004–05 and to the Title Transfer Facility (TTF) hub for 2006 (provided by ENDEX).
- *CO_2 emission allowances*   Carbon prices for EUAs (expressed in €/tCO_2) refer to forward prices Cal05, Cal06 and Cal07 (for delivery in December 2005, 2006 and 2007, respectively, as provided by PointCarbon and NordPool).

MWh of electricity, while a *spark* spread refers to the difference between the power price and the costs of *gas* to produce a MWh of electricity. If, subsequently, the carbon costs of power production are also subtracted, these indicators are called 'clean dark/spark spreads', respectively.[3]

Figures 5.3 and 5.4 present trends in year-ahead power spreads over 2004–06 in Germany and the Netherlands, respectively, based on the forward market trends in power prices and fuel/carbon costs discussed above. Whereas Figure 5.3 depicts trends in (clean) dark spreads for the off-peak period in Germany, Figure 5.4 shows similar trends in the (clean) spark spread during the peak hours in the Netherlands. In addition, these figures illustrate the opportunity costs of CO_2 allowances to cover the emissions per MWh produced by a coal- or gas-fired power plant, with an emission factor of 0.97 and 0.51 tCO_2/MWh, respectively.

For the off-peak hours in Germany, Figure 5.3 shows that there is a close relationship between the dark spread and the emission costs of a coal-fired power station, at least up to April–May 2006 when the year-ahead (Cal07) price of an EUA suddenly collapsed and – after a short recovery plus stabilization phase – declined steadily during the latter part of 2006. The dark spread in Germany, however, fell less in April–May 2006, and more or less stabilized during the latter part of 2006, resulting in a growing disparity between the spark spread and the emission costs of coal-generated power per MWh. This suggests either that declining carbon costs are passed through to a lesser extent (or less quickly) than rising carbon costs (that is, asymmetric pass-through) or that changes in power prices/spreads are largely due to other factors than changes in fuel/carbon costs, for instance due to growing power market scarcities and related increasing market power of electricity suppliers to set sales prices.

A similar, but even stronger picture of the delinking between the trends of the power spreads and related carbon costs – particularly since Spring 2006 – can be observed in Figure 5.4, which presents these trends during the peak period of 2004–06 in the Netherlands. While the gas-related carbon costs declined from about 15 €/MWh in April/May 2006 to approximately 5 €/MWh in late 2006, the clean spark spread improved substantially from about 30 to 45 €/MWh over this period.

In addition to the trends in power spreads, Figures 5.3 and 5.4 also provide trends in *clean* spreads over 2004–06 in Germany and the Netherlands, respectively (by subtracting the full carbon emission costs from the 'normal' spreads). If it is assumed that (i) fuel and carbon costs are passed through more or less fully and directly to power prices, and (ii) other generation costs are more or less stable during the period considered, then the trend of the clean dark spread would be represented by a straight

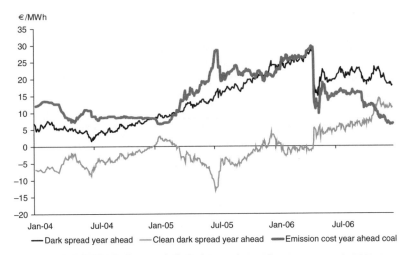

Figure 5.3   *Trends in power spreads and carbon costs on forward markets in Germany during off-peak hours, 2004–2006*

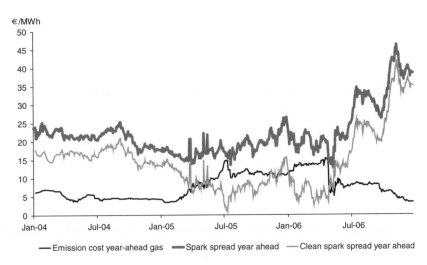

Figure 5.4   *Trends in power spreads and carbon costs on forward markets in the Netherlands during peak hours, 2004–06*

horizontal line at a certain level (say 10 or 20 €/MWh in order to cover the other generation costs, including profits).

Figure 5.3 and 5.4 show that, in general, clean spreads fluctuated significantly at a certain level in 2004–05, while they increased substantially during 2006. For instance, the clean spark spread during the peak hours in the Netherlands (i) was rather stable in 2004, fluctuating at a level of about 18 €/MWh, (ii) declined during the first part of 2005 (due to rising fuel/carbon costs that were not fully passed through), (iii) fluctuated at a level of approximately 15 €/MWh between mid-2005 and Spring 2006, and (iv) increased rapidly from about 10 €/MWh in April 2006 to more than 35 €/MWh in late 2006, implying that trends in peak power prices have diverged by some 25 €/MWh over this period from trends in fuel/carbon costs.

During the off-peak period, a similar but far less striking increase in clean dark spreads can be observed since April/May 2006 on the year-ahead power markets of Germany. Note, however, that these spreads are generally low, even in 2006, and that they were actually negative during most of the time in 2004 and 2005 (see Figure 5.3). The latter is surprising as it raises the question why coal operators would generate power at prices which do not even cover the opportunity costs of fuel and carbon allowances and, hence, would earn more by selling the fuel and carbon allowances straight on the market rather than using them for generating power.

The incidence of negative clean dark spreads, as observed in Figure 5.3 during the off-peak period in Germany, could be due to several reasons. First, the calculation of these spreads is based on an assumed fuel efficiency of 35 per cent for a coal station setting the price. However, if this efficiency is higher, both the fuel and carbon costs per MWh will be lower and, hence, the clean spread will be higher. Second, operators of coal stations may decide to continue power generation during off-peak hours at lower prices if it saves start-up costs for producing electricity during the peak period at more attractive prices.

Third, the calculation of the clean dark spreads is based on the assumption that off-peak prices in Germany are set by (domestic) coal plants. During certain off-peak hours, however, power prices in Germany are set by lignite plants which, overall, may have lower fuel and carbon costs (depending on the relative prices and efficiencies of the fuels and carbon used).

Finally, the observation that during certain off-peak periods the clean spreads are negative and, hence, that it would be more profitable to sell contracted fuels and (freely) obtained carbon allowances directly on the market rather than using them for generating power assumes that (i) fuel markets are liquid and, hence, contracted fuels can readily and without major costs be resold at the market, and (ii) power generators aim to maximize their profits. However, sometimes it is hardly possible or rather costly to resell contracted fuels at current market prices. Moreover, rather than maximizing profits, power generators may try to achieve other (short-term) objectives – for instance, to maintain certain market shares – or accept a certain satisfying profit margin, in particular if free allocation of carbon allowances results in a 'normal' spread that is already relatively high.

Statistical Estimates of CO_2 Cost PTRs

This subsection provides and discusses some statistical estimates of PTRs of CO_2 emission trading cost to power prices on forward wholesale markets in Germany and the Netherlands for 2005–06. The basic assumption of these estimates is that during the observation period (say 'peak 2005' or 'off-peak 2006') changes in the year-ahead power prices can be explained by variations in the fuel and carbon costs of the price-setting technology over this period. Hence, it is assumed that during this period other costs, for instance capital, operational or maintenance costs, are constant and that the market structure did not alter over this period (that is, changes in power prices cannot be attributed to changes in technology, market power, generation capacity, risks or other factors).

Based on these assumptions, the relationship between power prices (P), fuel costs (F) and CO_2 costs is expressed by equation (5.1), where superscripts c and g indicate coal and gas, respectively. Likewise, the term CO_{2t} is the CO_2 cost associated with coal and gas at time t. Thus, it is equal to the product of the CO_2 allowances price at time t and the time-invariant CO_2 emission rate of coal or gas generators. For the present analysis, fuel costs are assumed to be fully passed on to power prices. This is equivalent to fixing the coefficient β_2 at unity:

$$P_t = \alpha + \beta_1 CO2_t^{c,g} + \beta_2 F_t^{c,g} + \varepsilon_t. \qquad (5.1)$$

By defining Y_t as the difference between power price and fuel cost, equation (5.2) becomes the central regression equation of which the coefficient β_1 has been estimated. In fact, Y_t represents the dark spread for coal-generated power and the spark spread for gas-generated power:

$$Y_t = (P_t - F_t^{c,g}) = \alpha + \beta_1 CO2_t^{c,g} + \varepsilon_t. \qquad (5.2)$$

The first (constant) term on the right-hand side of the equation represents the fixed component of the power spread, comprising the fixed cost elements of power generation and the other, less quantifiable but stable, elements. The second term refers to the opportunity costs of the CO_2 allowances needed for the generation of power per MWh multiplied by the PTR (β_1). The last variable, the error term, represents all other non-stable components of the power spread.

In order to establish the applicability of the so-called 'ordinary least squares' (OLS) regression method to estimate the unknown variables of equation (5.2), the stationarity of the relevant data time series has to be determined. In the case of the relevant power spreads and carbon costs, all series appeared to be non-stationary. After first differencing of the data, stationarity was established and, thus, all series were found to be integrated of order one. None of the relevant series, however, appeared to be co-integrated. Therefore, by differencing the relevant time series the OLS method was applied to the following regression equation:

$$\Delta Y_t = \Delta(P_t - F_t^{c,g}) = \beta_1 \, \Delta CO2_t^{c,g} + u_t \qquad (5.3)$$

where Δ refers to the difference between sequential data observations and u_t represents the error term.

Table 5.1 presents the results of the estimated regression equation, notably of the estimated PTRs of carbon costs to electricity prices on the year-ahead power markets of Germany (DE) and the Netherlands (NL) during the peak and off-peak periods in 2005–06. The major findings of this table include:

- In those cases where the price-setting technology is assumed to be coal (DE-peak, DE-off-peak and NL-off-peak), the estimated PTRs vary between 40 and 60 per cent, while in the gas-fired production case (NL-peak), the estimated PTRs are slightly above 1, that is, 1.3 in 2005 and 1.1 in 2006. These estimates seem to suggest that in the latter (gas) case the PTRs are substantially higher than in the former (coal) cases, although in an absolute sense the emission factor and, hence, the carbon costs of gas are significantly lower compared to coal.
- All estimated PTRs are statistically significant at the 1 per cent level with, in general, small confidence intervals. However, the indicator for the 'goodness of fit' of the estimated regression equation (R^2) is generally low (although far from bad for a single variable equation), implying that only a small part – about 30 per cent – of the changes in power prices/spreads can be attributed to changes in carbon costs.

These findings, however, have to be interpreted with some caution due to the following considerations.

First, as noted, the estimated PTRs are based on the fundamental assumption that changes in power prices are predominantly caused by changes in the underlying costs of fuels and CO_2 emission allowances, and that all other generation costs and factors affecting power prices are more

*Table 5.1   Empirical estimates of carbon cost PTRs on year-ahead power
markets in Germany and the Netherlands, 2005–2006**

		DE		NL	
		Peak	Off-peak	Peak	Off-peak
	Price-setting technology	Coal	Coal	Gas	Coal
	Fuel efficiency (%)	35	35	40	35
2005	PTR	0.60	0.41	1.34	0.40
	Interval (Δ)	±0.06	±0.04	±0.14	±0.04
	R^2	0.29	0.32	0.28	0.34
2006	PTR	0.57	0.64	1.10	0.38
	Interval (Δ)	±0.05	±0.04	±0.14	±0.03
	R^2	0.36	0.38	0.20	0.38

Note: *Based on a first-difference regression of power spreads versus carbon costs. All
estimated PTRs are statistically significant at the 1% level.

or less fixed during the observation period (that is, for instance, the peak
period in 2005 or the off-peak period in 2006). However, as observed in the
previous two subsections, this assumption seems to hold for certain periods
(for example, the off-peak 2005) but not for others (notably during the peak
period of the second half of 2006). The other generation costs and factors
refer not only to maintenance or fixed costs, but also to items such as
changes in scarcity of generation capacity, market power, risks and so on.
Due to a lack of data, however, it is not possible to account quantitatively
for the impact of these other changes in power prices, which may lead to
biased results of the estimated PTRs.

Second, the estimated PTRs are based on the assumption that during the
observation period, power prices are set by a single (marginal) technology
with a fixed, generic fuel efficiency. In practice, however, peak or off-peak
prices during a particular year (or even a particular month, week or day)
may be set by a variety of technologies (with different or changing fuel
efficiencies), depending on the specific load hour, the maintenance or
outage schedule of the generation park, daily changes in relative
fuel/carbon prices and so on. Once again, due to a lack of data, it is not
possible to account quantitatively for these technological factors, which
may lead to (additional) biases in the estimated PTRs.

Third, the estimated PTRs depend on (that is, are sensitive to) the
assumed generic (fixed, average) fuel efficiency rates, which in all relevant
cases amount to 35 and 40 per cent for coal and gas, respectively. However,
for specific cases, for example, NL-off-peak, these rates may be too low. As

indicated by Sijm et al. (2005), the estimated PTR increases significantly if a higher fuel efficiency rate is assumed, notably when the fuel costs of the marginal technology account for a major share of the power price and, hence, for a relatively low power spread.[4]

Finally, the estimated PTRs are based on the use of daily price data for fuels traded on (inter)national, rather liquid markets, assuming that these data reflect the changes in the opportunity costs of the fuels used by the marginal, price-setting technology in either Germany or the Netherlands (for details, see Box 5.1). In practice, however, power generators may use another (or adjusted) fuel price indicator for their operational and bidding strategies as they usually rely on long-term fuel supply contracts with specific marketing and pricing conditions. Moreover, in particular the gas market is often less liquid and, hence, the 'opportunity costs' of gas becomes a dubious concept as power companies are less flexible in trading gas surpluses or shortages due to contract fines and other, high balancing costs of trading gas flexibly. Therefore, the estimated PTRs depend on the assumptions made with regard to the fuel price data.

Nevertheless, although the exact value of the estimated PTRs is hard to determine, there is sufficient (both theoretical and empirical) support for the conclusion that in liberalized power markets, such as in Germany and the Netherlands, generators include the opportunity costs of (freely allocated) CO_2 emission allowances in their pricing strategies. In addition to the empirical analyses outlined above – as well as in several other studies – this support includes interviews, presentations and other statements by representatives of the power sector confirming that they do indeed incorporate these costs in their wholesale price bidding and other operational decisions.[5]

Power producers, however, are not able simply to set wholesale power prices in liberalized, competitive markets or to pass through carbon costs to these prices as price setting and cost pass-through in the power sector are determined by a complex set of wholesale market forces. In general, it is hard to assess the impact of CO_2 allowance costs on power prices as these prices are set by a large variety of factors, including fuel prices, the €/US$ exchange rate, available production capacity, investment costs, imports, weather conditions, heat demand ('must runs'), fuel contract inflexibilities, risks, expectations and sentiments of market players, and so on. Moreover, the extent to which CO_2 costs are passed through to power prices depends on factors such as power market structure, demand responsiveness, changes in the merit order or specific (free) allocation provisions (Sijm et al., 2008).

Therefore, although in liberalized, competitive markets power producers include the opportunity costs of (free) CO_2 emission allowances in their price bidding and other operational decisions, due to a large variety of factors affecting power prices and carbon cost pass-through it is hard to determine empirically the exact PTR and, hence, the exact impact of emissions trading costs on electricity prices.

Carbon Cost Pass-through on Retail Power Markets

In the previous sections, the analysis focused on the impact of CO_2 emissions trading on (year-ahead) *wholesale* power prices in Germany and the Netherlands over the 2005–06 period. This raises the question whether and to what extent there is already some empirical evidence on the pass-through of carbon allowances costs to *retail* power prices in these countries during this period. In order to address this question, data have been gathered from Eurostat on average, semi-annual power prices for two categories of electricity end-users:

- households, with an annual consumption of 3.5 MWh (of which 1.3 MWh at night); and
- industry, in particular large industrial end-users with an annual consumption of 24,000 MWh (maximum demand 4 MW and 6,000 annual load hours).

Figure 5.5 presents the changes in the average, annual electricity prices for these two categories of power consumers in Germany and the Netherlands over 2004–06. It shows that retail power prices in Germany and the Netherlands have increased significantly for both households and industrial consumers. For instance, including taxes, power prices for large industrial end-users in Germany rose from 86 €/MWh in 2004 to 105 €/MWh in 2006 (+ 21 per cent), while household electricity prices in the Netherlands increased from 183 to 211 €/MWh over this period (+ 15 per cent). To some extent, these changes in retail prices are affected by changes in energy taxes (including value-added taxes). Between 2004 and 2006, for instance, taxes on industrial power prices in Germany were raised from 24 to 27 €/MWh, resulting in an increase in these prices, excluding taxes, from 62 to 78 €/MWh (+ 25 per cent), while taxes on household power prices in the Netherlands were raised from 80 to 89 €/MWh, leading to an increase in these prices, excluding taxes, from 103 to 122 €/MWh (+ 18 per cent). Hence, whereas changes in energy taxes can explain a major part (about one-third) of the increase in household power prices in the Netherlands over 2004–06, they are less important (about one-sixth) in accounting for differences in industrial power prices in Germany during this period.

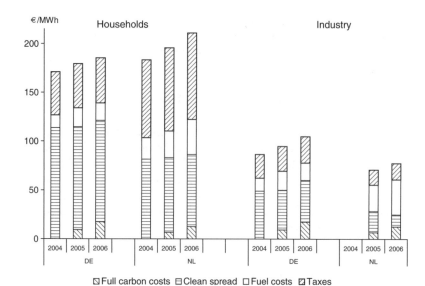

Figure 5.5 *Changes in cost components of electricity prices for households and industry in Germany and the Netherlands, 2004–2006*

In order to assess the possible impact of CO_2 emissions trading on (changes in) retail power prices in Germany and the Netherlands during 2005–06, the carbon costs passed through on the retail power markets have been estimated according to three different methodologies:

1. Estimation of the carbon costs passed through based on the change in the so-called 'retail power spread' (defined as the difference between the average, annual power price, excluding taxes, and the average, annual fuel costs of power generation per MWh). This approach assumes that changes in this spread can be solely attributed to changes in carbon costs passed through on the retail market (and, hence, that changes in retail power prices can be explained by changes in these carbon costs, fuel costs and taxes), while other costs or determinants of retail power prices are fixed over this period (2004–06). According to this approach, the estimated carbon costs passed through are assumed to be equal to the difference in the average, annual retail power spread during a certain year after emissions trading (2005 or 2006) and the year before emissions trading (that is, 2004).[6]
2. Estimation of the carbon costs passed through on retail markets based on the estimated PTRs on related wholesale power markets. This approach assumes that for each specific case (say Germany in 2005) the

same rate (or amount) of carbon costs is passed through on both the wholesale and retail power markets. According to this approach, the estimated carbon costs passed through on the retail market are assumed to be equal to the weighted average of the estimated CO_2 costs passed through on the wholesale market during the peak and off-peak periods.

3.   Estimation of the carbon costs passed through on retail markets based on the so-called 'full carbon costs' of the marginal technologies setting the power price. This approach assumes that the costs of these technologies are fully passed through on the retail markets. According to this approach, for each specific case, the estimated carbon costs passed through are assumed to be equal to the weighted average of the CO_2 emission costs of the marginal technologies setting the power price during the peak and off-peak periods.

The results of the three methodologies outlined above are summarized in Table 5.2, where the three approaches are briefly denoted as 'retail', 'wholesale' and 'full carbon costs', respectively.[7] First, the upper part of this table shows the estimated amounts of carbon costs passed through according to these three methodologies. For instance, following the first approach (retail), the amounts of carbon costs passed through to households in Germany are estimated at 1.0 €/MWh in 2005 and 7.7 €/MWh in 2006, while for the large industrial users these costs amount to 0.9 and 11.0 €/MWh, respectively. However, according to the second methodology (wholesale), the estimated amounts are significantly higher for both German households and industrial users, that is, 4.8 and 9.0 €/MWh in 2005 and 2006, respectively. These amounts are even higher if it is assumed that the carbon costs of the price-setting technologies are fully passed on to these consumers (that is, following the third, full carbon costs approach). Note that, in general, the estimated amounts of carbon costs passed through to retail power prices are substantially higher in 2006 than in 2005. This is due to the fact that, while the estimates for 2005 are based on year-ahead prices of CO_2 emission allowances in 2004 (to be delivered in 2005) and estimates for 2006 on year-ahead carbon prices in 2005, these prices have been, on average, significantly higher in 2005 than in 2004.

Table 5.2 then presents the estimated PTRs according to the three different methodologies (where the PTR is defined as the estimated amount of carbon costs passed through divided by the full carbon costs of the price-setting technologies, as discussed above). Following the 'retail' approach, the PTRs are estimated at 11 per cent in 2005 and 44 per cent in 2006 in the case of German households, at 24 and 38 per cent, respectively, for German industry, and at 10 and 63 per cent, respectively,

Empirical analyses

Table 5.2   Summary of estimated carbon cost PTRs on retail power
markets in Germany and the Netherlands, 2005–2006

Approach	Households				Industry			
	DE		NL		DE		NL	
	2005	2006	2005	2006	2005	2006	2005	2006
Estimated amount of carbon costs passed through in (€/MWh)								
Retail	1.0	7.7	1.6	4.8	0.9	11.0	N.A.	N.A.
Wholesale	4.8	9.0	5.2	9.9	4.8	9.0	5.2	9.9
Full carbon costs	9.2	17.4	6.7	12.6	9.2	17.4	6.7	12.6
PTR (% of full carbon costs)								
Retail	11	44	24	38	10	63	N.A.	N.A.
Wholesale	52	52	78	78	52	52	78	78
Full carbon costs	100	100	100	100	100	100	100	100
Share of carbon costs passed through (% of retail power prices, including taxes)								
Retail	1	4	1	2	1	10	N.A.	N.A.
Wholesale	3	5	3	5	5	9	7	13
Full carbon costs	5	9	3	6	10	17	9	16
Share of carbon costs passed through (% of change in retail power prices, including taxes, compared to 2004)								
Retail	12	52	13	18	9	60	N.A.	N.A.
Wholesale	58	62	42	35	63	49	N.A.	N.A.
Full carbon costs	111	120	53	45	121	95	N.A.	N.A.

Note: Some estimates for Dutch industry are not available (N.A.) since Eurostat data on
power prices for large industrial power consumers in the Netherlands are missing prior to
2004. All estimated PTRs are statistically significant at the 1% level.

for Dutch households (while similar estimates for Dutch industry are not
available since data on power prices for large industrial end-users in the
Netherlands are lacking up to 2004). On the other hand, assuming that
the PTRs on the retail markets would be similar to the estimated PTRs on
the wholesale markets, these rates amount to 52 per cent in Germany and
78 per cent in the Netherlands for both consumer groups in both 2005 and
2006.[8]

The results following from the retail approach suggest that the pass-
through of CO_2 emission costs on the retail markets in Germany and the
Netherlands was rather low in 2005, but increased substantially in 2006.
The low figures for 2005 may be due to time lags in retail price setting or
other (marketing) constraints in passing through carbon costs fully or
immediately to retail power consumers. The estimated PTRs according to

this approach, however, have to be interpreted with due care as they are based on the assumption that changes in retail power spreads result only from changes in carbon costs passed through – and, hence, both changes are equal – but not from changes in other price determinants (besides taxes, fuel costs and carbon costs) such as distribution or marketing costs or growing market scarcities.

Finally, in order to get an indication of the relevance of carbon costs passed through for both the absolute levels of the retail prices and the changes of these prices in Germany and the Netherlands during 2005–06, the lower part of Table 5.2 presents these costs as a share or percentage of both these absolute levels and price changes. In general, the table shows:

- as the carbon costs passed through on the retail market according to the retail approach are generally much lower compared to either the wholesale or – even stronger – the full carbon costs approach, the shares of these costs in (changes of) retail power prices are consequently much lower for the retail approach than the other two methodologies;
- as the retail prices are usually much higher for households than for industrial power consumers, the shares of carbon costs passed through to these prices are consequently much lower for households than for industrial users;
- as the estimated carbon costs passed through on retail markets are generally much higher for 2006 than for 2005, the shares of these costs in (changes of) retail prices are consequently much higher in 2006 than in 2005; and
- as short-term changes in retail power prices are usually a minor part of the total or absolute levels of these prices, the shares of carbon costs passed through on retail markets are consequently much higher when expressed as a percentage of the changes in retail prices rather than as a share of the absolute levels of these prices.[9]

More specifically, Table 5.2 shows that when the carbon costs passed through are estimated according to the retail approach, the share of these costs in total retail prices is relatively low in 2005–06, that is, in general less than 4 per cent. The only exception concerns the case of German industry in 2006, where the carbon costs passed through account for about 10 per cent of the retail power price concerned. Even if one assumes that the full carbon costs are passed through to retail power prices, these costs account generally for only a small part of these prices, although in the case of the large industrial power users in both Germany and the Netherlands the share of the full carbon costs in the electricity prices for these consumers amounted to about 16–17 per cent in 2006.

On the other hand, when the (estimated or assumed) carbon costs passed through are expressed as a percentage of the changes in retail power prices, these rates are generally much more significant. For instance, if it is assumed that the changes in the retail power spreads are solely due to the pass-through of carbon costs (that is, the retail approach), the shares of these costs in the changes of the retail prices in 2005–06 (compared to 2004) range from 13–18 per cent for Dutch house-holds, 12–52 per cent for German households, and 9–60 per cent for German industry (where the first percentage mentioned refers to 2005 and the second to 2006, see Table 5.2). This implies that the remaining shares of the price changes in these cases can be attributed to changes in fuel costs and/or energy taxes.

However, if it is assumed that the carbon costs passed through on the retail market are similar to either the carbon costs passed through on the wholesale market (that is, the wholesale approach) or the full carbon costs of the price-setting technologies (that is, the full carbon costs approach), Table 5.2 shows that the shares of these costs in the retail price changes are usually much higher.

To conclude, if it is assumed that over the 2004–06 period changes in the retail power spreads – defined as retail power prices excluding taxes and fuel costs – are solely due to carbon costs passed through, the impact of the EU ETS on (changes in) retail power prices was still relatively low in 2005 due to relatively low year-ahead carbon prices in 2004 and, perhaps, some time lags or other (marketing) constraints in passing through these costs to retail prices. In 2006, however, this impact seems to be already more significant, notably in Germany, due to relatively higher forward carbon prices in 2005 and, presumably, an increasing share of carbon costs passed through. Moreover, if it is assumed that the carbon costs passed through on the retail market are similar to either the carbon costs passed through on the whole-sale market or the full carbon costs of the price-setting technologies, the impact of these costs – and, hence, of the EU ETS – on retail power prices becomes generally even more significant. These findings, however, have to be treated with due care as, to some extent, they depend on the assumptions made to estimate the carbon costs passed through, in particular the assumption that the changes in the retail power prices over the 2004–06 period are solely due to changes in taxes, fuel costs and carbon costs and, therefore, that other determinants of these prices – such as distribution/marketing costs or the incidence of market scarcity/power – have been stable over this period.

5.3   THE ISSUE OF WINDFALL PROFITS

The pass-through of the opportunity costs of EUAs to power prices has raised the issue of the so-called 'windfall profits'. As power companies receive most of the allowances to cover their emissions for free during the first and second trading periods (2005–12), the value of these free allowances cannot be considered as truly paid costs but rather as the transfer of a lump-sum subsidy (or 'economic rent') enhancing the profitability of these companies (depending on the output price and sales volume effects of passing through the opportunity costs of the EUAs). In addition, even if companies have to pay fully for all allowances needed, some infra-marginal producers may benefit (or lose) from emissions trading, depending on the ETS-induced increase in power prices set by the marginal producer versus the EUA costs of the infra-marginal producer (where both the marginal and the infra-marginal producers can be either a high-, low- or non-CO_2 emitter).

Estimates of the incidence of windfall profits due to the EU ETS vary widely, depending on the countries or companies considered and the under-lying assumptions made.[10] For instance, based on an EUA price of 20 €/tCO_2, estimates of windfall profits accruing to power producers in Germany are estimated at €4–8 billion per annum, that is, about 8–17 €/MWh produced, depending on whether either a gas or coal station is assumed to set the power price (WWF, 2006).[11] Similar estimates for the Netherlands vary from €19 million (Frontier Economics, 2006), €250–600 million (Sijm et al., 2006b) or even more than €1 billion per annum (Kesisoglou, 2007), depending primarily on the assumptions/estimates with regard to the PTRs and the shares of allowances obtained for free versus those purchased at the market by power producers. With an annual production of about 100 TWh in the Netherlands, these estimates imply an average pass-through amounting to 0.2, 2.5–6 and 10 €/MWh, respectively.

Several qualifications, however, can be added to the issue of EU ETS-induced windfall profits in the power sector. First, the term 'windfall profits' is often poorly defined and understood, notably in the context of emissions trading in the power sector. Literally (or originally), the term seems to refer to the fruit that falls from the tree due to the wind. Hence, it relates to something one gets for free, that is, an extra bonus without having to make an additional effort and which, usually, one did not expect to receive. Therefore, in the context of EU emissions trading in the power sector, the term defined broadly refers to the changes in generators' profits (either positive or negative) due to the implementation of the EU ETS which these generators had not expected once they made their investment decisions. Consequently, windfall profits have a bearing only on existing installations – that is, 'incumbents' or, more precisely, on investments made before the policy decision to introduce (or change the fundamental conditions) of emissions trading – but not on new investments as the level and kind of these investments (including those in more expensive, but low- or non-CO_2-emitting installations) are based on the new policy conditions and the attendant profit expectations.

Moreover, as indicated above, changes in incumbents' profits due to policy decisions on the fundamentals of emissions trading (that is, windfall profits, defined broadly) can or should be distinguished into the following two categories:

A.   *Changes in incumbents' profits due to ET-induced changes in production costs, power prices and sales volumes*   This category of profit changes (denoted as 'windfall A') occurs irrespective of whether eligible companies have to purchase all their allowances at an auction or market or receive them for free. The impact of changes in generation costs, power prices and sales volumes on incumbents' profits can vary significantly among companies (or even countries) and can be positive or negative, depending on the fuel generation mix of these companies (or countries), the price of an emission allowance, and the ETS-induced changes in power prices set by the marginal installation versus the ETS-induced changes in generation costs and sales volumes of both marginal and infra-marginal operators (where these operators can be either a high-, low- or non-CO_2 emitter). For instance, if the power price is set by a coal (high-emitting) installation, an operator of such a plant may either break even – if the change in carbon and other generation costs is passed fully to the power price, while sales volumes do not change – or make a loss if price changes are lower than cost changes or if sales volumes drop due to (i) lower, price-responsive demand levels or (ii) lower load hours resulting from a loss of competitiveness and an attendant change in the merit order of power supply. However, in such a situation, infra-marginal operators of a low- or non-CO_2-emitting station may benefit from a higher profit margin and higher load hours (that is, sales volumes) due to gains in competitiveness. On the other hand, if the power price is set by a gas (low-emitting) or nuclear (non-emitting) plant, the operator of such an installation may more or less break even, whereas infra-marginal producers operating a higher-emitting station will make a loss as the increase in their carbon cost is not covered by a similar increase in power revenues.[12]

B.   *Changes in incumbents' profits due to the free allocation of emission allowances*   This category of profit changes (denoted as 'windfall B') is an addition to or compensation for the first category of windfall profits/losses to the extent to which allowances are obtained for free – rather than purchased – by eligible companies. These changes in incumbents' profits are usually positive, but can vary significantly among companies (or even countries), depending on the fuel generation mix of their installations, the price of an emission allowance, the amount of free allowances received, and the impact of specific free allocation provisions on the power price.[13] For instance, if carbon prices are high and emissions are covered largely by allowances allocated for free in a fuel-specific way (that is, high polluters such as coal or lignite plants get more free allowances), companies – or countries – with a relative high share of high-emitting installations in their generation mix benefit most, in an absolute sense, while low- or non-CO_2-emitting installations will profit less or not at all from free allocation.

The distinction between the two categories of windfall profits is relevant not only to indicate the differences in the underlying causes or mechanisms of these profits (or in differences in the incidence of these profits at the installation, sectoral or national level) but also to discuss the differences of these two categories in terms of investment incentives and policy implications. Whereas the first category (windfall A) encourages investments in especially low- or non-CO_2-emitting installations, the second category (windfall B) induces investments in particularly high-emitting technologies (provided that allowances are allocated for free to both incumbents and new entrants, in particular in a fuel- or technology-specific way, it implies a capacity subsidy that benefits and, hence, promotes notably more carbon-intensive generation plants). In addition, if for one reason or another one wants to tackle the incidence of generators' windfall profits due to the EU ETS, one has to make a distinction between the two categories of these profits as some policy options affect only the first category but not the second, or vice versa (as discussed in Section 5.4, below).

Third, the term, 'windfall profits' has a negative connotation, mainly because it is associated with either 'unfair' or 'unjustified' practices resulting in higher power prices for small and less-benevolent end-users and, hence, in a transfer of wealth from these end-users (or the public sector) to privileged stakeholders of large, private power companies filling their pockets. However, the pass-through of the opportunity costs of (free) emission allowances into power prices is a rational and intended effect from both a business economics and an environmental policy perspective. If someone is to blame for the resulting windfall profits one should primarily look at the policy makers who decide to allocate these allowances for free (rather than at the power producers whose actions are governed by rational, profit-maximizing motives and, hence, could be expected). Moreover, a major part of the windfall profits in the power sector accrues to public hands, as these profits are subject to public taxation while, in addition, in several EU countries a large number of the power companies are still owned by the public sector (including municipalities, provinces or federal states). Finally, if one wants to avoid the negative connotation of windfall profits, one could use the term 'changes in generators' profits' or, even better, 'changes in producer surplus'.

A fourth and last qualification is that estimates of windfall profits have to be treated with due care since it is very hard to estimate these profits empirically in an exact and reliable way, in particular at the company level or in the long run. Most estimates of windfall profits are based on estimates (or sometimes even on assumptions) of the EUA cost PTR on a certain market during a certain period (for example, the wholesale forward market in Germany during the peak or off-peak period in 2006). As outlined above, however, it is very difficult to estimate these PTRs empirically, not only on forward markets but even more on spot markets as power prices on these markets are affected by a large variety of factors besides fuel/carbon costs (Sijm et al., 2008). Hence, in practice, it is very hard to estimate what the power price would have been without emissions trading. It is even more difficult to estimate changes in generators' profits due to emissions trading as, besides changes in power prices, these profits are affected by changes in carbon or other generation costs and changes in sales volumes (due to lower, price-responsive power demand and carbon price-induced changes in the merit order or other abatement measures). Moreover, ET-induced changes in sales volumes – or other variables affecting profits – may vary significantly at the company level, depending on their fuel generation mix, making it even more complicated to estimate the incidence of windfall profits at the company level.

In addition, in the long run, the price elasticity or responsiveness of power demand to ET-induced increases in power prices may become more significant (that is, reducing windfall profits) while ET-induced investments in new capacity will further affect changes in power prices, cost structures, sales volumes and, hence, generators' (windfall) profits. Another complicating factor is that estimates of windfall profits are usually based on transactions and PTRs on the wholesale power market, while at the retail level transactions, PTRs and other factors influencing profits of (integrated) power companies are often affected by the incidence of time lags, long-term contracts or other considerations besides maximizing short-term profit such as maintaining or reaching a certain market share. Hence, due to all these factors and changes it is hard to make a reliable, empirical estimate of windfall profits, notably of the first category ('windfall A') at the company level or in the long run.

At first sight, it seems easier to estimate the second category of windfall profits (B), since this can be done quite straightforwardly through multiplying the amount of allowances obtained for free by their (average) price, resulting in their market value or 'economic rent'. However, in the case of specific free allocation provisions – such as (i) updating, (ii) closure rules or (iii) free allocation to new entrants – this category is also rather hard to estimate empirically, notably in the long run, as these provisions have contrary, long-term effects on power prices on the one side (that is, reducing the ET-induced increases in these prices) and on carbon prices on the other (that is, raising these prices and, hence, the carbon cost passed through to power prices). Therefore, these provisions have contrary, indeterminate effects on changes in generators (windfall) profits, which are, hence, difficult to estimate empirically.

Nevertheless, despite all the qualifications and complications involved, rough/conservative estimates of ETS-induced windfall profits in the power sector can be made in order to get a feeling of the order of magnitude concerned. For instance, at an (average) price of 15 €/tCO$_2$, the market value or economic rent of the allowances allocated for free during 2005–06 is equal to some €700 million per annum in the Netherlands and approximately €5 billion in Germany (and at least €15 billion in the EU ETS as a whole). Or, assuming an ET-induced increase in (average) power prices of only 3 €/MWh in 2005–06 (while average generation costs and sales volumes are supposed to be more or less similar to 2004), windfall profits in the power sector due to the EU ETS amount to about €300 million per annum in the Netherlands and almost €2 billion in Germany (and more than €9 billion in the EU ETS as a whole). For the short run, these are rough but rather conservative estimates, implying that they may be significantly higher if the (average) carbon price or the (average) pass-through is higher. However, even conservative estimates of windfall profits raise questions on the socio-political acceptability of the EU ETS, in particular if this system does not lead to significant emission reductions or if it results in higher electricity prices for small households and power-intensive industries which may not always be able to pass on these higher energy costs to their customers. These questions will be addressed further in the next section, including policy implications and options to deal with the incidence of windfall profits and other concerns regarding the pass-through of the opportunity costs of EU emission allowances.

5.4   POLICY OPTIONS AND IMPLICATIONS

As supported by economic theory and empirical evidence, power producers in competitive, unregulated electricity markets pass through (part of) the opportunity cost of CO_2 emissions trading, even if they receive carbon allowances for free. From a climate policy perspective, internalizing the costs of CO_2 emissions is a rational and intended effect, enhancing the efficiency of emissions trading by incentivizing end-users to reduce their consumption of carbon-intensive goods. Hence, from such a perspective, the pass-through of these costs should be supported and promoted rather than discouraged – even if the allowances are granted for free – by creating conditions for competitive power markets and avoiding measures or threats to regulate price formation or carbon cost pass-through on these markets.

Nevertheless, as indicated above, the pass-through of CO_2 emissions costs – notably in the case of free allocations – may raise certain questions or concerns affecting the socio-political acceptability of the EU ETS. In particular, these questions or concerns refer to:

- *Windfall profits – that is, more surpluses – for power producers*   As noted, the pass-through of carbon costs to electricity prices results in windfall profits for power producers, which may be quite substantial even in the case where all allowances have to be purchased at an auction or a market. To some extent, windfall profits – and losses – for (infra-)marginal producers due to ETS-induced changes in power prices, generation costs and sales volumes ('windfall A') can be accepted as the outcome of normal, everyday changes in economic conditions (which in the case of policy-induced losses can justify some free allocations or other – temporary – compensation measures). However, in countries with a large share of nuclear/hydro installations as base-load capacity (such as France or Sweden), this category of windfall may not only be substantial but also raise questions and concerns about these profits: why should end-users such as small households or power-intensive industries pay more for their electricity consumption, resulting in additional profits for (well-to-do) stakeholders who often made their nuclear/hydro investment decisions a few decades ago when these profits did not lead to significant CO_2 reductions, for instance due to all kinds of constraints limiting the further expansion of non-CO_2 power generation? Similar questions and concerns are raised even more outspokenly in the case of windfall profits due to free allocations ('windfall B'), in particular (i) if these profits – or the EU ETS as a whole – do not lead to significant carbon abatements in the power sector or, through fuel-specific free allocation provisions to new entrants, even encourage investments in CO_2-intensive power generation, and (ii) if these profits actually imply a wealth transfer from the public sector or (private, less benevolent) electricity end-users to (private, privileged) stakeholders of power companies, raising income distributional or equity concerns (see also next point below).

- *Higher prices – that is, fewer surpluses – for electricity consumers*
The pass-through of CO_2 emission costs of power generation leads to higher prices for electricity end-users, regardless of whether the carbon allowances are allocated for free or not. As noted, this is a rational, intended/expected effect of emissions trading enhancing the carbon abatement efficiency of the EU ETS and, therefore, it can be regarded as an acceptable, necessary or unavoidable effect. In some particular cases, however, the ETS-induced increases in end-user electricity prices raises questions and concerns from either a competitiveness or equity point of view. For instance, some industrial end-users face higher power prices but, in turn, are not able to (fully) pass on these higher costs themselves due to outside competition or relatively high price responsiveness of demand for their output products, resulting in a loss of competitiveness, market shares, sales volumes or profits. Although this issue has sometimes been exaggerated, notably by some business associations, there are indeed some power-intensive industries or specific products that are disadvantaged by this effect (such as the aluminium industry or the production of copper). In addition, higher electricity prices have a negative purchasing-power effect and a regressive income-distribution effect as they affect notably low-income households which spend a relatively high share of their budget on power consumption. These effects may be particularly relevant for some EU countries, for instance in Eastern Europe, where the incidence of low-income households is relatively higher and which may have other, more attractive options to meet their mitigation commitments than reducing power-related emissions through higher end-user prices. Moreover, in some countries – for instance, the Netherlands – households already pay a substantial amount of environmental levies on their electricity consumption, which may lead to 'double taxation' of these households once the costs of emissions trading are passed through to the end-user prices. Finally, it should be noted that the above-mentioned concerns with regard to the potential adverse effects of higher power prices on industrial competitiveness, household income and equity would be even stronger if (i) the future prices – and, hence the cost pass-through – of carbon allowances

were significantly higher, (ii) the abatement effect of the EU ETS was modest, notably the price-induced demand effect on power-related emissions, and (iii) the windfall profits for power producers were high due to, in particular, free allocations and a high pass-through of carbon costs.

In order to address the (either putative or real) concerns outlined above, policy makers, analysts, industrial stakeholders or other interest groups have suggested a wide variety of options, including options to change the allocation system, both inside and outside the EU ETS. More specifically the suggested options include:

1. auctioning;
2. allocating free allowances to power consumers;
3. benchmarking;
4. reducing carbon prices;
5. regulating power prices;
6. encouraging competitive power markets; and
7. taxing windfall profits.

These options are evaluated briefly below in terms of (i) their impact on power prices, (ii) their impact on windfall profits in the power sector, distinguished between 'windfall A' and 'windfall B' categories, (iii) their impact on the competitiveness of power-intensive industries, (iv) some other major effects (or advantages and disadvantages) of these options, and (v) the overall performance of these options in terms of socio-political acceptability, feasibility and addressing the concerns related to carbon cost pass-through outlined above.

Auctioning

The first and most widely suggested option to address in particular the EU ETS-induced windfall profits is to sell the CO_2 emission allowances at an auction (or market) rather than allocating them for free. In the two ideal (or textbook) types of allocation, that is, auctioning versus perfect free allocation (based on either grandfathering or benchmarking), both types have the same effects in terms of environmental effectiveness, economic efficiency, cost pass-through and output prices. The only difference concerns the distribution of the market value or 'economic rent' of the CO_2 emission allowances in the sense that this value accrues to the auctioneer (or public sector) in the case of auctioning and that it is transferred as a kind of lump-sum subsidy to eligible companies in the case of free allocations, thereby enhancing the profits of these companies (compared to a situation of emissions trading with auctioning). Therefore, in the ideal situation, auctioning eliminates only the windfall profits due to the free allocations of emission allowances (windfall B) by abolishing the transfer of the market value of these allowances to eligible companies. It should be noted, however, that auctioning in itself does not reduce, let alone eliminate, the windfall profits due to the ETS-induced changes in power prices, generation costs and sales volumes (windfall A).

In addition, the present system of free allocations in the EU ETS does not meet the ideal type of perfect grandfathering or perfect benchmarking as it is characterized by some specific free allocation provisions called 'updating' as a result of periodic allocation decisions, instead of more permanent provisions, including the loss of free allowances in the case of plant closures and the allocation of free allowances to new entrants. The implication of these provisions is that they have a depressing effect on power prices (and, hence, on generator profits), which may vary not only by country but also in the short, medium or long term, depending on (i) the scope and force of these provisions in the countries concerned, (ii) the impact of these provisions on the present and future (fuel mix of) generation capacities or on the relevant opportunity costs of emission allowances for participating producers (which influences the impact on power prices in the short, medium or long run), and (iii) the demand responsiveness of electricity consumers to changes in power prices, the technology or fuel-specific character of the free allocation provisions, and the EU ETS cap versus the limits on the inflow of joint implementation and clean development mechanism (JI/CDM) credits (which influences the impact of these provisions on total CO_2 emissions and, hence, the demand for carbon allowances, the price of these allowances, the opportunity costs of the allowances passed through and, ultimately, the resulting changes in power prices and generators' profits).[14]

The outcome or balance of these contrary effects on power prices and generators' profits is an (unknown) empirical issue, depending on the factors mentioned above. In a closed ETS with a fixed CO_2 budget (that is, with a fixed cap and a binding limit – or strict ban – of JI/CDM and other offset credits), the depressing effects of the specific free allocation provisions on power prices may largely cancel out, implying that – on balance or over time – these prices hardly change if the allocation system changes. However, in a more open ETS with a flexible CO_2 budget (for instance, with a flexible, price-dependent inflow of offset credits), the specific free allocation provisions – notably for new entrants – have a depressing impact on power prices in the long run which is not cancelled out by a similar upward-pressing effect on EU carbon prices (due to the inflow of offset credits).

This implies that in the case of auctioning – that is, abolishing these provisions and effects – power prices and related (windfall) profits may be higher in the long run.

Similarly, empirical estimates of carbon cost PTRs on power markets are often less than 1.0 in the short run, but little is known about the actual reasons why these rates are less than 100 per cent (let alone the values and determinants of these PTRs in the medium or long term). For instance, is the value of these estimates influenced by the effects of the specific free allocation provisions and, if yes, what is – on balance – the impact of these provisions (or abolishing these provisions by means of auctioning) on the power prices and generators' profits in the long run? Moreover, the pass-through of the opportunity costs of carbon allowances is based on the assumption that power producers try to maximize their profits. However, in the case of free allocation, producers may perhaps sacrifice some of the resulting windfall profits – by reducing the amount of carbon cost pass-through – in order to achieve other short-term objectives such as reaching or maintaining a certain (retail) market share. In the case of auctioning, however, producers lack these windfall resources and, hence, they may increase the amount of carbon cost pass-through. Therefore, in these examples, shifting from free allocation to auctioning not merely abolishes the windfall profits due to the economic rent of allocating allowances, but may also affect (that is, increase) power prices and, hence, windfall profits due to other factors than transferring economic rents of free allocations.

To conclude, shifting from perfect free allocation to auctioning implies that windfall profits due to the transfer of economic rents will disappear, but it will have no impact on electricity prices or other factors affecting generators' profits, including windfall profits due to ETS-induced changes in these prices and other factors (assuming that power producers try to maximize their profits). However, if emissions trading is characterized by specific free allocation provisions (such as updating, plant closure rules or free allocation to new entrants) a shift towards auctioning may imply that, in the long term, power prices – and, hence, related windfall profits – may be higher, notably when additional emissions due to these provisions result in an extra inflow of JI/CDM credits rather than an increase in the price of an EU carbon allowance and a corresponding pass-through of the allowance costs into power prices.

Other effects of auctioning
In addition, auctioning of emission allowances has some other effects.[15] A major advantage of auctioning is that it raises revenues which can be used (i) to finance public expenditures on carbon abatement or other useful, social objectives, (ii) to reduce taxation and related efficiency distortions

('double dividend'), or (iii) to compensate power-intensive industries and other electricity consumers for the ETS-induced increases in power prices. Recycling of auction revenues, however, raises all kinds of new allocation issues (Sijm et al., 2006b). For instance, if these revenues are recycled by reducing income and business taxation in a general way, it may particularly benefit better-off households and firms which are affected relatively less by the ETS-induced increases in power prices.[16] On the other hand, if auction revenues are recycled in a specific, targeted way in order to compensate consumers for the ETS-induced increases in power prices, it may lead to an overcompensation of some industrial end-users (that is, those able to pass on the higher power costs into higher output prices) or all kinds of perverse effects on CO_2-related power consumption (similar to the distortive effects of specific free allocation provisions on CO_2-related power production).[17]

The main disadvantage of auctioning is that it raises the (true, actual) costs for eligible firms which reduces their competitiveness, profitability, sales volumes and/or market shares if these costs cannot be fully passed on to their output prices due to the fact that (i) eligible firms face competition from outsiders not subject to similar carbon costs, (ii) infra-marginal generators face higher carbon costs than marginal, price-setting producers, or (iii) companies are faced by a significant demand response to ETS-induced price increases (notably in the medium or long run).[18] To some extent, however, these issues can be relieved by (a) restricting auctioning to those eligible firms that are unlikely to face outside competition (such as power companies), while applying free allocations to other, 'exposed' participants, (b) limiting or differentiating the extent of auctioning (say 70 or 90 per cent of allowances needed) for firms facing issue ii or iii, and (c) recycling auction revenues to improve industrial competitiveness in general or to (partly) compensate firms affected by auctioning (while observing the qualifications made above on the recycling of auction revenues). With regard to the power sector, however, one may question whether limiting the extent of auctioning or recycling auction revenues can be justified after 2012 since, by that time, it has already benefited, in general, from generous free allocations and ETS-induced increases for more than eight years (2005–12).

Overall, to conclude, auctioning of emission allowances seems to be a proper option for the power sector after 2012 in order to address the issue of windfall profits due to free allocations up to 2012 and the efficiency distortions of some specific free allocation provisions. Eliminating these provisions, however, may lead to some increases in power prices and related windfall profits. Moreover, auction revenues from the power sector could be used to finance expenditures for useful, social objectives or to reduce taxation in order to improve industrial competitiveness in general or to compensate certain consumer groups in particular for ETS-induced increases in power prices.

Allocating Free Allowances to Power Consumers

Rather than allocating free allowances directly to power producers, these allowances could be allocated indirectly to power consumers while power producers are still obliged to cover their emissions by submitting allowances to the emission authority. This would imply that these consumers could sell these allowances while the producers have to buy them.

Basically, the option has the same effects as auctioning in terms of abolishing the windfall profits of power producers due to free allocations and, if present, eliminating the effects of specific free allocation provisions on power prices and related generators' surplus. The major difference is that electricity consumers are compensated directly for the ETS-induced increases in power prices (rather than the auction revenues accruing to the public sector).

However, if allocation of allowances to individual power consumers depends on their decisions on the quantities of electricity purchased, it may have a perverse, that is, stimulating effect on power consumption and related CO_2 emissions (similar to the effects of recycling auction revenues in a direct, targeted way as discussed above). In addition, it may lead easily to an overcompensation of at least some of the consumers, in particular those able to pass on higher power costs into higher output prices. Moreover, besides an adjustment of the present EU ETS directive and current practice of allocating allowances directly to power producers, it may imply a significant increase in transaction costs if allowances have to be allocated to hundreds of millions of end-users and, subsequently, sold on the market.

To some extent, the problems or disadvantages outlined above can be relieved by restricting allocations to end-users who cannot pass on the costs of higher electricity prices, or by allocating allowances to local distribution companies or to an independent trustee who could sell the allowances to power producers and use the revenues to rebate consumers on a per capita or household basis independent of the quantities of electricity purchased by each consumer.[19] Nevertheless, although this option may at first sight seem attractive, its overall performance seems to be low compared to the first option of auctioning discussed above and using the auction revenues in more general ways (including appropriate means to compensate end-users who actually need it without having an adverse effect on their power consumption decisions).

Benchmarking

Benchmarking implies allocating emission allowances for free based on a standard emission factor (that is, the benchmark) multiplied by a certain quantity or activity level (for instance, a certain input, output or capacity level). While the benchmark itself is usually fixed *ex ante* (but can vary per activity, technology, country or period considered), the quantity or activity level can be either fixed *ex ante* (that is, before the actual operational decisions are taken, resulting in a fixed cap-and-trade system) or adjusted *ex post* (that is, after the actual activity level is realized, resulting in a relative cap-and-trade system).

If a similar amount of free allowances is allocated in a benchmarking system with a similar fixed cap as in a grandfathering system, it has the same performance in terms of environmental effectiveness, economic efficiency, carbon prices, cost pass-through, output prices and overall (windfall) profits. However, in terms of distributing the economic rent of the free allocations – and, hence, the related windfall profits – it may result in a different outcome among the sectors or installations involved, depending on the specifics of the benchmarking system. This applies in particular to a 'perfect' benchmarking system (compared to a 'perfect' grandfathering system), that is, a free allocation system with a fixed cap and no updating – including no specific free allocation provisions for new entrants or plant closures – but also to a benchmarking system with a fixed cap and updating provisions (compared to a similar, less perfect grandfathering system).

On the other hand, in a benchmarking system with a relative (*ex post*) cap, the allocation of free allowances acts as a production subsidy which reduces the opportunity costs of emissions trading and, hence, reduces the amount of these costs passed through and the related windfall profits proportionally (compared to a situation of perfect free allocation – either grandfathering or benchmarking – with no updating). Depending on the level (stringency) of the benchmark and the actual emissions of the price-setting technology, the opportunity costs passed through and the resulting changes in power prices and windfall profits for marginal producers may even reduce to zero. Infra-marginal generators, on the contrary, may realize either windfall profits or losses depending on any possible change in output prices and sales volumes, as well as on the balance between their actual emissions and the allowances received for free (that is, the balance of allowances to be bought or sold on the market).

The main disadvantage of benchmarking with a relative cap, however, is that it also reduces the environmental effectiveness and/or economic efficiency of the ETS as the implicit output subsidy (and the resulting lower output prices) lead to more (price-responsive) demand, more production,

less carbon efficiency, more emissions, extra demand for emission allowances, higher allowance prices and/or higher inflows of JI/CDM credits.
For exposed sectors (that is, those facing outside competitors without
similar carbon costs) benchmarking with a relative cap could to some
extent be considered as a possible option, depending on weighing the trade-
off in the performance of such a benchmarking system versus the performance of an alternative allocation system with a fixed cap (either
auctioning or free allocation). However, for the power and other sheltered
sectors (that is, those lacking outside competitors) benchmarking with a
relative cap is not an attractive option from an efficient climate policy perspective as it results in more emissions, higher abatement costs or both.
Moreover, besides uncertainty on meeting the overall emission target of the
EU ETS (and, hence, of the EU mitigation commitments), a relative cap
system is fundamentally different from the present fixed system, requiring
a basic change of the EU ETS, which is not a politically feasible or acceptable option for the European Commission.

Reducing the Price of an Emission Allowance

In addition to changing the allocation system, there are some other options
for addressing concerns related to the ETS-induced increases in power
prices and generators' profits, for instance by reducing the price of an emission allowance. In theory, this carbon price reduction can be achieved by
(i) increasing the EU ETS cap, (ii) setting a binding maximum carbon price,
(iii) increasing the inflow of JI/CDM and other offset credits, (iv) implementing other policies besides emissions trading that reduce emissions of
the ETS sectors, and (v) encouraging carbon-saving technologies.

In general, by lowering the price of an allowance, and, hence, the amount
of carbon costs passed through, these options do indeed reduce the ETS-
induced increases in power prices and both categories of windfall profits (A
and B), at least in an absolute sense. For a variety of reasons, however, these
options have some restrictions or other drawbacks, which make them either
less attractive or feasible from an efficient carbon policy point of view. For
instance, increasing the EU ETS cap is not possible within a current trading
period, while probably neither carbon efficient nor politically acceptable as
it implies that the EU will not reach its mitigation objectives or, most likely,
that the non-ETS sector would have to abate at higher overall costs.
Similarly, setting a binding maximum carbon price is also not a politically
acceptable, feasible option partly because it is a kind of market regulation
which is nowadays unpopular among both policy makers and private
traders, and partly because it has implications in terms of mitigation targets
and abatement costs similar to the option of increasing the EU ETS cap

outlined above. Moreover, although there may be some rational considerations for introducing a maximum ETS price ('safety valve'), one may question whether addressing concerns related to ETS-induced increases in power prices and windfall profits is an appropriate justification for such a safety valve.

Increasing the inflow of offset credits (JI/CDM), on the contrary, could be a rational and attractive option to reduce EUA prices. It should be noted, however, that such a strategy only makes sense when there is no equilibrium between EUA and carbon offset prices or, more precisely, when the differential between these prices is significantly higher than the difference in risks and transaction costs between these alternative options to cover emissions of EU ETS installations. Moreover, the supply of these credits may be hard to increase due to a variety of political, technical, socio-economic and other project-related constraints in the home countries concerned. In addition, the EU prefers to limit the inflow of these credits into its ETS to ensure that a major part of the mitigation commitments are met domestically and to maintain a certain EUA price level that furthers domestic innovation purposes.

Implementing other climate or energy policies besides emissions trading – for instance, policies to promote renewables or energy saving – may lead to fewer emissions in the ETS sectors and, hence, to lower EUA prices. If these policies are implemented largely for other reasons than mitigation objectives – for instance, to enhance energy security – attendant outcomes in terms of lower ETS emissions or EUA prices could be welcomed (although it would probably make more sense to lower the ETS cap according to the lower ETS sector emissions due to these policies). On the other hand, if these policies are implemented solely to reduce ETS sector emissions or EUA prices, they can be questioned from a socially efficient climate policy perspective as, if effective, they generally replace cheaper abatement options (induced by emissions trading) by more expensive options (Sorrell and Sijm, 2003).

Finally, encouraging, carbon-saving technologies to reduce the price of a CO_2 emission allowance can be a sensible option, depending on the time perspective considered and the means applied to achieve this objective. If such (existing) technologies are subsidized heavily from public resources just to reduce short-term carbon prices for private operators, it does not seem to make sense from a socially efficient climate policy perspective. On the other hand, if certain market imperfections in the R&D stages of new carbon-saving technologies are overcome by adequate public support in a socially optimum way, it can be a highly justified option to keep carbon prices affordable in a process of growing mitigation ambitions. However, this option, if successful, will only control carbon prices in the long run rather than reducing them in the short term.

Regulating Power Prices

Another option to reduce ETS-induced increases in power prices and generators' profits due to free allocation is to have these prices regulated by an external authority, for instance the national transmission system operator (TSO) or the energy market surveillance authority. In practice, this option would imply that power producers are allowed to pass through only the (average) costs of carbon allowances bought on an auction or market (and the abatement costs of reducing power-related CO_2 emissions, or other changes in generation costs due to emissions trading) but not the opportunity costs of the allowances obtained for free. Besides limiting increases in electricity prices in favour of end-users, including small firms and low-income households, a related advantage of this option is that it reduces the deterioration of the international competitiveness of some power-intensive industries.

Regulating power prices, however, has some serious drawbacks. First, this option is nowadays not popular among EU policy makers as it does not fit in the current process of market liberalization, privatization and deregulation in order to achieve competitive, efficient power markets. Second, it may be hard and administratively demanding to determine (*ex ante*) the (average) costs of purchasing the necessary allowances over a certain trading period or the abatement costs (and other changes in generation costs) due to emissions trading, notably in the case of setting wholesale spot or forward prices.

Third, if effective, and assuming power demand to be price responsible – notably in the medium and long terms – this option implies higher power production, and, hence, higher sector-related emissions, thereby forfeiting an efficient strategy to meet future mitigation commitments. Moreover, lower power prices imply fewer incentives for investments in more-expensive, but carbon-saving technologies such as renewables.

Finally, one may question the effectiveness of this option to reduce power prices. As noted above, if effective, this option would result in more power demand, fewer carbon-saving technologies and, hence, more power production by CO_2-intensive plants. However, as operators of these plants are not allowed to pass through the opportunity costs of allowances obtained for free, they are inclined to reduce their production and sell the allowances on the market, resulting in serious power market scarcities and induced higher (rather than lower) electricity prices. Therefore, for a variety of reasons, regulating power prices does not seem to be a cost-effective or politically attractive option to reduce ETS-induced increases in electricity prices or generators' profits due to free allocations of allowances.

Encouraging Competition in the Power Sector

It is sometimes suggested that the ETS-induced increases in power prices and windfall profits resulting from free allocations are due to a lack of competition in the power sector and, hence, that encouraging this competition would reduce these increases in prices and profits. However, although encouraging power market competition may increase sector efficiency or reduce the incidence of market power – and, hence, reduce power prices – one may question whether this option is effective in reducing ETS-induced increases in power prices and generators' profits due to free allocations.

First, as supported by economic theory and empirical evidence, in competitive markets power producers also pass through the opportunity costs of carbon allowances into their price bids (even up to 100 per cent), regardless of whether they have purchased these allowances or obtained them for free. Moreover, depending on the specific characteristics of noncompetitive market structures and power demand (that is, a constant elasticity or linear demand curve), the carbon cost PTR on a monopolistic or oligopolistic market may be either significantly higher or lower than 100 per cent (Sijm et al., 2008). Therefore, encouraging competition in the power sector will not eliminate ETS-induced increases in power prices and windfall profits due to free allocation (on the contrary), but may even result in a higher carbon cost PTR and, hence, to even higher increases in these prices and profits.

In addition, a similar or related suggestion is that free allocations to new entrants lead to earlier investments in additional generation capacity and, perhaps, even in more power producers actively supplying on the market, resulting in less market scarcity, less market power or more competition and, therefore, in reducing or compensating the ETS-induced increases in power and windfall profits due to free allocation to existing producers. However, although to some extent these effects may occur, several qualifications can be made to free allocations to new entrants (in addition to the qualifications made above with regard to the impact of market competition on cost pass-through and power prices).

First, this option is only effective if it indeed leads to additional, earlier investments in generation capacity, which in the power sector may take at least several years to implement. Second, due to a variety of technical, economic and other constraints, investments in new generation capacity are usually conducted by existing firms rather than by newcomers. Third, as already noted for similar options reducing power prices, if effective, and assuming power demand to be price-responsive, this option implies higher power production and, hence, higher sector-related emissions, thereby giving up an efficient strategy to meet mitigation targets. Moreover, lower power prices imply less incentive for investments in more-expensive, but carbon-saving technologies such as renewables. This applies particularly if free allowances to new entrants are allocated in a fuel-specific or technology-biased way (that is, high polluters get more, while non-CO_2 emitters receive nothing), thereby undermining the ETS incentive structure towards carbon-saving investments. Finally, if one is interested in increasing generation capacity or power market competition, there are most likely more socially efficient measures than free allocations to new entrants, such as introducing capacity markets or direct capacity payments to power producers, including newcomers, or separating power network structures from production and marketing activities. Therefore, for a variety of reasons, encouraging competition in the power sector – notably by allocating allowances for free to new entrants – is highly questionable as a cost-effective option to reduce ETS-induced increases in power prices and windfall profits.

Taxing Windfall Profits

Another major, final option to address the issue of windfall profits due to the EU ETS is skimming these profits through taxation, either fully or partially. Compared to auctioning, a major advantage of taxation is that it can address both categories of windfall profits, that is, not only category B but also category A. Another advantage of taxing windfall profits is that it raises revenues that can be either recycled or used to finance public expenditures (although recycling tax revenues raises similar problems as recycling auction revenues, discussed above).

The major problem of taxing windfall profits is that, in practice, it is hard to estimate them reliably just as it is rather difficult to estimate empirically exact, reliable PTRs and, hence, to estimate what power prices (or sales volumes, generation costs, and so on) would have been without emissions trading (as discussed in Section 5.3). This applies in particular to estimating windfall profits at the individual company level, or to estimating such profits when free allocation provisions such as updating or free allocations to new entrants reduce ETS-induced increases in power prices and windfall profits in the medium or long run. An additional complicating issue is whether only ETS-induced windfall profits in the power sector should be taxed or also similar profits in other sectors, and how to determine these profits in a fiscal–juridical correct way (and what about any possible windfall losses due to emissions trading?).

Another, related problem concerns the definition of windfall profits, notably whether they refer to category A or B, or both categories, and whether they are related only to existing producers or also to new entrants (see Section 5.3). While in some EU ETS countries the issue of windfall profits in the power sector refers almost solely to category B (that is, windfall profits due to free allocations), in other countries it is related primarily to category A (that is, windfall profits due to ETS-induced changes in power prices, sales volumes and generation costs).

In addition, while some observers refer the issue of windfall profits to both existing and new producers, others relate it solely to incumbents, arguing that new entrants have based their investment decisions on profit expectations *after* the policy decision to introduce emissions trading. Moreover, taxing windfall category A to new entrants would imply that the incentive to invest in carbon-saving technologies would be reduced. On the other hand, however, taxing windfall category B accruing to new entrants would mean that the incentive to invest in CO_2-intensive technologies and the distortive effects on output prices and abatement efficiency would be reduced, notably if the free allocation to new entrants is applied in a fuel-specific or technology-biased way.

To some extent, the dilemmas outlined above could be relieved by restricting taxation to the full or partial (average) market value of the allowances allocated for free to both incumbents and new entrants in the power and other sheltered sectors of the EU ETS. However, a similar and, perhaps, even simpler solution would be to auction the corresponding amount of allowances to these sectors. In addition, a problem of full, that is, 100 per cent, taxation (or auctioning) is that it may lead to 'overtaxation' of windfall profits due to free allocations – depending on the actual PTR and the ETS-induced changes in sales volumes – while, as noted, it is hard to estimate the right tax rate to break even, notably at the company level or in the long run. Moreover, taxing only windfall category B would not solve the issue of windfall category A, which is not only more important in some EU ETS countries but, in addition, would deny these countries the potential revenues to address some concerns related to the ETS-induced increases in electricity prices such as losses in purchasing power of low-income households or losses in international competitiveness of some exposed, power-intensive industries.

Another option would be no taxation but auctioning of carbon allowances to all power operators (and other sheltered producers) and, as far as category A of windfall profits to existing, private companies is a relevant problem in some countries, these profits can be taxed by these countries – based on a conservative, prudent estimate of the size of windfall A – while the revenues can be used at their own discretion.

5.5 CONCLUSION

Power prices on forward (that is, year-ahead) wholesale markets in Germany and the Netherlands have generally increased substantially between early 2005 and mid-2006. In those cases where these prices have been set predominantly by coal-fired stations, notably during the off-peak period, this increase cannot be ascribed to the impact of fuel costs – as coal prices were rather stable over this period – whereas there seems to be a close relationship between the price and carbon costs of coal-generated power. However, in the case of gas setting (peak) power prices, the increase in these prices is mainly due to rising fuel costs, while the impact of gas-related carbon costs is less significant. Moreover, after the collapse of the carbon price in April/May 2006 and, particularly, during the latter part of 2006 (when both carbon and gas prices declined steadily), the link between power prices and fuel/carbon costs is far less clear, suggesting that other factors – such as growing capacity scarcities or market power – have become more important in affecting power prices.

Empirical estimates of carbon cost PTRs on forward wholesale power markets in Germany and the Netherlands vary from 0.4 to more than 1.0 in 2005–06. These estimates have to be interpreted with due care as, to some extent, they depend on (shortcomings of) the data and the methodologies used or the assumptions made, in particular that during the observation period power prices are set by a single (marginal) technology with a fixed, generic fuel efficiency, or that changes in power prices are predominantly caused by changes in the underlying costs of fuels and CO_2 emission allowances, and that all other generation costs and factors affecting power prices are more or less fixed.

Power prices on retail markets for either households or industrial users in Germany and the Netherlands have also increased significantly in 2004–06. However, since retail electricity prices in these countries are generally 2–4 times higher than wholesale power prices – due to high energy taxes, in particular for households, and high distribution or other marketing costs – the role of carbon costs passed through seems to be less relevant to account for (changes in) power prices on retail markets in Germany and the Netherlands in 2005–06.

More specifically, if it is assumed that over the 2004–06 period changes in the retail power spreads – defined as retail power prices excluding taxes and fuel costs – are solely due to carbon costs passed through, the impact of the EU ETS on (changes in) retail power prices was still relatively low in 2005 due to relatively low year-ahead carbon prices in 2004 and, perhaps, some time lags or other (marketing) constraints in passing through these costs to retail prices. In 2006, however, this impact seems to be already more significant, notably in Germany, due to relatively higher forward carbon prices in 2005 and, presumably, an increasing share of carbon costs passed through. Moreover, if it is assumed that the carbon costs passed through on the retail market are similar to those passed through on the wholesale market, the impact of these costs – and, hence, of the EU ETS – on retail power prices becomes generally even more significant. These findings, however, have to be treated cautiously as, to some extent, they depend on the assumptions made to estimate the carbon costs passed through.

For 2005–06, empirical estimates of windfall profits in the power sector of Germany and the Netherlands vary from, on average, 0.2 to 17 €/MWh or, in total, from €20–1000 million for the Netherlands and €4–8 billion in Germany. Similarly to the above-mentioned findings on carbon cost pass-through on wholesale and retail power markets, however, these estimates have to be treated with caution as EU ETS-induced windfall profits are hard to estimate precisely, depending on the time period considered and the assumptions made, including the definition of windfall profits.

Passing through the opportunity costs of (freely allocated) CO_2 emission allowances to power end-user prices is a rational and intended effect from an efficient carbon abatement policy perspective, while generators' windfall profits may result from free allocations and/or increases in these prices set by marginal fossil-fuelled stations (which also or mainly benefit infra-marginal, less-carbon-intensive plant operators). Nevertheless, the supposed ETS-induced increases in power prices and generators' profits have raised questions and concerns affecting the legitimacy or acceptability of the present EU ETS, including concerns regarding its impact on the international competitiveness of some power-intensive industries, the purchasing power of electricity end-users such as small households or, more generally, the distribution of social welfare among power producers and consumers. As a result, in several countries – including Germany and the Netherlands – policy makers and stakeholders of industrial or other interest groups have suggested a variety of options to address these concerns, including changing the emissions trading allocation system, taxing windfall profits or controlling market prices of EU carbon allowances, electricity or both. A summary of the performance of the major options suggested to address the above-mentioned concerns is provided in Table 5.3. The table shows that the performance of options to control or reduce carbon/power prices – either directly or indirectly – is generally low to medium, partly depending on the means to achieve these objectives, because either they barely address the ETS-related concerns mentioned above or they have certain disadvantages or other side-effects which make these options not attractive or acceptable to policy makers.

Table 5.3 Performance of options to address concerns regarding ETS-induced increases in output prices and windfall profits in the power sector

Option	Impact on power prices	Impact on windfall profits A	B	Impact on competitiveness of power-intensive industries	Other main effects (including major advantages and disadvantages)	Overall performance
1. Auctioning	0/+?	0/+?	–	0/–?	Raising auction revenues May reduce competitiveness of specific firms	High
2. Allocation to power consumers	0/+?	0/+?	–	0/–?	Direct compensation Perverse consumption effect Overcompensation of sheltered industries	Medium
3. Benchmarking:						
• Fixed (*ex ante*) cap	0	0	0	0	Effects are similar to grandfathering with fixed cap	Low
• Variable (*ex post*) cap	–/0?	–/0?	–	+/0?	Losses of economic efficiency and environmental effectiveness	Low
4. Reducing EUA price by:						
• Increasing ETS cap	–	–	–	+	Overall, lower CO_2 reductions and/or higher costs	Low
• Setting maximum prize	–	–	–	+	Idem + interferes with free market	Low
• Increasing JI/CDM credits	–	–	–	+	Technical, socio-economic and/or political limitations	Medium
• other carbon-reducing policies	–	–	–	+	Neither abatement effective nor efficient	Low

						Mainly effective in the long run	Medium/high
• *Encouraging carbon-saving technologies*	–	–	–	+		Mainly effective in the long run	Medium/high
5. Regulating power prices	–	–	+			Interferes with liberalization of competitive markets More demand/emissions Fewer carbon-saving investments More market scarcities	Low
6. Encouraging market competition	–/+?	–/+?	+/–?			Effects depend mainly on level of PTR of more vs. less competition	Medium
• *By free allocation to new entrants*	–/0?	–/0?	+/0?			Abatement inefficiency Undermines EU ETS incentives	Low
7. Taxing windfall profits	0	–	0			Windfall profits are hard to define or to estimate precisely in a fiscal–juridical way	Medium

Note: '+' indicates that prices or profits increase (or competitiveness improves), while '–' indicates that prices or profits decrease (or competitiveness deteriorates) due to the policy option.

For similar reasons, the overall performance is also low to medium for free allocation-related options such as free allocation of allowances to power consumers or free allocation based on benchmarking with either a fixed (*ex ante*) or a flexible (*ex post*) cap. On the other hand, the overall performance of auctioning allowances to power producers is considered to be rather high as it enhances the carbon efficiency of the EU ETS, eliminates the windfall profits due to free allocations, while it raises revenues that can be used (i) to finance public expenditures on carbon abatement or other useful, social objectives, (ii) to reduce taxation and related efficiency distortions ('double dividend'), or (iii) to compensate power-intensive industries and other electricity consumers for the ETS-induced increases in power prices.

Auctioning, however, does not reduce generators' windfall profits due to ETS-induced increases in power prices – in particular for infra-marginal, less-carbon-intensive plant operators – and may even result in an increase in such profits (notably when it implies the termination of free allocation to new entrants, leading to higher power prices in the medium or long run). As far as such profits are a major point of concern in some EU countries, these profits can be taxed by these countries, while the revenues can be used at their own discretion (similar to recycling auction revenues).

NOTES

1. This chapter is largely based on a study conducted by the Energy research Centre of the Netherlands (ECN) on behalf of the European Commission (see Sijm et al., 2008). It should be emphasized, however, that the views expressed here are those of the authors and do not necessarily reflect those of the European Commission.
2. Unless stated otherwise, the forward market refers to the year-ahead market where, for instance, electricity or fuel delivered in 2006 is traded during every day of 2005. (For a discussion of the data used for the empirical analyses, see Box 5.1.)
3. These spreads are indicators for the coverage of other (non-fuel/carbon) costs of generating electricity, including profits. For the present analysis, however, these other costs (for instance, maintenance or capital costs) are ignored as they are assumed to be constant for the period considered (although they may vary for the different country/load periods analysed) and, hence, they are assumed to not affect the PTRs of carbon costs estimated below in Section 6.2.
4. For instance, for the Netherlands over the period from January to July 2005, Sijm et al. (2005) show that if the assumed *gas* efficiency rate is raised from 40–45 per cent, the estimated PTR in the peak hours jumps from 0.27 to 0.55 while, if the assumed *coal* efficiency rate is raised from 35 to 40 per cent, the estimated PTR in the off-peak period increased from 0.47 to 0.55.
5. For a detailed discussion of the theoretical and empirical support for the pass-through of the opportunity costs of emissions trading to power prices, see Sijm et al. (2008).
6. For more details on the methodologies applied, see Sijm et al. (2008).
7. See also Figure 5.5, which presents a decomposition of the retail power prices into (a) energy taxes, (b) fuel costs, (c) full carbon costs, and (d) clean spreads, defined as the difference between the 'normal' (or 'dirty') retail power spreads and the full carbon costs

of the technologies setting power prices. Hence, by adding the full carbon costs to the clean spreads presented in Figure 5.5, one gets an indication of the absolute levels of these (normal/dirty) spreads in 2004–06 and the changes of these spreads over this period.

8. Note that the estimated PTRs according to the 'wholesale' approach vary by country but are similar in both 2005 and 2006 for both consumer groups in each country. This is due to the assumptions of this approach, notably that (i) for each country, the estimated carbon costs passed through on the wholesale market are equal to those passed through on the retail market, regardless of whether the electricity is sold to households or industrial consumers, and (ii) the PTRs for the year-ahead wholesale markets in 2004 (that is, power produced/consumed in 2005) are equal to the PTRs estimated for the forward markets in 2005 (as estimates of year-ahead PTRs for 2004 are lacking). In addition, note that the estimated PTRs according to the 'wholesale' approach for Germany and the Netherlands in 2006 (as recorded in Table 5.2) are actually the averages of the estimated PTRs of these countries on the year-ahead power markets during the peak and off-peak periods in 2005 (weighted by the shares of each period in total annual power sales), as recorded in Table 5.1. This follows from the assumption that the carbon costs passed through on the wholesale year-ahead markets in 2005 (with delivery in 2006) are subsequently passed through on the retail markets in 2006.

9. Note that in some cases of the 'full carbon costs' approach, the share of carbon costs passed through as a percentage of the changes in retail power price is more than 100 per cent. This may be due to the fact that (i) the carbon costs passed through are actually overestimated by the 'full carbon costs' approach, and/or (ii) the net change in retail power prices is small compared to the carbon costs passed through because (the increase in) these costs are compensated by a decrease in fuel costs or energy taxes.

10. See Sijm et al. (2008) for a review and discussion of estimates of windfall profits due to EU emissions trading.

11. VIK (2005) has made a similar estimate of EU ETS-induced windfall profits for the German power sector amounting to €5 billion per year, that is, approximately 10 €/MWh generated.

12. Note that these changes in profits of (infra-)marginal producers due to changes in relative carbon costs are similar to profit changes resulting from changes in fuel or other generation costs.

13. See Sijm et al. (2008) for a discussion of the power price impact of specific free allocation provisions, including (i) upgrading of free allocation, (ii) free allocation contingent on minimum production levels ('plant closures'), and (iii) free allocation to new entrants.

14. For a more detailed discussion of the effects of free allocation provisions on power prices, see Sijm et al. (2008).

15. For a broader discussion including design options, advantages and disadvantages of auctioning emission allowances, see Hepburn et al. (2006), Burtraw et al. (2007), Matthes and Neuhoff (2007) and Harrison et al. (2007).

16. In countries where end-users already pay relatively high environmental levies or value-added taxes on their power consumption, auction revenues could be used to reduce these levies/taxes or, perhaps even better, to reduce the taxes on those environmentally friendly commodities consumed by small households and firms in order to compensate them for the regressive income distribution effect of ETS-induced increases in retail power prices.

17. These perverse effects can be avoided if power users are compensated by a fixed, lump-sum amount which is independent of their current or future consumption decisions, but as soon as updating – including 'firm closures' and 'new entrants' – is included in the compensation scheme, it has a perverse effect on these decisions.

18. Another 'disadvantage' of auctioning is that governments cannot use free allocations to achieve other objectives besides carbon abatement efficiency, such as promoting security of supply or certain technological innovations (Harrison et al., 2007). However, such objectives can also – or even better – be achieved by using auction revenues accordingly.

19. For a further discussion of these approaches, see Burtraw and Palmer (2006).

REFERENCES

Burtraw, D., J. Goeree, C. Holt, K. Palmer and B. Shobe (2007), *Auction Design for Selling CO$_2$ Emission Allowances under the Regional Greenhouse Gas Initiative*, Phase 1 Research Report, Resources for the Future, Washington, DC.

Burtraw, D. and K. Palmer (2006), 'Comments for Senate Discussions on Climate Policy (Question 2. Allocation)', Resources for the Future, Washington, DC.

Frontier Economics (2006), *CO$_2$ Trading and Its Influence on Electricity Markets*, Final report to DTe, Frontier Economics Ltd, London.

Harrison, D., P. Klevnas, D. Radov and A. Foss (2007), *Complexities of Allocation Choices in a Greenhouse Gas Emissions Trading Program*, Report to the International Emissions Trading Association (IETA), NERA Economic Consulting, Boston, MA.

Hepburn, C., M. Grubb, K. Neuhoff, F. Matthes and M. Tse (2006), 'Auctioning of EU ETS Phase II allowances; how and why?', *Climate Policy*, **6** (1), 137–60.

Kesisoglou, I. (2007), 'Mitigating the windfall profitability of the power sector due to the European Emissions Trading Scheme', Master Thesis, Delft University of Technology, The Netherlands.

Matthes, F. and K. Neuhoff (2007), *Auctioning in the European Union Emissions Trading Scheme*, Final Report commissioned by World Wildlife Fund, Öko-Institut e.V, Berlin, and University of Cambridge, UK.

Sijm, J., S. Bakker, Y. Chen, H. Harmsen and W. Lise (2005), *CO$_2$ Price Dynamics. The Implications of EU Emissions Trading for the Price of Electricity*, ECN-C-05-081, Petten.

Sijm, J., Y. Chen, M. ten Donkelaar, S. Hers and M. Scheepers (2006a), *CO$_2$ Price Dynamics. A Follow-up Analysis of the Implications of EU Emissions Trading for the Price of Electricity*, ECN-C-06-015, Petten.

Sijm, J., K. Neuhoff and Y. Chen (2006), 'CO$_2$ cost pass-through and windfall profits in the power sector', *Climate Policy*, **6** (1), 49–72.

Sijm, J., S. Hers, W. Lise and B. Wetzelaer (2008), *The Impact of the EU ETS on Electricity Prices*, Final report to the European Commission, DG Environment, conducted and published by the Energy research Centre of the Netherlands (ECN), Petten/Amsterdam.

Sorrell, S. and J. Sijm (2003), 'Carbon trading in the policy mix', *Oxford Review of Economic Policy*, **19** (3), 420–37.

VIK (Verband der Industriellen Energie- und Kraftwirtschaft) (2005), *VIK-Berechnungen zu den Windfall Profits der Strombranche durch den CO$_2$-Emissionshandel* (Assessments of windfall profits in the power sector due to Co$_2$ emissions trading), Verband der Industriellen Energie- und Kraftwirtschaft e.V., Essen.

WWF (World Wildlife Fund) (2006), *Gewinne aus der Einpreisung der CO$_2$-Kosten im Verhaltnis zu den angekundigten Investionen von RWE, E. ON* (Profits from the pass-through of CO$_2$ costs related to announced investments by RWE, EO.N), *Vattenfall Europe, EnBW und STEAG*, Berlin.

6. A vector error correction model of the interactions among gas, electricity and carbon prices: an application to the cases of Germany and the United Kingdom

Derek W. Bunn and Carlo Fezzi

6.1 INTRODUCTION

The European Emissions Trading Scheme (EU ETS), started on 1 January 2005, has been a substantial initiative of the European Union (EU) to fulfil its carbon abatement targets following the Kyoto Protocol. According to the ETS directive (European Commission, 2003), tradable allowances are allocated to industrial emitters of carbon dioxide, specifying the amount of CO_2 they can emit each year. Since companies are allowed to trade permits freely with one another within the EU, the scheme should ensure not only that overall emissions are reduced, but also that the cuts are made by those firms that provide lower abatement costs. Therefore, the economic impact of reducing CO_2 emissions should be minimized.

Prior to the emergence of actual evidence from carbon trading in practice, extensive theoretical and simulation analyses have speculated upon its effects, in particular on the energy sector (for example, Böhringer, 2002; Barreto and Kypreos, 2004; Böhringer and Lange, 2005). Although capable of providing normative and policy insights, these theoretical models are not appropriate for explaining carbon price dynamics on a daily basis. Indeed, as soon as the first market data became available, empirical, econometric models were developed to explain CO_2 price behaviour. For example, Mansanet-Bataller et al. (2007), using several regression models, identify weather and energy price variables (in particular oil price) as the main determinants of CO_2 price changes during 2005. However, their analysis does not provide a complete picture of the interactions between energy and carbon prices but focuses on the dynamics of CO_2 prices only, in a single-equation framework. For this reason, electricity price is not included explicitly in the model, but represented by weather-related variables, and gas price is assumed exogenous a priori. The extent to which gas prices may follow carbon and electricity prices has, however, been an open question (mostly in the UK where a substantial part of the domestic gas demand has been from power generation), particularly as the EU ETS is intended to promote fuel switching in the short term, for example, from coal to gas.

In this chapter we address this collective price formation process in detail by proposing a modelling framework that jointly analyses, as endogenous, the electricity, gas and carbon price interactions on high-frequency, day-ahead data. In specific terms we estimate a vector error connection model (VECM) on UK and German data, which encompasses both short-run and equilibrium relations. From this, we can estimate the transmission of shocks between gas, carbon and power prices, and thereby address questions on the short-term economic impact and potential efficiency of the scheme. In particular, we estimate the dynamic pass-through of carbon price into the electricity prices of both countries.

6.2 CARBON PRICE FORMATION AND THE ENERGY MARKETS

As for any other freely traded product, the fundamentals influencing the carbon market are supply and demand. During Phase I of the EU ETS (2005–07) the supply of carbon allowances is essentially fixed, and determined by the national allocation plans (NAPs) of the EU member states.[1] On the other hand, demand is primarily influenced by four factors: (a) the allowance allocation, (b) the carbon abatement costs, (c) the CO_2 emissions, and (d) expectations about the future price. Given this unique environment, at the official launch of the EU ETS on 1 January 2005, only a few market analysts and academics would have expected the dynamics that the carbon price series subsequently demonstrated (Convery and Redmond, 2007).

As shown in Figure 6.1, in the first half of 2005, carbon allowances were traded at about 7€/tonne, rising steadily to a peak over 29 €/tonne in July, before falling back to around 20 €/tonne a month later and fluctuating around that level during the rest of 2005. By April 2006, daily prices had again risen to over 30 €/tonne, falling precipitously during three days at the end of the month to below 10 €/tonne when the first annual settlement news appeared and it became apparent that the market was long by several million of allowances and that far less abatement was needed. Given this dramatic fall, it is plausible to conclude that not many expected such a surplus in the allowances allocation. Shocks of that magnitude affect the

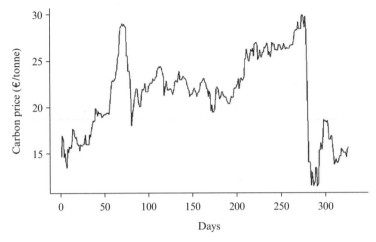

Source: EEX.

Figure 6.1   Carbon allowances price, 1 April 2005 to 30 June 2006

asset values of power companies since they substantially reduce the wind-fall profits originating from the grandfathering of the allowances. For example, British Energy lost 5 per cent of its stock market value during those three days in April 2006.

The strong linkage between the ETS and the power markets relates to the carbon emissions generated by the electricity production process, which have to be covered by carbon allowances. Of course, even though most of the allowances were freely allocated to the power producers according to the different NAPs, the ETS price of carbon is still part of the short-run power generation cost as it is a clear opportunity cost associated with the combustion of fossil fuel (see, among others, Sijm et al., 2006). Furthermore, the main short-run carbon reduction option available to portfolio power generators is switching production to a less carbon-intensive facilities. For example, a power producer burning coal can roughly reduce by 40 per cent its carbon emissions per MWh by switching to natural gas. Since this coal to gas switch was seen as likely to be an important short-term response in the first phase of the EU ETS, the price of carbon is potentially an important determinant of the gas demand and a shifter of the electricity supply function.

Furthermore, gas and electricity are now fully liberalized commodities in most of the European countries, and they are actively traded daily. Their prices have been characterized by extremely high volatility and, in particular for electricity, it is not uncommon to observe a variation of 200

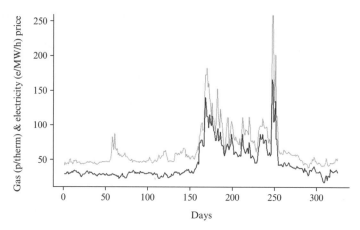

Source: Platts.

*Figure 6.2   Day-ahead electricity (grey line) and gas (black line) prices in
the UK, 1 April 2005 to 30 June 2006*

per cent on a weekly basis. As shown in Figure 6.2, the prices of these two
commodities are closely related in the UK, where almost 40 per cent of
the energy is produced by gas-fired power plants. The relationship
between gas and electricity is less obvious in Germany (Figure 6.3), where
a substantial amount of power is produced by burning coal or lignite,
although gas may still be influential as a marginal price setter. It is still
uncertain how fluctuations in gas and power prices are transmitted to
carbon prices, since carbon allowances need to be settled only annually,
and this therefore offers much more temporal arbitrage than electricity,
which is substantially non-storable, and gas, with rather limited storage.
On the other hand, CO_2 price is potentially a determinant of electricity
and gas prices, which are already interrelated. Indeed, previous research
by Mansanet-Bataller et al. (2007) suggests that gas and oil prices are
indeed capable of influencing CO_2 prices. However, in their regression
models, gas price is an exogenous factor and electricity price is not considered at all. Those assumptions remain open questions, therefore, given
the mutual influence that gas, electricity and carbon prices might have on
one another.

In this chapter we study the interactions among the electricity, gas and
carbon markets by developing a VECM model in which all three commodity prices are modelled jointly as endogenous. The model is estimated
separately for Germany and the UK. The time series of the endogenous
variables (see Figures 6.1–3) present a drifting behaviour, some with a

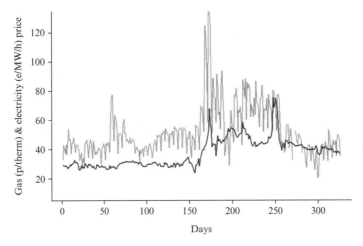

Source: Platts.

Figure 6.3   Day-ahead electricity (grey line) and gas (black line) prices
in Germany, 1 April 2005 to 30 June 2006

Table 6.1   Unit root test on the endogenous variables (in natural
logarithms)

Variable	Trend	Lags[a]	Levels		First differences	
			ADF	KPSS	ADF	KPSS
P_{carbon}[b]	Yes	4	−2.57	0.586**	−7.91**	0.149
$P_{electricity\ UK}$	No	1	−3.15*	0.731**	−15.2**	0.051
$P_{gas\ UK}$	No	3	−2.33	0.706**	−10.1**	0.069
$P_{electricity\ GE}$	No	5	−3.91*	0.684**	−8.58**	0.054
$P_{gas\ GE}$	No	1	−2.12	0.510**	−12.4**	0.054

Notes:
*   = significant at 5 per cent, ** = significant at 1 per cent against the asymptotical critical
     values in Davidson and MacKinnon (1993) and Kwiatkowski et al. (1992).
a   Number of lags selected with the Hannan and Quinn (1979) criterion.
b   For carbon price the ADF test has to be augmented to take into account the level shift at
     the end of April 2006. Therefore, we implemented the ADF test with exponential level
     shift introduced in Lanne et al. (2002) and Saikkonen and Lütkepohl (2002).

smooth annual seasonality and possibly following a trend. We investigate
their stationarity using the augmented DF (ADF: Dickey and Fuller, 1979;
Said and Dickey, 1984) unit root test and the KPSS (Kwiatkowski, Phillips,
Schmidt and Shin, 1992) stationarity test on their logarithms[2] (Table 6.1).

For gas and carbon prices, both tests support the presence of a unit root, while for electricity they give opposite indications since the null hypotheses of unit root and of stationarity are both rejected. This behaviour is typical of electricity price series, which often present dynamics which are indeterminate between stationary and unit root processes (Koopman et al., 2007). On the other hand, there is strong evidence that the first differences of all the endogenous series are stationary. Therefore, we model all series as non-stationary following Hendry and Juselius (2000, p. 21), who suggested that 'even though a variable is stationary, but with unit root close to unity . . . it is often a good idea to act as if there are unit roots to obtain robust statistical inference'.

6.3   THE MODEL

As discussed in the previous section, there are economic reasons why energy commodity prices and carbon price can mutually influence each other. As a result, in a modelling framework, none of these variables can be assumed exogenous a priori. Therefore, our approach starts from a VAR (Vector Autoregressive Model) where electricity, gas and carbon prices are jointly modelled as endogenous. Introduced in Sims (1980), VAR models rapidly became one of the most popular tools in applied macroeconomics, providing a coherent and credible approach to data description and forecasting. In the classical, reduced-form VAR, all the variables are considered as endogenous, and modelled as a linear function of their own lagged values. When it is possible to identify some further (exogenous) variables that influence the endogenous ones but are, themselves not, directly affected by them, the model can be augmented by adding current and lagged values of those exogenous variables.

In this framework, the endogenous variables consist of electricity, gas and carbon prices, while the exogenous variables include oil and coal prices, three dummies to encompass the carbon price shift following the 'news' shock in April 2006, and atmospheric temperature, as a proxy for electricity and gas demand. Temperature has to be transformed before entering the model, since its relationship with electricity demand (and hence, price) is non-linear and 'U'-shaped (for an illustration, see Engle et al., 1986). A possible way to linearize this relation is to define two thresholds. When the temperature is lower than the first one, electricity and gas are used mainly for heating purposes and the relation has a negative slope; between the two thresholds the temperature effect on electricity and gas demand is at its lowest level and almost constant; above the second threshold electricity is used for air conditioning, hence the relation with temperature is positive, while gas demand roughly remains constant.[3] These exogenous variables are crucial in explaining the dynamics of the dependent variables and encompass most of the exogenous shocks that affect the prices formation process. Therefore, all the remaining correlations between the endogenous variables are indeed to be attributed to the mutual influences among themselves, and not, for example, to simultaneous correlations with unmodelled variables.

While this modelling approach, in general, often provides an accurate statistical representation of the dynamic behaviour of the system of variables, its main drawback may be the lack of economic interpretability of its parameters. In fact, VAR models are reduced forms, since the instantaneous interactions of the endogenous variables are not modelled explicitly, but are included in the covariance matrix of the residuals (for a critique of VAR models, see Cooley and Le Roy, 1985). However, structural relations can be estimated from VARs when the variables in the system are non-stationary, as happens to be the case for the specific electricity, gas and carbon price time series we are considering (see the analysis in the previous section). Thus, even though the endogenous variables considered *per se* are not stationary, that is, they are I(1), there may exist linear combinations of them which are stationary. Those are called 'cointegrating vectors', and are long-run relations that hold the variables together over time. From a statistical point of view they are equilibrium states 'to which the system is attracted, other things being equal', (Banerjee et al., 1993). Furthermore, they can be interpreted as long-run behavioural relationships, with direct structural economic meaning (Johansen, 1995; Davidson, 1998). Of course, 'long run' has to be interpreted in the context of the time span in the data set analysed. Typically, only I(1) variables linked over time by such structural economic relationships prove to be cointegrated.[4]

In this chapter we use the maximum likelihood (ML) methodology, introduced in Johansen (1991) and Johansen and Juselius (1994) to test for cointegration and eventually estimate the cointegrating vector(s). This technique starts from a reduced-form VAR and derives the corresponding Vector Error-Correction Model (VECM) specification, expressed in first differences, in which all the variables are stationary. Indicating with $y_t = [p_{el}, p_{gas}, p_{carb}]$ the vector of endogenous variables containing the natural logarithms of electricity, gas and carbon prices and with $z_t = [1, t_{cold}, D_{cold}, t_{hot}, D_{hot}, p_{oil}, p_{coal}]$ the vector of exogenous variables (with t_{cold} the temperature below the first threshold and with D_{cold} its indicator dummy variable, t_{hot} the temperature above the second threshold and with D_{hot} its dummy, p_{oil} and p_{coal} logarithms of oil and coal prices) and with $x_t = [y_t, z_t]$ the VECM can be written as:

$$\Delta y_t = \Gamma_0 \Delta z_t + \Gamma_1 \Delta x_{t-1} + \Gamma_2 \Delta x_{t-2} + \dots + \Gamma_{k-1} \Delta x_{t-k+1} + \alpha \beta' y_{t-1} + u_t,^5$$

$$(6.1)$$

where u_t is the residual term, serially uncorrelated and distributed as $N(0,\Sigma)$, and k is the number of lags in the reduced form VAR large enough to ensure absence of autocorrelation. This model encompasses both short-run, reduced-form relations and structural, long-run interactions. The first terms are expressed by the parameters Γ_i ($i = 0, \dots, k - 1$) which contain the effects of the exogenous and the lagged endogenous variables. The latter are given by the cointegrating vectors $\beta' y_{t-1}$: the long-run equilibrium relationships towards which the system is attracted over time. The vector α contains the error-correction coefficients, which represent the speed of adjustment of each endogenous variable towards each cointegrating vector. If the endogenous variables are not linked over time by any long-run relationships, $\alpha\beta'$ will not be significantly different from zero, that is, the product matrix will have rank $= 0$.

As shown in Chapter 4 of Johansen (1996), model (6.1) can be rewritten to express the variation in the endogenous variables as a function of the current and lagged residuals. This representation can be interpreted as reflecting the responses to impulse shocks on the system. For instance, it provides the dynamic response of electricity price to a shock on carbon price. In effect, this is an estimate of the dynamic pass-through of the carbon price into the electricity market. In the next section we estimate model (6.1) separately for Germany and the UK, and deriving the impulse response function (IRF) of electricity and gas prices to a shock on the carbon market.

6.4   THE EMPIRICAL ANALYSIS[6]

The model outlined in the previous section is estimated on the day-ahead electricity and gas prices for the UK (UKPX and NBP) and Germany (EEX and TTF) and the European carbon emission price (EEX) illustrated in Figures 6.1–3. Atmospheric temperature is represented by the daily average temperature in London (for the UK model) and in Munich (for the German model), available from the archive provided by the University of Dayton (http://www.engr.udayton.edu/weather/). The oil price is represented by the Brent Oil Index and the coal price by the ARA (Amsterdam-Rotterdam-Antwerp) forward price, both provided by Platts. We transform the commodity price variables (electricity, gas, carbon, coal and oil prices) into their natural logarithms to reduce variability, and thus obtain directly the elasticity values from the parameter estimates. We estimate model (6.1)

Table 6.2   Cointegrating vector estimates and cointegration test[7]

Ho		United Kingdom		Germany	
r	p–r	LR	p–value	LR	p–value
0	2	35.38	0.001	47.09	0.000
1	1	9.17	0.161	6.80	0.351
2	0	2.75	0.115	1.47	0.262
		Beta	t–ratio	Beta	t–ratio
$P_{electricity}$		1	–	1	–
P_{gas}		−0.65	−11.89	−0.49	−3.22
P_{carbon}		−0.33	−2.94	−0.52	−3.06
Constant		−0.73	−2.19	−0.58	−0.87

with one lag in both the endogenous and exogenous variables (HQ (Hannan-Quinn) criterion), and test for the number of cointegrating vectors using the trace test introduced in Saikkonen and Lütkepohl (2000). We restrict the intercept to lie in the cointegration space since we do not find evidence of a trend in the dynamics of the variables.

The results, reported in the top panel of Table 6.2, strongly support the presence of just one cointegrating vector in both countries. In the lower panel, therefore, the single cointegrating equations for the UK and Germany are presented. Observing the cointegrating coefficients, we are reassured that all the estimates have plausible signs. The coefficients can be interpreted as price elasticities, implying, for instance, that a gas price rise of 1 per cent in the UK, would, in equilibrium, be associated with an electricity price rise of 0.65 per cent. Furthermore, since all the coefficients are strongly significant, all the price variables are important to define the equilibrium vector, that is, both carbon and gas prices are crucial to define the level to which electricity price is attracted over time. However, differences exist between the two countries. In the UK, where the marginal fuel is often natural gas, the relationship between gas and electricity price is significantly stronger than in Germany, where a substantial fraction of the power is produced by burning coal or lignite. On the other hand, and as a consequence of this, the relation between electricity and carbon price is stronger in the German market, with the equilibrium coefficient of carbon price being approximately 1.60 times larger than that of the UK. Reassuringly, the carbon content of natural gas is indeed roughly 60 per cent of that of coal per unit of electricity produced, and so the estimated co-integrating relationships do present plausible economic interpretations and inter-market differentiation.

Even though they are useful to understand the equilibrium price of electricity in the 'long run', the cointegrating vector does not contain any information regarding the short-term interactions of those prices (matrixes Γ_i in equation (6.1)) or how fast each of the variables moves towards the equilibrium (matrix α). In order to analyse these issues we estimate model (6.1) using 3SLS (3 stage least squares) and eliminate the non-significant coefficients through a recursive procedure, that is, sequentially excluding the regressors with the lowest t-ratio and ultimately minimizing the HQ criterion (see Brüggemann and Lütkepohl, 2001). The final estimates are reported in Table 6.3. All the overidentifying restrictions are not rejected according to the likelihood ratio, chi-square test (p-values 0.99 and 0.76) and there is no evidence of unmodelled serial correlation. However, there is a significant ARCH (autoregressive conditional heteroskedastic) component in the residual variance. This could be expected, given the high and time-varying volatility that characterizes the endogenous price series (for an analysis of this issue in electricity price modelling, see, for example, Koopman et al., 2007), but it is not likely to be a major problem in our cointegration analysis (Gonzalo, 1994).

According to the adjustment coefficient values (see, for instance, Johansen, 1991) there is evidence of long-run weak exogeneity of carbon and gas prices in both markets. In other words, when the system is out of equilibrium, only electricity prices revert towards the long-run cointegrating relationship. However, carbon price is influenced by lagged gas price in both markets and by the gas price in the UK, even though the significance levels are not very high. One reason for this 'weak effect' is that CO_2 allowances are traded on an international market covering the whole of the EU and, therefore, shocks coming from distinct national markets alone (even though large, like Germany and the UK) are not always strong enough to affect significantly the EU carbon price. Furthermore, in line with Mansanet-Bataller et al. (2007), oil price seems to be one of the major factors influencing CO_2 price dynamics, given its strong connection with the gas contracts in most of the European countries (Convery and Redmond, 2007). Finally, temperature affects both electricity and gas prices in a non-linear fashion, but not carbon prices directly. This is consistent with carbon allowances, although traded daily, being subject to annual settlement. Overall, the consistency of the specifications for Germany and the UK, and the plausible differences due to their gas/coal fuel mix differences, suggests that the above model is providing satisfactory insights and estimates.

Finally, we analyse the dynamic pass-through of carbon price into electricity price by computing the IRF of a shock on carbon price in both countries. Even though it is not generally correct to give to the forecast IRF a

Table 6.3   VECM final estimates

	United Kingdom			Germany		
	$\Delta p_{electricity}$	Δp_{gas}	Δp_{carbon}	$\Delta p_{electricity}$	Δp_{gas}	Δp_{carbon}
Error $_{t-1}$	−0.25	−0.07	−0.01	−0.19	0.01	0.01
	(−4.77)	*(−1.38)*	*(−0.33)*	*(−5.82)*	*(0.89)*	*(0.45)*
$\Delta p_{electricity,t-1}$	−0.13	–	−0.04	–	–	−0.03
	(−2.44)		*(−1.62)*			*(−1.64)*
$\Delta p_{gas,t-1}$	0.20	–	0.06	–	–	–
	(3.59)		*(2.37)*			
$\Delta p_{oil,t}$	–	–	0.39	–	–	0.41
			(3.48)			*(3.63)*
$\Delta p_{coal,t}$	–	−0.75	–	–	–	–
		(−2.05)				
$\Delta p_{oil,t-1}$	–	–	–	−0.75	–	–
				(−2.09)		
$\Delta p_{coal,t-1}$	–	–	–	0.86	–	–
				(1.60)		
$\Delta t_{hot,t}$	0.01	−0.01	–	0.01	–	–
	(2.45)	*(−4.17)*		*(1.50)*		
$\Delta t_{cold,t}$	–	−0.01	–	–	−0.01	–
		(−2.16)			*(1.4)*	
$D_{fest,t}$	–	–	–	−0.10	–	–
				(−2.5)		
$D_{carb,t}$	–	–	−0.12	–	–	−0.13
			(−3.32)			*(−3.4)*
$D_{carb,t-1}$	–	–	−0.30	–	–	−0.29
			(−7.92)			*(−7.70)*
$D_{carb,t-2}$	–	–	−0.27	–	–	−0.27
			(−7.21)			*(−7.28)*
Restrictions[a]						
χ(32) & χ(36)	–	14.5 [0.99]	–		27.8 [0.76]	–
AR(4)[b], χ(36)	–	50.9 [0.06]	–		44.1 [0.16]	–
ARCH (4)[c],χ(4)	4.05 [0.40]	4.30 [0.37]	[29.8] [0.00]	15.8 [0.00]	24.8 [0.00]	30.18 [0.00]

Notes
[a]   LR (likelihood ratio) test for overidentifying restrictions.
[b]   Breusch–Godfrey LM (Lagrange multiplier) test for vector-autocorrelation (e.g., Lütkepohl and Krätzig, 2004).
[c]   ARCH LM test for conditional heteroskedasticity in the residuals (Lütkepohl and Krätzig, 2004).

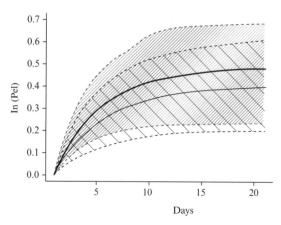

Note: Bootstrapped 90 per cent confidence intervals (dashed lines) according to Hall (1992).

Figure 6.4   *Forecasting the IRF of electricity price on a shock on gas price Germany in grey and UK in black*

structural interpretation (for a discussion, see Cooley and LeRoy, 1985; Blanchard and Quah, 1986) in this specific framework it is possible to give economic meaning to the response to a shock on the carbon price equation because of the low and not significant cross-correlation of the carbon equation residuals with the gas and electricity ones (results not reported in Table 6.3 but available on request from the authors).

The dynamic impact of a 1 per cent carbon price increase on the UK and German electricity prices is shown in Figure 6.4. Clearly, even though the estimated effect is higher for Germany, which is characterized by a more 'carbon-intensive' power sector than the UK, the difference between the two countries is not significant. This is caused by the wide confidence interval bands which reflect the high variability characterizing the two electricity price time series. However, in both markets the response to a carbon shock takes some time to be fully passed through into the electricity price.

6.5   CONCLUSIONS

Using a cointegrated VECM, we show how carbon price is important in formulating the equilibrium price of electricity in the UK and Germany. Furthermore, it is also a function, itself, of the underlying energy prices in each country. This is a diffused effect, as distinct national markets alone are not always strong enough to affect significantly the price of carbon, which is traded on an EU level. The empirical evidence, therefore, supports the structural expectations for the joint interaction of electricity, gas and carbon, and suggests that the markets may well be following fundamentals.

We also estimate the dynamic pass-through of carbon price into electricity prices, concluding that, eventually, a 1 per cent shock in carbon translates on average into a 0.33 per cent shock in the UK electricity price and a 0.52 per cent shock in the German one. This is consistent with the greater proportion of coal in the German fuel mix. Further, even though the linkage between electricity and gas prices is significant in both countries, we do not find any influence of carbon price on gas prices. This might have been because the price of carbon during the period analysed was not high enough to stimulate substantial switching from coal to gas in power plants and, therefore, did not increase significantly the demand for gas. Another reason might be that the fraction of gas demand attributable to power generation, across the EU as a whole, may, at that time, not have been sufficient to make a significant effect on short-term gas price formation, especially with the strong contractual links of gas to oil price in place. Overall, the results of the model suggest a consistent picture and indicate an electricity market responding rather well to the fundamentals of fuel and carbon prices. As for the fundamental behaviour of the carbon prices themselves, a longer-term perspective is clearly needed to assess the success of the market signals for actual carbon abatement.

NOTES

1. In practice it is possible to create allowances by undertaking certain types of environmentally friendly investment in developing countries. However, The EU ETS has limited the inclusion of these 'offset' projects, and the effect of these was not substantial in the early years of the scheme.
2. We model logarithms instead of the original series for two reasons: first the logarithmic transformation reduces variability and kurtosis, and second, it allows us to interpret the model parameters directly as elasticities.
3. Through a preliminary exploratory analysis we define 54° F (12 °C) as the lower threshold and 60° F (16° C) as the upper threshold.
4. A further elaboration of cointegration is beyond the scope of this text. For an extensive analysis we refer to the wide literature available, among others, by Engle and Granger (1987), Johansen (1991, 1995), Banerjee et al. (1993), Davidson (1998), Maddala and Kim (1998) and Juselius (2006).
5. The two variables Δt_{cold} and Δt_{hot} included in Δx_t are not simply the first difference of t_{cold} and t_{hot}. In fact, in order to linearize a relation in the first differences, one has to consider whether, during the intra-period variation, the relationship with quantity is reversed if the temperature crosses the threshold. To overcome this problem we define as Δt_{hot} all the variation of the temperature that occurs above the upper threshold and as Δt_{cold} all the variation that occurs below the lower one.

6. All the empirical analysis, including the unit root tests in Section 6.2, has been implemented in JMULTI (Lütkepohl and Krätzig, 2004, http://www.jmulti.de/).
7. We also tried a specification with the coal price included in the cointegrating vector, but it resulted in being not significant.

REFERENCES

Barreto, L. and Kypreos, S. (2004), 'Emission trading and technology deployment in an energy-system "bottom-up" model with technology learning', *European Journal of Operational Research*, **158**, 243–61.
Banerjee, A., J.J. Dolado, J.W. Galbraith and D.F. Hendry (1993), *Co-integration error-correction and the econometric analysis of non-stationary data*, Advanced Test in Econometrics, Oxford:
Blanchard, O.J. and Quah, D. (1986), 'The dynamic effects of aggregate demand and supply disturbances', *American Economic Review*, **79** (4), 655–73.
Böhringer, C. (2002), 'Industry-level emission trading between power producers in the EU', *Applied Economics*, **34** (4), 523–33.
Böhringer, C. and Lange, A. (2005), 'On the design of optimal grandfathering schemes for emission allowances', *European Economic Review*, **49**, 2041–55.
Brüggemann, R. and Lütkepohl, H. (2001), 'Lag selection in subset VAR models with an application to a U.S. monetary system', in R. Friedmann, L. Knüppel and H. Lütkepohl (eds), *Econometric Studies: A Festschrift in Honour of Joachim Frohn*, Münster: LIT Verlag, pp. 107–28.
Convery, F.J. and Redmond, L. (2007), 'Market and price development in the European Emissions Trading Scheme', *Review of Environmental Economics and Policy*, **1** (1), 88–111.
Cooley, T. and LeRoy, S. (1985), 'Atheoretical macroeconometrics: a critique', *Journal of Monetary Economics*, **16**, 283–306.
Davidson, J. (1998), 'Structural relations, cointegration and identification: some simple results and their application', *Journal of Econometrics*, **87**, 87–113.
Davidson, R. and MacKinnon, J. (1993), *Estimation and Inference in Econometrics*, Oxford: Oxford University Press.
Dickey, D.A. and Fuller, W.A. (1979), 'Distribution of the estimators for autoregressive time series with a unity root', *Journal of the American Statistical Association*, **74**, 427–31.
Engle, R.F. and Granger, C.W.J. (1987), 'Co-integration and error correction: representation, estimation and testing', *Econometrica*, **55** (2), 251–76.
Engle, R.F., Granger, C.W.J., Rice, J. and Weiss, A. (1986), 'Semiparametric estimates of the relation between weather and electricity sales', *Journal of the American Statistical Association*, **81**, 310–20.
European Commission (2003), *Directive 2003/87/EC of the European Parliament and of the Council of 13 October 2003 establishing a scheme for greenhouse gases emission allowance trading within the Community and amending Council Directive 96/61/EC-OJ L275*.
Gonzalo, J. (1994), 'Five alternative methods of estimating long-run equilibrium relationships', *Journal of Econometrics*, **60** (1), 203–33.
Hall, P. (1992), *The Bootstrap and Edgeworth Expansion*, New York: Springer.
Hannan, E.J. and Quinn, B.G. (1979), 'The determination of the order of an autoregression', *Journal of the Royal Statistical Society*, **41**, 190–95.

Hendry, D.F. and Juselius, K. (2000), 'Explaining cointegration analysis: Part I', *The Energy Journal*, **21**, 1–42.

Johansen, S. (1991), 'Estimation and hypothesis testing of cointegrating vectors in Gaussian vector autoregressive models', *Econometrica*, **59** (6), 1551–80.

Johansen, S. (1995), 'Identifying restriction of linear equations with application to simultaneous equations and cointegration', *Journal of Econometrics*, **69**, 111–32.

Johansen, S. (1996), *Likelihood-based Inference in Cointegrated Autoregressive Models*, 2nd edn, Oxford: Oxford University Press.

Johansen, S. and Juselius, K. (1994), 'Identification of the long-run and short-run structure. An application to the ISLM model', *Journal of Econometrics*, **63**, 7–36.

Juselius, K. (2006), *The Cointegrated VAR Model: Methodology and Application*, Oxford: Oxford University Press.

Koopman, S.J., Ooms, M. and Carnero, M.A. (2007), 'Periodic seasonal reg-ARFIMAGARCH models for daily electricity spot prices', *Journal of the American Statistical Association*, **102**, 16–27.

Kwiatkowski, D., Phillips, P.C.B, Schmidt, P. and Shin, Y. (1992), 'Testing the null hypothesis of stationarity against the alternative of a unit root', *Journal of Econometrics*, **54**, 159–78.

Lanne, M., Lütkepohl, H. and Saikkonen, P. (2002), 'Comparison of unit root tests for time series with level shifts', *Journal of Time Series Analysis*, **23**, 667–85.

Lütkepohl, H. and Krätzig, M. (2004), *Applied Time Series Econometrics*, Cambridge: Cambridge University Press.

Maddala, G.S. and Kim, I.M. (1998), *Unit Roots, Cointegration and Structural Change*, Cambridge: Cambridge University Press.

Mansanet-Bataller, M., Pardo, A. and Valor, E. (2007), 'CO_2 prices, energy and weather', *The Energy Journal*, **28** (3), 73–92.

Said, S.E. and Dickey, D.A. (1984), 'Testing for unit roots in autoregressive moving average models of unknown order', *Biometrika*, **71**, 599–608.

Saikkonen, P. and Lütkepohl, H. (2000), 'Testing for the cointegration rank of a VAR process with an intercept', *Econometric Theory*, **16**, 373–406.

Saikkonen, P. and Lütkepohl, H. (2002), 'Testing for a unit root in a time series with a level shift at unknown time', *Econometric Theory*, **18**, 313–48.

Sijm, J., Neuhoff, K. and Chen, Y. (2006), 'CO_2 cost pass-through and windfall profits in the power sector', *Climate Policy*, **6**, 47–70.

Sims, C. (1980), 'Macroeconomics and reality', *Econometrica*, **48** (1), 1–48.

7. Impacts of the European Emissions Trading Scheme on Finnish wholesale electricity prices

Juha Honkatukia, Ville Mälkönen and Adriaan Perrels[1]

7.1 INTRODUCTION

The immediate and anticipated effect of the European Emissions Trading Scheme (EU ETS) has been an increase in electricity prices. The basic effect of emissions trading on unit costs is clear enough; however, it is not straightforward to assess with a reasonable degree of precision by what amount the electricity wholesale price has risen as a result of price rises in the EU ETS. This chapter overviews the industrial organization aspects of how the ETS affects electricity pricing and empirically examines the developments in the first two years of emissions trading.

The goals of the study are twofold. First, the theoretical section (Section 7.2) explains the pricing mechanisms that may be relevant at the Nordic electricity markets and how the ETS should affect the prices under different assumptions about the market structures. Second, the empirical section (Section 7.3) involves econometric estimations of the extent to which EU ETS permit prices affect wholesale electricity prices in Finland. The results from the empirical section will then be discussed in the light of the results illustrated in the theoretical section.

Section 7.2 shows that under perfectly competitive markets the carbon price is passed on to the spot-market price only in times of peak demand when the market-clearing price exceeds the generators' cost of switching to fossil-fuel power. Comparing these results with the empirical observations in the NordPool spot market where the price closely follows the ETS price at all times, implies that simple theoretical models of perfect competition fail to capture all the properties observed in the Nordic markets.

The models of imperfect competition with capacity constraints exhibit features similar to those observed in the Nordic markets. In particular, the oligopoly model derived informally has equilibria where the changes in the production cost of fossil-fuel power, such as the price of the an ETS permit, will be passed on to the prices in full, regardless of the demand levels. These properties clearly imply that oligopoly models might be useful in understanding the Nordic markets.

The estimation results of Section 7.3 indicate that compensation of the cost effects of the EU ETS is indeed occurring, although with variations, mainly depending on the levels of power demand. On average, about 50–100 per cent of the price changes in the EU ETS are passed on to the Finnish NordPool spot price. It should be noted that usually, less than 50 per cent of the electricity sold via the spot market is based on fossil fuels. Although several theoretical models imply that capacity utilization can be used as an instrument to sustain higher electricity prices under imperfectly competitive markets, the current study does not assess the degree of competition in the markets in depth. Consequently, no definite conclusions can be made on this point, because price levels above marginal cost may well emerge in perfectly competitive markets due to high demand combined with insufficient capacity.

In the empirical section we employ time-series models considered plausible for estimating and predicting prices in electricity spot markets. The first model is a standard error correction model, where we find that 54 per cent of the price changes in the EU ETS are passed on to the Finnish NordPool spot price. The estimation results of the error correction model are plausible, but the model has its limitations as it does not fully capture some of the issues specific to the Nordic markets. In particular, the model fails to take into account that the pass–through rate of the ETS crucially depends on the cost structure (merit order) of the electricity system, which has several sources of variations. On the demand side, the electricity demand is largely dependent on the season, as the demand for electricity tends to be higher in the winter months. On the supply side, the generators' supply functions depend on the filling rate of the hydro reservoirs, which also has seasonal components. These effects are often specific to a situation of the electricity system as a whole and cannot be measured appropriately in terms of variations in time, because it is the levels of the variables that determine the state of the system.

The chapter's second empirical model takes into account the effects of the state of the system on the electricity prices and the pass-through rate of the ETS. To this end, we estimate the prices using an AR-GARCH model controlling for the information about the state of the system (demand levels, transmission capacity and capacity utilization). The results show that on average about 50–100 per cent of the price change in the EU ETS ended up in the Finnish NordPool spot price, but the estimation results involve seasonal variation. The pass-through rate exhibits strong seasonal variation with respect to the state of the power system.

The chapter is organized as follows. Section 7.2 describes the Nordic electricity markets and derives relatively non-formal theoretical results on electricity pricing under perfect and imperfect competition. Section 7.3 involves the empirical estimation of the Finish electricity prices. Section 7.4 concludes.

7.2   THEORETICAL VIEWPOINTS ON THE ETS AND ELECTRICITY PRICING IN THE NORDIC MARKETS

In this section we illustrate the key elements in the Nordic electricity market and derive theoretical explanations for some observations made in the markets. In particular, we describe common outcomes derived in models of imperfect competition considered plausible in modelling electricity markets. While the structure of the model is simple, it is built so that it resembles the Nordic markets in the key aspects illustrated in the previous section.

We proceed as follows. First, we illustrate some key elements in the Nordic markets, define the concept of the use of market power and show that prices above marginal costs of production do not necessarily imply imperfect competition. Second, we illustrate some stylized models, which capture the basic properties of capacity-constrained markets under perfect and imperfect competition. Here, we keep the analysis relatively informal and focus only on a certain class of oligopoly models used in the analysis of electricity markets. Third, we employ the ideas put forward in these models to analyse the impacts of the ETS on electricity prices, discuss the results of the model in the light of the recent developments in the Nordic markets and discuss the policy implications.

Nordic Markets

The Nordic electricity markets operate via NordPool which is the spot market for electricity. In liberalized energy markets where the product is homogeneous and the producer is a price taker, equilibrium prices should reflect the marginal cost, unless there is insufficient production capacity. Electricity, however, is an unconventional product with special properties, which might generate frictions in the market.

The first friction is generated by the property that electricity is non-storable, as it has to be produced at the moment it is needed. In a system of several production regions, an efficient operation of the market thus requires sufficient transmission capacity to mitigate congestion. Second, generators have access to several production units with different production technology, capacity and cost. In the Nordic market a key technology is hydro power, which is storable in hydro reservoirs. This means that the system is vulnerable to seasonal and stochastic capacity variation. Finally, partly due to the lumpy nature of the generation investments, the number of generators is often limited in electricity markets. This has raised concerns that in liberalized energy markets the generators might be able to sustain prices above competitive levels. In a market where the generators are effectively price takers, this can be accomplished through capacity withholding.

The key in understanding the Nordic electricity market is the merit order of production units and the so-called 'marginal units', which produce only in periods when there is sufficient demand to justify their operation. Figure 7.1 provides an approximation of the merit order.

The figure illustrates the approximate cost per MWh of Finnish capacity for situations with abundant hydro reserves ('wet years') and strained hydro reserves ('dry year'). Hydro power obviously complicates the analysis of the markets and the merit order. The reason is that although hydro energy is basically costless to produce, the hydro capacity has option value, because the generators optimize the use of hydro power in a dynamic environment where the present value of a unit of hydro production equals the price of electricity minus the future value of the unit. Since the sizes of the hydro reservoirs are heterogeneous and the future filling rates include stochastic elements, considering the present value of hydro capacity would considerably complicate the analysis. We, therefore, do not consider the issues regarding the hydro valuation, but acknowledge that our results might be affected by this factor.

Determination of the marginal unit depends on the cost structure just described and the capacity up to which the generators can produce with a certain fuel. Since the NordPool is a system of four countries (Finland, Denmark, Sweden and Norway) interconnected by a transmission grid, the marginal unit which determines the equilibrium price depends on the generation capacities of each of the four countries and the transmission capacity. Table 7.1 provides an overview of the installed generation and transmission capacity in Finland and the other NordPool countries as of 31 December 2004.

Figure 7.2 illustrates the utilization rates of the generation capacities, and Figure 7.3 illustrates the demand levels. Here, it is important to note that in 2005 there was a strike in the paper industry, which is clearly reflected in the consumption and production figures. From Figures 7.2 and 7.3, it can be inferred that demand developments can be predicted to some extent, but a large number of daily and hourly 'disturbances' need a constant accommodation to actual demand levels.

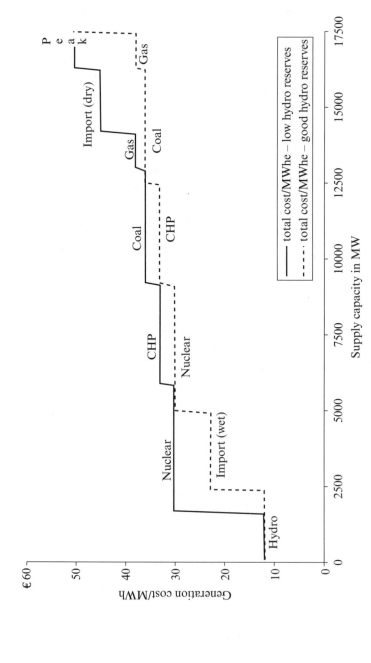

Note: CHP = combined heat and power.
    DH = district heat.

Figure 7.1   Illustration of approximate cost per MWh of various types of capacity in Finland

Table 7.1   Installed production capacity by generation type and cross-border transmission capacity in the NordPool area (in MW)

Generation type	Finland	Denmark	Sweden	Norway	NordPool
Nuclear	2,671	0	15,274	0	17,945
CHP-DH (fossil)	6,627	8,237	3,863	8	18,735
CHP-industry (fossil)	996	381	317	49	1,743
Other fossil (BP; CC)	800	270	1,623	64	2,757
Waste	131	271	153	27	582
Biofuel	2,198	418	1,545	96	4,257
Hydro	2,986	11	16,137	27,925	47,059
Wind	79	3,122	442	158	3,801
Total installed	16,488	12,710	39,354	28,327	96,879
Import capacity	To Finland	To Denmark	To Sweden	To Norway	To non-NordPool
From Finland	–	–	1,800	100	0
From Denmark	–	–	2,400	1,000	1,900
From Sweden	2,200	2,100	–	3,300	1,200
From Norway	100	1,000	3,600	–	50
From non-NordPool	1,500	1,500	1,200	50	–

Note: BP = Back Presure
　　　　CC = Combined Cycle

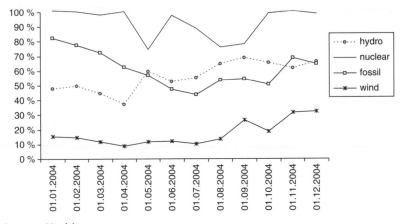

Source: Nordel.

Figure 7.2   Utilization rates by month of various types of capacity in the Finnish system, 2004

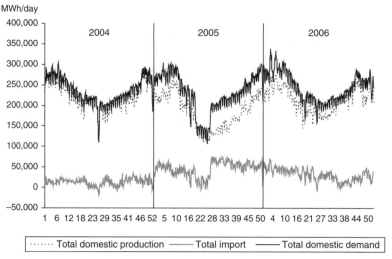

MWh/day

Note: numbers along the x-axis denote sequence numbers of weeks.

Source: NordPool.

Figure 7.3   Daily consumption and production of electricity in Finland and daily net import to Finland (MWh) (× 100,000)

Perfectly and Imperfectly Competitive Equilibria in Capacity-constrained Electricity Markets

This subsection characterizes imperfectly and perfectly competitive equilibria emerging in electricity markets which have a similar structure as the Nordic markets. The Nordic electricity markets operate via NordPool which is the spot market for electricity. In the spot market the generators first announce (bid) their supply function to an auctioneer (NordPool). The bids are price and quantity pairs to which the generators are committed.[2] Given the generators' bids and the demand, the auctioneer then selects a market-clearing price which satisfies the demand and the corresponding supply functions.[3]

Perfect competition benchmark

As a general rule, competition is considered imperfect when a producer can affect the market price through its output decisions. This means that a producer is not a price taker. In the spot market for electricity, this means that a single generator can affect the market-clearing price through its bid.

Assume now that there are *n* generators, which, for simplicity, have two generation technologies: non-fossil-fuel power and fossil-fuel power.

The non-fossil-fuel power consists of hydro and nuclear power. In what follows, we refer to the non-fossil-fuel power as a clean power. We further presume that the marginal cost of production is lower for clean power and increases discontinuously when the generator switches to fossil-fuel power (see Figure 7.4). When the generation capacity of the clean power is limited to, say, an amount $\overline{Q}$ the marginal cost function of a generator *i* is given by:

$$MC_i(s) = \begin{cases} C_h & \text{for} & Q_i \leq \overline{Q} \\ C_c + s & \text{for} & Q_i > \overline{Q} \end{cases}$$

where MC_i denotes the marginal cost of the last unit generated. The property that the marginal cost of production increases discontinuously implies an imperfect capacity constraint $\overline{Q}$, because we assume that $C_c > C_h$. This assumption states that the unit cost of producing clean power is lower than that of fossil-fuel power. The parameter *s* denotes the price of an emission permit per unit of output, which obviously increases the cost difference. This makes the marginal cost of electricity a piecewise linear but globally convex function.

Here, the difference between the marginal costs of the fuels is interpreted as an imperfect capacity constraint. The reason is that a higher marginal cost of the fossil fuels generates a vertical segment on the generators' cost function at $\overline{Q}$, which is the maximum generation level of clean power for the generators. In markets with perfect constraint, the generators cannot increase the output beyond $\overline{Q}$. In the present framework, a perfect capacity constraint emerges in a situation where $C_c \to \infty$, which implies that extending output beyond $\overline{Q}$ is economically infeasible. In a model of capacity-constrained oligopoly, Kreps and Scheinkman (1983) illustrate how capacity constraints can be used strategically to mitigate competition. Essentially, in the present framework we illustrate that when the generators can choose $\overline{Q}$, Kreps and Scheinkman's results emerge as a special case, where the vertical segment of the *MC* function $C_c - C_h$, is infinitely high.

In a competitive equilibrium, the marginal cost functions constitute the optimal bids for the generators. Letting $\mathbf{Q} = Q_1 + Q_2 + \ldots + Q_n$ denote the total output quantity in the market, the generator *i* takes the demand function $P(\mathbf{Q})$ as given and posts a bid, $B(Q_i, P_i)$, to the auctioneer. When the demand function and the marginal cost functions are common knowledge and a perfectly competitive generator chooses Q_i so as to maximize:

$$\pi = P(\mathbf{Q}) * Q_i - MC_i(s) * Q_i.$$

Empirical analyses

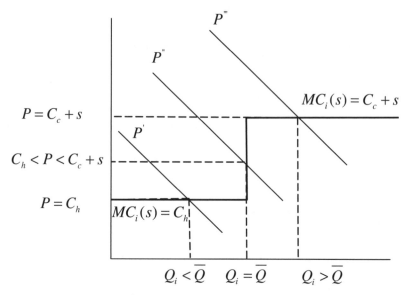

Figure 7.4   Equilibrium with capacity Q* under perfect competition

In equilibrium, profit maximization implies that marginal revenue of production equals the marginal cost, $MR = MC$. Perfect competition implies $dP(\mathbf{Q})/dQ = 0$, which gives the usual pricing rule $P = MC$. The equilibrium bids posted in the market thus equal $B(Q_i, P_i) = [Q_i, MC(Q_i)]$. Figure 7.4 illustrates this result under different demand levels. Function P' illustrates low demand level, P'' illustrates medium demand and P''' stands for peak demand.

Figure 7.4 readily illustrates that when the generators produce at capacity $Q^* = \overline{Q}$, but the demand for electricity is at a level P'', the price exceeds the marginal cost of the last unit produced. However, it is important to note that although the generators make a positive profit on the last unit produced, the generators have zero market power, as they cannot affect the market-clearing price through their output decisions.

Perfectly competitive equilibria exhibit the feature that the ETS price s passes through to the electricity price if and only if the demand level is high enough so that $P(n\overline{Q_i}) C_c + s$. In Figure 7.4, P''' illustrates such a demand function, which crosses the MC_i at $Q_i > \overline{Q}$. In this case, the optimal bid immediately implies that $dp/ds = 1$. If the demand function intersects the MC_i function at $Q_i < \overline{Q}$, the capacity constraint is binding for the generators, implying that a further increase in the marginal cost of fossil fuel does not affect the equilibrium prices, if the generators use non-fossil fuels.

The results just derived in the simple model thus imply that in perfectly competitive markets where a substantial share of the electricity can be produced with non-fossil fuels, the ETS passes on to prices only in times of relatively high demand. However, this is a simple example of the electricity markets as it does not take into account forward trading and/or endogenous valuation of hydro power as a function of the ETS. While these issues may affect the extent to which emissions trading affects electricity prices, they are beyond the scope of this study.

Imperfect competition benchmark

Further, we consider a duopoly where the firms first choose a capacity up to which they can produce clean and fossil-fuel power. We thus assume that before the actual bidding, the generators can establish a pre-commitment to a certain marginal cost function, on the basis of which they announce their bids.[4] Optimal bid, $B(Q_i^*, P_i^*) = [Q_i^*, P_i^*]$ maximizes:

$$\pi = P(Q_i, Q_j)*Q_i - MC_i(s)*Q_i.$$

For a given Q_j the optimal bid for generators, i is such that the marginal cost of increasing production equals the marginal revenue of price cutting. Formally, this condition can be written as

$$P + [dP(Q_j + Q_i)/dQ_i]Q_i = MC_i.$$

Intuitively, the optimal bid can be understood with the help of Figure 7.5, which illustrates the property that a bid schedule which intersects the marginal revenue function at $\overline{Q}_i$ is optimal for the generator i. Although the generator is essentially a price taker in the market and the bid is essentially based on the marginal cost function, the generators' ability to establish a pre-commitment to a marginal cost function with endogenous $\overline{Q}_i$ allows for capacity withholding that shows up in higher prices and higher profits for the generators.

It can be shown that the optimal bid just illustrated constitutes an equilibrium, where both generators design their bids so that the supply function coincides with the marginal cost function where

$$P(\overline{Q}_j + \overline{Q}_i) = C_c + s - [dP(\overline{Q}_j + \overline{Q}_i)/dQ_i]\overline{Q}_i.$$

Vives (1985) and Maggi (1996) show that the equilibrium coincides with the standard Bertrand outcome when the cost difference is zero ($C_c - C_h = 0$) and approaches to the least competitive Cournot outcome when the cost difference increases. When the difference approaches infinity, the

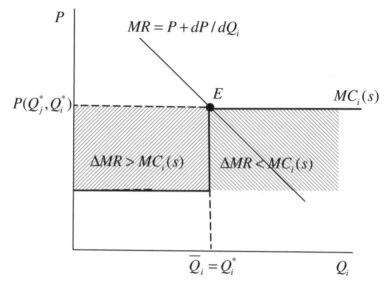

Figure 7.5   Equilibrium with capacity Q* under imperfect competition

equilibrium coincides with the Cournot outcome as shown by Kreps and Scheinkman (1983).

The equilibrium feature that $MR = C_c + s$ implies directly that when the price of the emission standard increases, the price of electricity increases, because:

$$\frac{dP}{ds} = 1 - [dP(\overline{Q}_j + \overline{Q}_i)/dQ_i]\frac{d\overline{Q}_i}{ds} > 0.$$

This expression implies that when the price of the ETS increases, the marginal revenue of increasing output increases. Thus, according to the equilibrium strategy, if the increase is small, the optimal response by the generators involves a reduction in output. This means that the price of electricity increases. If the demand is inelastic, the increase in the ETS price passes on to electricity prices in full. Comparing the results under different competitive environments, this result implies that the change in the marginal cost of fossil-fuel power also passes through to electricity prices in situations where the demand is lower. This goes against the result derived under perfect competition.

In this simplified example, the emissions trading cost s is a parameter which increases the convexity of the marginal cost function and therefore mitigates competition. The cost also implies the following properties which might be useful in understanding the market observations and empirical evidence on the Nordic electricity markets. First, the price correlates strongly with the marginal cost of production of the next unit of output, regardless of the demand level. In the present framework, this cost equals the marginal cost of fossil-fuel power. This result implies the second property: the market-clearing price is driven by the marginal cost of fossil-fuel power, but the production is mostly clean power. These results combined imply the third property: changes in the production cost of fossil-fuel power, such as the price of an ETS permit, will be passed on to the price of clean power in full.

The Nordic Markets and Theoretical Models of Electricity Pricing

Having provided a rough illustration of market outcomes in different competitive models of electricity markets, we discuss how the observations on the Nordic markets can be linked to the theoretical models. We first describe the key developments before and after the implementation of the ETS. Second, we illustrate how these developments can be explained with the models described above.

The wholesale electricity price in the NordPool area and in the Finnish sub-area went through several very high price periods in 2002 and the beginning of 2003. Since then up to the beginning of 2005, price variations have been more moderate. Figure 7.6 shows the daily weighted average spot prices for Finland and the entire NordPool area ('system price'), respectively, for the period from 1 January 2004 to 7 May 2006. The reason for the earlier high prices (in 2002/03) was the simultaneous occurrence of very cold winter weather and below-average reservoir fillings. During 2004, and even more so during 2005, the hydro reservoirs returned to long-term average levels, which mitigated the tensions regarding possible price rises.

Trading of EU ETS permits started in February 2005. There is a notation for each year in the first commitment period, 2005–07, as well as for permits for 2008–12. Figure 7.6 illustrates the price developments of EU ETS permits and wholesale electricity. While the basic effect of emissions trading on unit costs is clear enough, this figure tells little about the extent to which ETS prices pass through on to electricity prices.

There are several reasons for this. First, wholesale electricity prices vary for a host of reasons other than the EU ETS. Second, there are several types of wholesale markets, whose price formation is interlinked, but not identical. In this case, especially, the link between the spot market and forward/bilateral markets is important, as is possibly their share in the overall electricity trade. For example, distributors can decide to buy more via longer-term forward contracts in order to shed risks of the EU ETS-induced price peaks. In response, generators may decide to be more cautious in charging very high spot prices. Finally, since the fossil fuels are

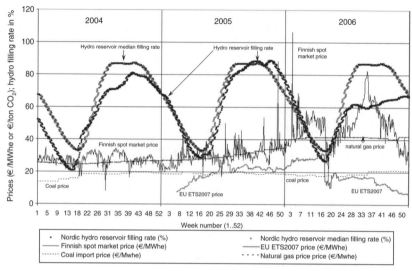

Figure 7.6   Development of key factors in the Finnish wholesale electricity market

the last generation units in the merit order, the theoretical models just described indicate that the pass-through rate might not be the same in all demand conditions.

To establish a link between the Nordic markets and the theoretical ideas presented in this section, observe that the Nordic market exhibits the following properties. First, the price of electricity correlates strongly with the cost of fossil-fuel energy and therefore with the price of the ETS. Second, most of the consumed energy is produced using non-fossil-fuel power, which is not subject to the emissions trading programme. These two properties and the equilibrium feature in the models that the ETS price can be used as a proxy of the degree of competition in the markets, serves as a link to the market observations and theoretical models.

We first show that the results derived in models of perfect competition might be less useful in describing Nordic electricity markets. To this end, observe that in Figure 7.4 the equilibrium outcome satisfies the stylized facts of the Nordic markets, if and only if at any given time the inverse demand function intersects the marginal cost function at point $(C_c + s, \overline{Q})$. Any other demand function would implement either an equilibrium with lower prices or a higher quantity with a fraction of output produced with fossil-fuel power. These properties imply that the features often observed in the Nordic electricity markets are feasible only in limited circumstances under perfectly competitive markets.

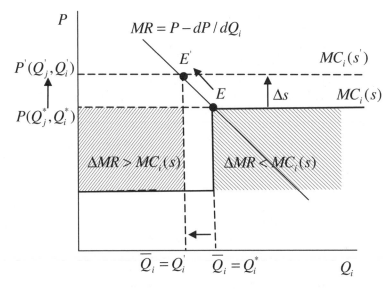

Figure 7.7   Increase in s increases prices and the use of 'clean' capacity

In the case of capacity-constrained oligopoly, the generators adjust their capacity to satisfy $MR = C_c + s$, which occurs when the generators produce exactly at capacity, that is, $Q_i = \overline{Q}$. Figure 7.5 shows that for any given demand level the capacity-constrained oligopoly model satisfies the stylized facts observed in the Nordic markets. That is, the spot market energy prices correlate strongly with the price of ETS permits even in times when no fossil fuels are used in production and the demand levels are relatively low.

The reason why the duopoly equilibrium satisfies these properties can be illustrated in Figure 7.7, which describes how an increase in s affects the equilibrium. In the figure, an increase in s makes the generators' pre-commitment to lower output level through capacity withholding more credible, because increasing production with fossil fuels becomes more expensive. In contrast to perfect competition, where an exogenous increase in s would not affect the equilibrium point E, a higher s reduces output, and consequently, increases prices. We can therefore infer that models of imperfect competition with capacity constraints exhibit three properties, which are similar to those observed in the Nordic markets. First, the price correlates strongly with the marginal cost of production of the next unit of output and the generators have a strictly positive price–cost margin for each unit produced. This result implies the second property: the market-clearing price is given by the marginal cost of fossil-fuel power, even though the production is to a very significant extent based on hydro and nuclear power. These results combined imply the third property: changes in the production cost of fossil-fuel power, such as the price of an ETS permit, will be passed on to the price of clean power in full.

These properties clearly imply that oligopoly models might be useful in understanding the Nordic markets. It should be noted, however, that these results do not provide any evidence of excessive market power employed by the generators, as it is essentially an empirical question. Section 7.3 provides some empirical results which lend some support to the analyses in this section. The results establish positive correlation between emission permit prices, production capacity and system prices on the spot market. These results are the same and statistically significant both under high and low demand periods.

Before moving to the empirical analysis, note that the analyses in this chapter, both theoretical and empirical, involve simplifications which should be taken into account. First, the theoretical model and the empirical evidence reported in this study do not provide a causal relationship between the observed prices and strategic behaviour.[5] Second, the analyses do not consider the dynamic valuation of hydro reserves. Contrary to other generation units, hydro reserves are storable and subject to stochastic variation, implying that generators must optimize the production dynamically. This increases the strategic dimension of the models and may affect the basic results just derived.

7.3   ECONOMETRIC ANALYSIS

The econometric analysis focuses on the impacts of price formation of spot market prices only. Neither the interaction between forward and spot markets, nor the interaction between input costs (coal, gas, EU ETS) has been assessed. The daily data on electricity prices, input prices, generation and transmission capacity utilization, and hydro-reservoir filling covers the period from 29 December 2003 to 31 December 2006 (1,100 consecutive days, of which 685 are for the EU ETS period.)[6] Appendix 7A contains more background information on the dataset. The time series of variables involved in the analysis were tested on stationarity. In as far as time series were not integrated, they often appeared to be nearly integrated.

From the discussion in Section 7.2, it can be inferred that likely significant variables are: emission price in the EU ETS, natural gas price, coal price, as well as indicators from within the electricity system (hydro-reservoir filling, utilization rate of production capacity and so on). Considering that the pricing of natural gas for large industrial users in

Finland is largely separate from the Western European market, whereas there is only a rudimentary secondary market for natural gas, the selection and use of gas price series remained somewhat problematic. Also, significant systematic differences in demand levels, such as working day versus weekend day, can be taken into account. Due to anticipatory elements in power capacity allocation, these structural demand variations have implications for the actually available capacity at a particular moment.[7]

In previous papers on electricity price formation and emissions trading, several models have been used. Here, we employ a vector error correction model (VECM) and an autoregressive conditional heteroskedasticity model (AR-GARCH). The VECM concerns a set of equations for the Finnish electricity spot price, the EU ETS 2007 price, the (Western European) coal price (ARA) and the (Western European) natural gas price (Zeebrugge day-ahead). In the other estimations the natural gas price series was dropped, whereas other variables representing information about the state of the system (load, utilization of import links, filling of Nordic hydro reservoirs and so on) were included.

Estimations with the VECM

We begin the empirical analysis with an error correction approach. Error correction models are convenient for the simultaneous analysis of long-run, equilibrium relationships between variables as well as for their adjustment to deviations from these equilibria in the short run. Their use can also be motivated methodologically when the time series to be analysed are non-stationary, as is often the case with economic data. Here, we concentrate on the direct effect of fuel – coal and gas – and allowance prices on Nordic spot electricity prices during ETS emissions trading. All of these variables appear to be non-stationary with a unit root when tested at the 1 per cent level, and all except the natural gas price appear so also at the 5 and 10 per cent levels (augmented Dickey–Fuller: ADS). The Johansen cointegration test indicates two cointegrating vectors at the most between electricity, fuel and allowance prices. We concentrate here on the case of only one cointegrating vector, but it is true that there may be cointegration not only between electricity, allowance and fuel prices, but also between allowance and fuel prices.

To facilitate the interpretation of the results, we have transformed coal and gas prices as costs in euros per MWh electricity produced in a steam condensing plant, the typical marginal unit, and the price of permits as euros per tonne CO_2 in a coal-fired condensation plant. Given this transformation we estimate the following error-correction model for the prices

Empirical analyses

of electricity and fuels (results for the full system are reported in Table 7.2. The test statistics are shown in Appendix 7B):

$$\Delta p_t^{elec} =$$

$$- A \times (\chi^{el} \times p_{t-1}^{elec} - \chi^{coal} \times p_{t-1}^{coal} - \chi^{gas} \times p_{t-1}^{gas} - \chi^{ETS} \times p_{t-1}^{ETS})$$
$$+ (b_{t-1}^{elect} \times \Delta p_{t-1}^{elec} + b_{t-1}^{coal} \times \Delta b_{t-1}^{coal} + b_{t-1}^{gas} \times \Delta P_{t-1}^{gas} + b_{t-1}^{ETS} \times \Delta p_{t-1}^{ETS})$$
$$+ (b_{t-2}^{elect} \times \Delta p_{t-2}^{elec} + b_{t-2}^{coal} \times \Delta P_{t-2}^{coal} + b_{t-2}^{gas} \times \Delta P_{t-2}^{gas} + b_{t-2}^{ETS} \times \Delta p_{t-2}^{ETS}) + \varepsilon_t,$$

where variables p denote price observations. The subscripts and super-scripts indicate the time and the type of fuel. The equation has the following interpretation. The error correction term, reported in parentheses in the first line, gives the long-run equilibrium relation between electricity prices, fuel prices and allowance prices, while the coefficient A for the error correction term indicates the adjustment of electricity prices to deviations from this equilibrium. The terms in the second and third lines give the effect of lagged electricity, allowance and fuel prices on the change of electricity prices.

We have estimated the system for three sample periods, the first covering 2005 and 2006, the second, only 2005, and the last, concentrating on 2006. The results for these samples are given in Table 7.2, and some conclusions can immediately be drawn. For the sample from 3 January 2005 to 29 December 2006, the estimates give a long-run relationship between electricity prices and allowance and fuel prices, where 54 per cent of allowance prices, 99 per cent of coal prices and 15 per cent of gas prices explain the electricity price. In the short run, however, only 7 per cent of the electricity price change is explained by an adjustment to deviations from this long-run equilibrium, 12 per cent by the changes in electricity prices in the previous period and 18 per cent in changes in the period prior to that. Generally, lagged fuel price changes do not have an effect on current electricity price changes.

Thus it is the long-run relationships and short-run pricing dynamics that appear to be driving the results. However, it leaves open a large part of the short-run dynamics. In the next subsection, we turn to possible reasons for short-run deviations stemming from demand and capacity utilization. In particular, we consider the possibility that variations in production capacity utilization and other features describing the state of the power system affect electricity prices. Here, we consider the stability of the long-run relationship by focusing on 2005 and 2006, in turn.

Several results are apparent. First, the cointegrating equation breaks down in 2006, leaving the history of electricity prices and allowance prices (but not the fuel prices, whose coefficients are not significant) to explain the development of electricity prices. It is apparent that this happens around

Table 7.2 VECM results

Sample		Cointegrating equation				Error correction								
		χ^{el}	χ^{ETS}	χ^{gas}	χ^{coal}	A	b^{elec}_{t-1}	b^{ETS}_{t-1}	b^{gas}_{t-1}	b^{coal}_{t-1}	b^{elec}_{t-2}	b^{ETS}_{t-2}	b^{gas}_{t-2}	b^{coal}_{t-2}
2005–06		1.000	−0.539	−0.151	−0.993	−0.066	−0.116	0.250	−0.005	0.016	−0.181	0.319	−0.014	−0.013
	Std error		0.222	0.0416	0.195	0.016	0.043	0.198	0.009	0.112	0.043	0.198	0.009	0.112
	t-stat		−2.431	−3.618	−5.085	−3.996	−2.662	1.263	−0.566	0.146	−4.183	1.609	−1.543	−0.117
2005		1.000	−0.354	−0.125	−1.014	−0.164	−0.027	−0.107	−0.014	0.036	−0.134	0.001	−0.038	0.011
	Std error		0.057	0.028	0.076	0.040	0.065	0.299	0.009	0.098	0.063	0.299	0.019	0.098
	t-stat		−6.258	−4.414	−13.27	−4.055	−0.411	−0.358	−1.543	0.368	−2.097	0.003	−1.935	0.107
2006		1.000	0.574	0.182	−3.613	−0.015	−0.149	0.497	0.003	−0.053	−0.192	0.497	−0.004	0.683
	Std error		0.899	0.081	0.944	0.018	0.063	0.277	0.011	0.908	0.062	0.277	0.012	0.906
	t-stat		0.638	2.237	−3.827	−0.848	−2.374	1.792	0.295	−0.058	−3.068	1.79	−0.353	0.753

Sample	2005–2006	2005	2006
R-squared	0.097923	0.123286	0.087979
Adj. R-squared	0.083717	0.094890	0.058794
Sum sq. resids	2956.922	1003.362	1940.889
S.E. equation	2.412615	2.015488	2.786316
F-statistic	6.893115	4.341721	3.014563
Log likelihood	−1184.379	−538.0878	−628.3275
Akaike AIC	4.616554	4.274123	4.921448
Schwarz SC	4.690505	4.398758	5.045045
Mean dependent	0.022445	0.014772	0.039059
S.D. dependent	2.520422	2.118506	2.872024
Determinant residual covariance	187.1082	41.76641	23.19188
Log likelihood	−4268.597	−1912.377	−1858.823
Log likelihood (d.f. adjusted)	−4286.756	−1930.701	−1877.143
AIC	16.73793	15.39610	14.80419
Schwarz criteria	17.06660	15.95003	15.35351

mid-2006, until which date the VAR (vector autoregression) model appears to explain the equilibrium relationship very well. This, of course, reflects the actual events in the allowance markets, where the prices plummeted from unexpected heights to rock bottom during the second quarter of 2006. Second, the VAR model explains the equilibrium relationship between electricity prices, fuel prices, and allowance prices nicely in 2005. Third, the coefficient for the error correction equation is larger for 2005 than for the whole period, implying that the long-run equilibrium relationship drove electricity prices more in 2005 than it did for the whole of the sample period.

We also studied the effects of exogenous variables in the VAR model. It appears that variables that explain the state of the supply improve the fit of the model markedly, pointing to the necessity of studying more closely the relationship between electricity prices and its supply and demand. In the next subsection, we shall turn to these issues.

Estimations with the AR-GARCH Model

In this subsection we estimate the electricity prices using levels instead of differences and include information about the state of the system (demand levels, transmission capacity and capacity utilization). The empirical method is AR-GARCH, using logarithmic transformations as far as possible.[8] This combination of accounting for autocorrelation, reduction of the effects of heteroskedasticity and the logarithmic transformation results in good fits. However, the attribution of effects to various variables remains relatively sensitive for the period modelled. In comparison to earlier estimations for a 15-month period (Honkatukia et al., 2006), the changes in parameter values of the prices of emission permits and coal, respectively, are larger. A plausible explanation for this is that the longer period covered in the estimations discussed here went through more regime changes such as changes in ETS prices and hydro availability.

For the estimation of the entire period (14 February 2005 to 31 December 2006), the equation is the following:

$$p_t^{elec} = a + b[b^{ETS} \times \ln(p_{t-1}^{ETS}) + b^{ETS} \times \ln(p_{t-1}^{coal})] +$$
$$[b^{tm_t} \times \ln(tmcap_t) + b^{pc_t} \times \ln(pcap_t) + b^{pc_{t-1}} \times \ln(pcap_{t-1})$$
$$+ b^{dr_t} \times \ln(dresfil_{t-1}) + b^{tmp_t} \times \ln(dtemp_t)]$$
$$+ [b^{wknd} \times wknd + b^{hld} \times hld] + \eta,$$

where a constant and the fuel prices enter in the first line on the RHS of the equation. The second and third lines contain the variables describing the state of the system. Here, *tmcap_t* indicates the utilization of the transmission capacity between Finland and Sweden at time *t*, *pcap_t* indicates the utilization of the production capacity. Variables *dresfil_{t-1}* and *dtemp_t* denote the deviations from the long-term median Nordic reservoir filling rates and average daily temperatures. The last line contains the weekend and holiday dummies and the error term η_t includes the AR(1 2 5)-GARCH(1) processes.

Figure 7.8 provides an illustration of the fit of the regression in terms of estimated and observed electricity prices, and Table 7.3 provides an overview of the estimation results. The estimation results are reported for the first two years of EU ETS (February 2005 to December 2006), the period from February 2005 to April 2006 (ending just after the price collapse), as well as 2005 and 2006 separately.

The parameter values for variables representing aspects of capacity utilization and short-term equilibration via lagged power prices do vary to some extent, but the overall pattern remains similar (as does the number of variables that is significant). Obviously for periods that have a large share of winter days the significance of the generation capacity utilization tends to be high. The much larger differences in parameter values for the main inputs (category 1) across the estimations illustrate that these input markets have been in quite different states during the considered period (the variables swap between critical and uncritical positions).

The state of the power system affects the sensitivity of the spot price with respect to passing on input cost, including the price of EU ETS emission allowances (see also next subsection). If the system is significantly less strained, the parameter value of the emission price goes down. However, the parameter value of the permit price for pure winter periods and more extended periods do not seem to differ significantly. Similar indications were obtained from the ARIMA (Autoregressive Integrated Moving-Average) estimations reported in Honkatukia et al. (2006).

The main results of this study are the following. First, ignoring summer periods and the period after the ETS price collapse, the pass-through rate of the EU ETS price on the Finnish NordPool spot price was high, as expected. In the AR-GARCH model the coefficient for the emission price is 0.4 and statistically significant. This result is in line with any given theoretical prediction, because in times of high demand, the carbon-intensive units are more likely to become the marginal units, which set the equilibrium price of the system.

Second, although the extent to which the fuel costs affect the prices depends on the state of the power system, the effect of the ETS on electricity price is also positive and significant in periods when the demand is lower and the carbon-intensive units are less likely the price-setting units.

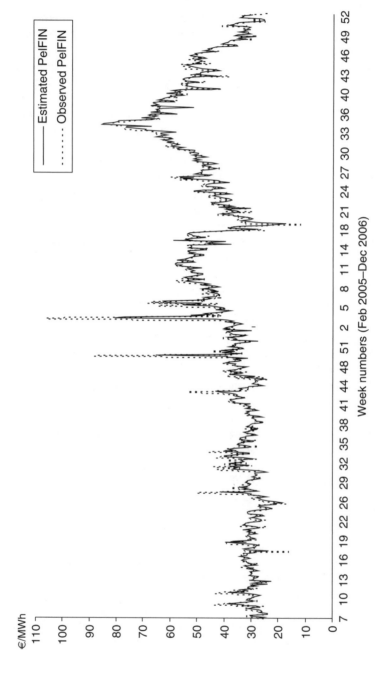

Figure 7.8 Comparison of observed and estimated electricity prices (€/MWh) for the Finnish NordPool area using the AR(1 2 5)-GARCH(1) model

Table 7.3 *AR(1 2 5)-GARCH(1) estimates for various periods (dependent variable is the daily average electricity price in the Finnish NordPool area)*

Variable	14–2–2005 to 31–12–2006	14–2–2005 to 7–5–2006	2005	2006	8–5–2006 to 31–12–2006	Winter months 2005 & 2006
a	1.167	1.300	3.442**	2.295**	3.11**	3.071**
$\ln(p_{t-1}^{ETS})$	0.109*	0.490**	0.333**	0.047	0.088	0.401**
$\ln(p_{t-1}^{coal})$	0.737**	0.462	−0.150	0.460*	0.175	0.008
$\ln(tmcap_t)$	0.001	0.003	0.005	0.001	0.001	0.004
$\ln(pcap_t)$	0.683**	1.406**	1.433**	0.330**	0.613**	1.681**
$\ln(pcap_{t-1})$	−0.113*	−0.396**	−0.549**	0.029	−0.137	−0.356**
$\ln(dresfil_{t-1})$	0.010	−0.010	−0.017	0.013*	−0.011	−0.014
$\ln(dtemp_t)$	0.009**	−0.001	0.012**	−0.002	−0.002	−0.009*
weekend	−0.063**	−0.044*	−0.047**	−0.055**	−0.055**	0.012
holiday	−0.133**	−0.043	−0.198**	−0.068**	−0.061	−0.122**
AR[t−1]	−0.671**	−0.495**	−0.546**	−0.678**	−0.661**	−0.538**
AR[t−2]	−0.174**	−0.106	−0.135*	−0.206**	−0.250**	−0.231**
AR[t−5]	−0.145**	−0.083	−0.046	−0.113**	−0.083	−0.115**
ARCH0	0.004**	0.010**	0.005**	0.002**	0.002**	0.003**
ARCH1	1.314**	0.150	0.939**	1.789**	0.208	1.43**
n	684	447	320	364	235	378
Total R^2	0.87	0.82	0.55	0.83	0.95	0.82

Note: * significant at 95 per cent level; ** significant at 99 per cent level.

One explanation for this result is that the ETS price also affects the system price through the opportunity cost of hydro power. That is, an increase in the expected price of electricity increases the value of water in the hydro reservoirs, and therefore, the price for which the generators are willing to offer hydro power increases. Another potential explanation for the positive pass-through of the ETS price is related to the capacity withholding as illustrated in Section 7.2, where the equilibrium under imperfect competition exhibits positive pass-through rates even in times of relatively low demand. Here, we should bear in mind that these interpretations should be treated carefully, as we have no causal evidence on the links between these two explanations and the estimation results.

Third, the results are comparable to earlier results concerning other power markets (for example, by Sijm et al., 2006). Comparing the results, however, suggests that the bandwidth for pass-through can be quite large (50–100 per cent), varying between countries and periods. This implies that policy recommendations or assessments of the effects of the ETS on a

Table 7.4   Shares of the rise of the EU ETS allowance price passed on immediately to the spot price for different single-day ETS price increases for different typical load levels and different estimation periods

dETS in %	Low loads share of dETS passing		Medium loads share of dETS passing		High loads share of dETS passing	
	Entire ETS period	Oct–April	Entire ETS period	Oct–April	Entire ETS period	Oct–April
20%	0.09	0.44	0.16	0.99	0.20	1.47
50%	0.08	0.29	0.14	1.06	0.18	1.38

specific electricity market are likely to be misleading if they are based on research concerning another market.

ETS Pass-through and the State of the Power System

The results of the level estimates presented in the previous subsection allow us to simulate to what extent the passing on of EU ETS allowance prices varies when the state of the power system varies (and hence the wholesale price level). The procedure is as follows. We insert day increases of 20 and 50 per cent for the EU ETS price, assuming a baseline level of €19 per ton, which is the average price during the period analysed. The results are summarized in Table 7.4. For example, if the price of the ETS allowances increases by 20 per cent (in one day) during an autumn day with typical medium loads (~10,000 MW) the Finnish spot price is expected to rise by 0.99×20 per cent, which amounts to 4–5 €/MWh.

The simulations show that higher loads (indicated by higher prices) imply higher shares of EU ETS price increases passed on to the spot price. It is obvious that these higher load levels correspond to an increased use of fossil fuels in the marginally offered units and hence an increased need for covering emissions with allowances. The simulations also illustrate that the pass-through rate of the ETS price is also relatively high in times of medium and low loads. These findings might be viewed as evidence supporting the theoretical illustrations of emission price pass-through in an imperfectly competitive market, but we cannot establish a causal link between any given competitive model and the estimation results. Interpretations of the results could therefore be misleading. As such, the observed spot price rises are simply the product of a liberalized electricity market and cannot be deemed as abuse of market power. Such a judgement would need much more elaborate and detailed analysis.

As was indicated by the estimation results, price sensitivity shows seasonal variation. Figure 7.9 illustrates that the carbon intensity of Finnish generation varied considerably in the 2004–06 period. During 2005 (the first year of the EU ETS), carbon intensity seems to respond to the rising price of ETS allowances. In 2006 the pattern of carbon intensity is rather similar up to May, although at a somewhat higher level. From June 2006 onwards the carbon intensity rises, which coincides rather precisely with the collapse of ETS prices. The reduction of the carbon intensity in the last months of 2006 can be attributed to a return of hydro reservoirs to normal median levels in conjunction with modest winter demand levels due to high temperatures (given the season).

7.4   CONCLUSIONS

Theoretical explanations as to why the EU ETS allowance price increases prices in perfectly competitive electricity markets are straightforward. Strategic behaviour in an imperfectly competitive spot market requires a more detailed analysis where the pass-through rate can be used as a proxy for the degree of competition in the markets. In this chapter we first illustrate theoretically that in a perfectly competitive market, a full pass-through of the ETS prices should occur only in limited situations with high demand levels. Strategic behaviour, however, implies that the ETS also passes on to electricity prices during lower demand levels and may lead to pass-through rates close to one.

Empirical analysis of Finnish electricity markets in recent years indicates that the price rises can be significant despite a share of fossil fuels in domestic generation of well below 50 per cent. On average, about 50–100 per cent of a price change in the EU ETS is passed on to the Finnish NordPool spot price. Since the empirical analysis does not estimate the nature of the competition in the market, these results could be a logical market outcome of increasing demand in a power system where the price-setting units use fossil fuels. Therefore, the empirical results reported in this study should not be used as an indicator of imperfect competition in the Finnish electricity market or in the NordPool spot market.

At least in the near term, future developments of fuel prices and the EU ETS allowance prices will be closely related. Together, these rising input cost represent a significant costs effect. The fact that capacity utilization appears to affect the sensitivity of the spot price for input cost indicates

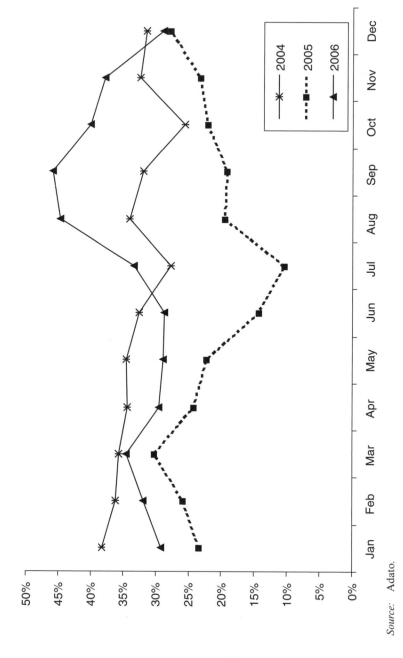

Source: Adato.

Figure 7.9 Approximate shares of fossil-fuel-based electricity generation (incl. peat) in total domestic production in Finland

that – other things being equal – future increases in demand for electricity will probably exacerbate the price effects of the EU ETS.

The NordPool spot price could be less affected by increasing prices of the EU ETS allowances if more non-fossil-fuel generation capacity were to be installed. This effect is not straightforward, however, as it depends on the particularities of market mechanisms driving the price formation in NordPool. Policy recommendations should therefore be based on a structural econometric analysis of the generators' behaviour in the spot market. A deeper understanding of competition on the power market requires more comprehensive data.In particular, data on active generation units and the actual bids posted in the market should be made available to help researchers gain an understanding of the market mechanism driving the electricity prices in different states of the power system.

APPENDIX 7A   BACKGROUND REGARDING THE DATASET

For the econometric assessment, data were obtained from:

- NordPool (daily and hourly observations for power prices, production, consumption, import/export for 2000–06);
- Nordel (reservoir filling);
- Statistics Finland (Finnish monthly wholesale prices of natural gas and coal);
- Argus (daily free on board coal prices for Baltic harbour destinations);
- Heren Energy (Zeebrugge node daily natural gas prices for day-ahead and forward markets); and
- Finnish Meteorological Institute (daily average temperature and the deviation from the long-term average for each day).

Two datasets were constructed for the period from 29 December 2003 to 7 May 2006. One contains daily records (861 consecutive days). The other contains three typical hourly observations per day: low load, daily plateau and peak hour (2,583 records).

Further data transformations and estimations were carried out in SAS ©.

APPENDIX 7.1: VECM ESTIMATION AND TEST RESULTS

Test statistics for samples. Standard errors are reported in ( ) and t-statistics in [ ].

Sample 1/06/2005–12/29/2006. Included observations: 517 after adjusting endpoints.

Cointegrating Eq:	CointEq1	Error correction:	D(PELNOR)	D(PCO2)	D(PGAS)	D(PCOAL)
χ^{el}	1.000000	A	-0.065839	-0.006650	0.098943	0.022363
			(0.01647)	(0.00371)	(0.07585)	(0.00648)
			[-3.99643]	[-1.79101]	[1.30453]	[3.45180]
χ^{ETS}	-0.538803	b^{elec}_{t-1}	-0.115600	0.008814	0.133350	0.010256
	(0.22157)		(0.04342)	(0.00979)	(0.19989)	(0.01707)
	[-2.43172]		[-2.66245]	[0.90065]	[0.66711]	[0.60067]
χ^{gas}	-0.150458	b^{elec}_{t-2}	-0.180634	0.004778	-0.275685	-0.009386
	(0.04158)		(0.04319)	(0.00973)	(0.19883)	(0.01698)
	[-3.61842]		[-4.18256]	[0.49080]	[-1.38657]	[-0.55265]
χ^{coal}	-0.993135	b^{ETS}_{t-1}	0.249754	0.330056	0.120077	0.038920
	(0.19530)		(0.19772)	(0.04456)	(0.91026)	(0.07775)
	[-5.08518]		[1.26317]	[7.40622]	[0.13192]	[0.50057]
Determinant res cov	187.1082					
Log Likelihood	-4268.597					
Log Likelihood	-4286.756					

(d.f. adjusted)
Akaike IC   16.73793
Schwarz C   17.06660

b_{t-2}^{ETS}	0.318894	-0.057427	0.186561	0.029429
	(0.19814)	(0.04466)	(0.91220)	(0.07792)
	[1.60944]	[-1.28588]	[0.20452]	[0.37769]
b_{t-1}^{gas}	-0.005363	-0.000342	-0.207558	0.002819
	(0.00948)	(0.00214)	(0.04363)	(0.00373)
	[-0.56590]	[-0.16013]	[-4.75721]	[0.75646]
b_{t-2}^{gas}	-0.014489	-0.002703	-0.276235	0.001324
	(0.00939)	(0.00212)	(0.04323)	(0.00369)
	[-1.54310]	[-1.27741]	[-6.39026]	[0.35851]
b_{t-1}^{coal}	0.016427	0.001025	0.366716	-0.000947
	(0.11235)	(0.02532)	(0.51725)	(0.04418)
	[0.14621]	[0.04049]	[0.70898]	[-0.02143]
b_{t-2}^{coal}	-0.013108	0.005130	0.385219	0.002762
	(0.11218)	(0.02528)	(0.51646)	(0.04411)
	[-0.11685]	[0.20288]	[0.74588]	[0.06261]
R-squared	0.097923	0.114308	0.113526	0.025133
Adj. R-squared	0.083717	0.100361	0.099565	0.009781
Sum sq. resids	2956.922	150.2193	62672.00	457.2631
S.E. equation	2.412615	0.543790	11.10721	0.948749
F-statistic	6.893115	8.195388	8.132078	1.637105
Log likelihood	-1184.379	-414.0989	-1973.778	-701.8516
Akaike Information Criteria	4.616554	1.636746	7.670320	2.749909
Schwarz Criteria	4.690505	1.710697	7.744271	2.823860
Mean dependent	0.022445	0.020008	0.094994	0.032819
S.D. dependent	2.520422	0.573319	11.70520	0.953423

187

Sample: 1/06/2005–12/29/2005. Included observations: 256 after adjusting endpoints.

Cointegrating equation

Cointegrating Eq:	CointEq1
χ^{el}	1.000000
χ^{ETS}	-0.353859
	(0.05655)
	[-6.25800]
χ^{gas}	-0.124833
	(0.02828)
	[-4.41444]
χ^{coal}	-1.014155
	(0.07642)
	[-13.2709]
Determinant res cov	41.76641
Log likelihood	-1912.377
Log likelihood	-1930.701
Akaike IC	15.39610
Schwarz C	15.95003

Error correction

Error correction:	D(PELNOR)	D(PCO2)	D(PGAS)	D(PCOAL)
A	-0.164207	-0.006100	0.436339	0.202036
	(0.04049)	(0.00870)	(0.13007)	(0.02410)
	[-4.05531]	[-0.70100]	[3.35473]	[8.38205]
b_{t-1}^{elec}	-0.026796	0.002476	0.263740	-0.073894
	(0.06514)	(0.01400)	(0.20924)	(0.03878)
	[-0.41135]	[0.17688]	[1.26045]	[-1.90567]
b_{t-2}^{elec}	-0.133579	0.004973	-0.250896	-0.090356
	(0.06368)	(0.01369)	(0.20455)	(0.03791)
	[-2.09763]	[0.36334]	[-1.22656]	[-2.38361]
b_{t-1}^{ETS}	-0.107116	0.183539	0.146660	0.096323
	(0.29948)	(0.06436)	(0.96197)	(0.17827)
	[-0.35768].	[2.85166]	[0.15246]	[0.54032]
b_{t-2}^{ETS}	0.000925	0.045148	0.348390	0.139282
	(0.29980)	(0.06443)	(0.96301)	(0.17846)
	[0.00309]	[0.70070]	[0.36177]	[0.78046]

b^{gas}_{t-1}	−0.017260	−0.002863	−0.286364	0.020072
	(0.02012)	(0.00432)	(0.06463)	(0.01198)
	[−0.85779]	[−0.66198]	[−4.43050]	[1.67576]
b^{gas}_{t-2}	−0.038174	−0.004010	−0.213241	0.011161
	(0.01972)	(0.00424)	(0.06335)	(0.01174)
	[−1.93547]	[−0.94598]	[−3.36587]	[0.95063]
b^{coal}_{t-1}	0.036357	0.005892	0.489956	−0.006340
	(0.09880)	(0.02123)	(0.31737)	(0.05881)
	[0.36797]	[0.27745]	[1.54379]	[−0.10779]
b^{coal}_{t-2}	0.010708	0.008578	0.348711	−0.002642
	(0.09859)	(0.02119)	(0.31668)	(0.05869)
	[0.10861]	[0.40484]	[1.10115]	[−0.04502]
R-squared	0.123286	0.027679	0.171012	0.224840
Adj. R-squared	0.094890	−0.003813	0.144162	0.199733
Sum sq. resids	1003.362	46.34397	10352.70	355.5333
S.E. equation	2.015488	0.433160	6.474085	1.199753
F-statistic	4.341721	0.878931	6.369193	8.955475
Log likelihood	−538.0878	−144.4852	−836.8259	−405.2888
Akaike IC	4.274123	1.199103	6.608015	3.236631
Schwarz Criteria	4.398758	1.323738	6.732650	3.361266
Mean dependent	0.014772	0.057906	0.142620	0.069376
S.D. dependent	2.118506	0.432336	6.998140	1.341141

Sample: 1/03/2006–12/29/2006. Included observations: 259.

Cointegrating equation   Error correction

Cointegrating Eq:	CointEq1	Error correction:	D(PELNOR)	D(PCO2)	D(PGAS)	D(PCOAL)
χ^{el}	1.000000	A	-0.015445	-0.005055	-0.194448	0.003308
			(0.01821)	(0.00417)	(0.09309)	(0.00125)
			[-0.84798]	[-1.21226]	[-2.08892]	[2.63630]
χ^{ETS}	0.574589	b^{elec}_{t-1}	-0.149267	0.015717	0.137748	0.003598
	(0.89937)		(0.06286)	(0.01439)	(0.32126)	(0.00433)
	[0.63888]		[-2.37455]	[1.09209]	[0.42877]	[0.83085]
χ^{gas}	0.182617	b^{elec}_{t-2}	-0.191717	0.005385	-0.210174	-0.005064
	(0.08161)		(0.06248)	(0.01431)	(0.31932)	(0.00430)
	[2.23770]		[-3.06837]	[0.37646]	[-0.65818]	[-1.17643]
χ^{coal}	-3.613214	b^{ETS}_{t-1}	0.449397	0.412750	-0.128738	0.018208
	(0.94419)		(0.27556)	(0.06309)	(1.40829)	(0.01899)
	[-3.82678]		[1.63085]	[6.54232]	[-0.09141]	[0.95906]
Determinant res. cov.	23.19188					
Log likelihood	-1858.823					
Log likelihood	-1877.143	b^{ETS}_{t-2}	0.497112	-0.106870	0.204622	0.000978
Akaike IC	14.80419		(0.27740)	(0.06351)	(1.41769)	(0.01911)
Schwarz C	15.35351		[1.79206]	[-1.68273]	[0.14434]	[0.05117]

190

b_{t-1}^{gas}	0.003488	0.001203	-0.183580	-0.000619
	(0.01182)	(0.00271)	(0.06042)	(0.00081)
	[0.29499]	[0.44445]	[-3.03832]	[-0.76030]
b_{t-2}^{gas}	-0.004157	-0.001829	-0.285667	-0.001210
	(0.01177)	(0.00270)	(0.06017)	(0.00081)
	[-0.35302]	[-0.67840]	[-4.74731]	[-1.49213]
b_{t-1}^{coal}	-0.052869	0.004230	1.689899	-0.079310
	(0.90844)	(0.20799)	(4.64275)	(0.06259)
	[-0.05820]	[0.02034]	[0.36399]	[-1.26716]
b_{t-2}^{coal}	0.682511	-0.011220	-0.846779	-0.020527
	(0.90609)	(0.20745)	(4.63071)	(0.06243)
	[0.75325]	[-0.05409]	[-0.18286]	[-0.32882]
R-squared	0.087979	0.160685	0.129099	0.049442
Adj. R-squared	0.058794	0.133827	0.101230	0.019024
Sum sq. resids	1940.889	101.7371	50693.86	9.212967
S.E. equation	2.786316	0.637925	14.23992	0.191968
F-statistic	3.014563	5.982760	4.632379	1.625410
Log likelihood	-628.3275	-246.4957	-1050.842	64.53492
Akaike IC	4.921448	1.972939	8.184107	-0.428841
Schwarz C	5.045045	2.096536	8.307703	-0.305245
Mean dependent	0.039059	-0.017297	0.048653	-0.003648
S.D. dependent	2.872024	0.685437	15.02047	0.193821

NOTES

1. The authors would like to thank senior adviser Pekka Tervo from the Ministry of Trade and Industry for comments, and gratefully acknowledge the assistance of Tarja Tuovinen in data collection and estimation.
2. In other words, the supply function determines the minimum prices for which a generator is willing to produce a specified quantity for the market.
3. The structure of the spot market thus closely resembles models derived in Vives (1985) and Klemperer and Meyer (1989).
4. There are several instruments that the generators can use to establish such precommitment. For instance, the generators can announce their plant-level generation capacity, which implicitly makes their supply function common knowledge.
5. An example of empirical examination of strategic behaviour in the electricity market can be found, for instance, in Hortacsu and Puller (2005).
6. Not all data were originally observed on a daily basis. For example, only the EU ETS prices have working day notations, whereas the reservoir filling is interpolated from weekly data (this may be a source of biases, see, for example, Sijm et al., 2006).
7. Some authors suggest skipping weekend and holiday observations. However, in the case of serial correlation for data at the daily observation level, this can easily cause other biases.
8. For variables that can include negative values, a conditional formulation was included to avoid division by zero when using the natural logarithm.

REFERENCES

Honkatukia, J., Mälkönen, V. and Perrels, A. (2006), 'Impacts of the European Emissions Trading Scheme on Finnish wholesale electricity prices', VATT Discussion Paper 405, Helsinki.

Hortaçsu, Ali and Steven L. Puller (2005), *Understanding Strategic Bidding in Restructured Electricity Markets: A Case Study of Ercot*, NBER Working Paper Series no. 11123, Cambridge: National Bureau of Economic Research.

Klemperer, Paul and Margaret Meyer (1989), 'Supply function equilibria in oligopoly under uncertainly', *Econometrica*, **57**, 1243–77.

Kreps, D. and Scheinkman, J. (1983), 'Quantity precommitment and Bertrand competition yield Cournot outcomes', *Bell Journal of Economics*, **14**, 326–37.

Maggi, G. (1996), 'Strategic trade policies with endogenous mode of competition', *American Economic Review*, **86**, 237–58.

Sijm, J., Neuhoff, K. and Chen, Y. (2006), 'CO_2 cost pass-through and windfall profits in the power sector', *Climate Policy*, **6**, 47–70.

Vives, X. (1985), 'Commitment flexibility and market outcomes', *International Journal of Industrial Organization*, **4**, 217–229.

8. The impact of the European Emissions Trading Scheme on power prices in Italy: the 'load duration curve approach'

Liliya Chernyavs'ka and Francesco Gullì

8.1 INTRODUCTION

The extent to which carbon price is passed through into power prices is one of the main questions concerning the impact of the EU ETS (European Emissions Trading Scheme) on the electricity sector. Nevertheless, the empirical literature does not provide clear enough answers to this question. Some authors argue in favour of a full (or almost full) pass-through.[1] Others find that the CO_2 costs have apparently not been fully passed into power prices[2] or that there is limited evidence that CO_2 is factored into the wholesale price.[3]

In this chapter we attempt to provide a further contribution in this field by estimating the impact of the EU ETS on power pricing in Italy. For this purpose, we use a heterodox methodology, the 'load duration curve approach', which allows us to examine how the pass-through varies continuously over time (that is, how it is dependent on the level of power demand).

The chapter proceeds as follows. Section 8.2 describes the main structural features of the Italian power market. Section 8.3 applies the theoretical model to simulate the pass-through rate in Italy.[4] Section 8.4 sets out the empirical analysis in the Italian context. The load duration curve approach will be used in order to check how well the observed pass-through curves match the estimated ones. Finally, Section 8.5 summarizes the main results of the analysis.

8.2 THE ITALIAN MARKET

The Italian market is a highly concentrated context in which Enel, the dominant firm, exerts a high degree of market power. Furthermore, it can be

Table 8.1   Structural features of the Italian sub-markets, 2005

	North	Macro-South	Macro-Sicily	Sardinia
Peak demand (MW)	28,800	18,000	3,800	1,900
Available installed capacity* (MW)	37,000	18,500	6,400	2,800
Share of capacity operated by the first company (%)	35	65	50	39
Share of capacity operated by the second company (%)	14	14	23	24

Note: *Including imported power.

Source: Our estimations and AEEG (2005).

split into four (macro) sub-markets (North, macro-South, macro-Sicily and Sardinia) which differ significantly in some important structural characteristics, namely in the maximum power demand, the available generation capacity and market concentration (Table 8.1).

Note that the North and macro-South sub-markets are characterized by a dominant firm facing a competitive fringe model while macro-Sicily and Sardinia might be characterized as being typical duopolistic models of competition (Sardinia more than macro-Sicily). In addition, in the North, the degree of market concentration is relatively low and there is excess generation capacity whereas in the macro-South, the degree of market concentration is very high and there are problems of scarcity of generation capacity.[5] In contrast, in both Sardinia and macro-Sicily there is excess capacity even though in this latter case the excess capacity is mostly due to inefficient plants operated by the dominant firm. Finally the Italian sub-markets differ significantly in the technology mix (Table 8.2). Thus, analysing them separately might allow us to understand how the impact of the ETS under market power depends on the different structural factors of the power market.

8.3   SIMULATIONS

Model Setting

This subsection describes the assumptions and the structure of the model that we use in order to simulate the carbon price pass-through in Italy.

Table 8.2   Technology mix in the Italian sub-markets, 2005 (%)

	North	Macro-South	Macro-Sicily	Sardinia
Gas turbine	2	1	0	0
Hydro	18	9	8	6
Oil-fired steam cycle	8	20	30	8
Gas-fired steam cycle	12	19	4	3
CCGT	45	33	57	36
Coal	13	12	0	44
Other	2	6	1	3
Total	100	100	100	100

With regard to power demand, and in line with most contributions on this topic, we assume that power demand is inelastic,[6] predictable with certainty and given by a typical load duration curve $D(H)$, where H is the number of hours (the reference time unit adopted here) in the reference time period (for example, the year) that demand is equal to or higher than D, where $0 \leq H \leq H_L. D_L = D(H_L)$ is the base-load demand (the minimum level) and $D_M = D(0)$ is the peak-load demand (the maximum level).

With regard to power supply, we model technologies by means of two distinctive elements: variable costs (essentially, fuel costs) and CO_2 emission rates (emissions per unit of electricity generated).

In particular, the CO_2 emission rate is $e \geq 0$ and the variable cost of production is $v \geq 0$ for production levels less than capacity, while production above capacity is impossible (that is, infinitely costly).

We restrict the analysis to two groups of plants, a and b, and assume that each group includes a very large number n of homogeneous generating units[7] such that:

$$K_j = \sum_{i=1,2,\ldots,n} k_j^i = n k_j, \ j = a, b \text{ and } v_j^i = v_j; \ e_j^i = e_j, \ \forall i, j,$$

where K_j is the total capacity of the group j, $v_j^i = v_j > 0$ and $k_j^i = k_j > 0$ are the variable cost and the capacity of the i-th unit belonging to the group j, respectively. Thus K_a and K_b are the installed capacity of groups a and b, respectively. We assume that $v_a < v_b$ and $K_a + K_b = K_T = D_M$, that is, the units of a and b are sufficient to meet the peak demand.

Emission abatement is deemed to be impossible or, equivalently, abatement cost is infinitely costly. This hypothesis is consistent with the time horizon of the analysis (short-term analysis of the ETS impact).

With regard to the wholesale market, we assume a typical day-ahead market, in line with the Italian case. Before the actual opening of the market (for example, the day ahead) the generators simultaneously submit bid prices for each of their units on an hourly basis. We ignore the existence of technical constraints such as start-up costs. The auctioneer (generally the so-called 'market operator') collects and ranks the bids by applying the merit order rule. The bids are ordered by increasing bid prices and form the basis upon which a market supply curve is derived.

In order to simulate market power in the electricity market, we adopt a dominant firm facing a competitive fringe model rather than the usual dupolistic–oligopolistic framework. This model is well suited to reflect the structure of the Italian market.

Given the regulatory framework described above, it is straightforward that price equilibria will depend on the power demand level. Since this latter varies continuously over time, a useful way of representing the price schedule is to derive the so-called 'price duration curve' $p(H)$, where H is the number of hours in the year that the power price is equal to or higher than p.

We assume that the allowance market is very large (in accordance with the extent of the European ETS) and that firms are price takers.[8] Therefore, the allowance price, p^{tp}, is given exogenously. Carbon emission allowances are allocated free of charge.[9]

Finally, we assume that firms' offer prices are constrained to be below some threshold level, $\hat{p}$, which can be interpreted in several ways.

It may be a (regulated) maximum price, $\bar{p}$, as officially introduced by the regulator or we can assume that it is not introduced officially, but simply perceived by the generators, that is, firms believe that the regulator will introduce (or change) price regulation if the price rises above the threshold. This latter interpretation fits well with the topic analysed here. In fact, firms might decide to bring down bid prices not only to avoid regulation in the wholesale electricity market but also to avoid a change in allowance allocation (for example, underallocation) or a change in taxation.[10] For these reasons we think that it is acceptable, assuming that the price cap is insensitive to the CO_2 price. This hypothesis is useful to describe the Italian situation where the dominant firm, Enel, restrains itself from increasing prices in order to maintain a specific profit target.

Alternatively, we can suppose that there is so much generation that price is never above the marginal cost of a peaker. In order to simulate this situation, we introduce a third technology, c, such that $v_c > \max [v_a, v_b]$ and $e_c > e_b$ and whose capacity is great enough, $K_c = \bar{K}_c$, that the dominant firm does not try to let it all run and drive the price up to the price cap. Instead, $K_c = 0$, is useful to simulate the situation in which there is no excess capacity in the market and prices can reach the price cap, $\bar{p}$. These latter assumptions are crucial for our analysis but not arbitrary. Technology c, in fact, can be interpreted as a typical peaking technology (in the Italian market, old oil-fired plants or gas turbine plants) whose electrical efficiency is generally much lower than that of the other plants (for example, combined cycle gas turbine (CCGT) plants, coal plants and gas-fired steam-cycle plants). Furthermore, this technology is generally more polluting than the CCGT and the gas-fired steam-cycle plants but cleaner than coal plants.

We shall briefly consider two cases of available capacity in the market, namely excess capacity ($K_c = \overline{K}_c$) and scarcity of generation capacity ($K_c = 0$). In the former case, the maximum price is the marginal cost of the technology c. In the latter case the maximum price is the price cap, $\overline{p}$.

In order to derive price equilibria in the form of price duration curves, we have to start from how the ETS impacts on marginal production costs. Given that an emission allowance represents an opportunity cost, the marginal cost of production is expected to include the full carbon opportunity cost, regardless of whether allowances are allocated free of charge. Formally,

$$MC_j^i = v_j^i + p^{tp}e_j^i, \tag{8.1}$$

where MC_j^i is the marginal cost of the i-th unit belonging to the group j of plants and $p^{tp}e_j^i$ is the corresponding carbon opportunity cost.

Given equation (8.1) and for the purpose of this analysis, the generating units belonging to the group j of plants are the most- (least-)efficient units if their marginal cost (including the carbon opportunity cost) is lower (higher) than that of the units belonging to the other group i.

Furthermore, if we assume that there is a trade-off in the plant mix, that is, the technology with lower variable cost is the worse polluter,[11] there exists an allowance price, the 'switching price' $p^{tp*} = (v_b - v_a)(e_a - e_b)$, such that the marginal cost of the plants of group a, MC_a, is equal to that of the plants of group b, MC_b. Allowance prices are defined as low if $p^{tp} \leq p^{tp*}$ and high if $p^{tp} > p^{tp*}$.

Finally, the marginal carbon opportunity cost is the price of the CO_2 emission allowance multiplied by the emission rate of the marginal production unit.

Given these definitions, the change (due to the ETS) in marginal production cost of the marginal unit is given by:

$$\Delta MC = \begin{cases} \overline{MC} - v_b & \forall D \in \,]D_M; \underline{K}] \\ \underline{MC} - v_a & \forall D \in \,]\underline{K}; D_L] \end{cases},$$

where:

$$\overline{MC} = \max\{MC_a = v_a + p^{tp}e_a; MC_b = v_b + p^{tp}e_b\}$$

$$\underline{MC} = \min\{MC_a = v_a + p^{tp}e_a; \; MC_b = v_b + p^{tp}e_b\}$$

and

$$\underline{K} = \begin{cases} \begin{cases} K_a & \text{if } p^{tp} \leq p^{tp*} \\ K_b & \text{if } p^{tp} > p^{tp*} \end{cases} & \text{when } v_a < v_b \text{ and } e_a > e_b \\[2em] K_a \quad \forall p^{tp} & \text{when } v_a < v_b \text{ and } e_a < e_b. \end{cases}$$

Note that ΔMC is equal to the impact of the ETS under perfect competition. In this case, in fact, prices equal the marginal cost of the marginal unit regardless of the power demand level.

We are now able to simulate the impact of market power[12] on power pricing. For this purpose, as previously pointed out, we adopt a dominant firm facing a competitive fringe model. The general formulation of the model assumes that the dominant firm owns and operates $z \in [0; 2n]$ units of both group a and group b, while the remaining units are operated by $2n - z$ firms behaving as a competitive fringe. Obviously, $z = 0$ corresponds to the case of pure competition while $z = 2n$ corresponds to that of pure monopoly.

In order to derive the price schedule in the form of a price duration curve, we introduce the following parameters.

The first parameter is $\delta \in [0; 1]$ representing the share of the total power capacity in the market operated by the dominant firm. Conversely, the competitive fringe operates the share $(1 - \delta)$ of the total power capacity. Thus, δ can be interpreted as a measure of the degree of market concentration.

The other parameters are $\mu^d \in [0; 1]$ and $\mu^f \in [0; 1]$ representing the share of own-power capacity that the strategic operator and the competitive fringe get in the most-efficient plants, respectively. Conversely, $\overline{\mu}^d = (1 - \mu^d)$ and $\overline{\mu}^f = (1 - \mu^f)$ are the shares in the least-efficient ones.

By facing the competitive fringe, the dominant firm has two alternative strategies: (i) bidding the price threshold ($\hat{p}$) and so accommodating the maximum production by the fringe or (ii) competing *à la* Bertrand with rivals in order to maximize its market share.

Let $\underline{K}^f$ be the installed capacity in the most-efficient plants operated by the competitive fringe. Thus $\underline{K}^f = \mu^f (1 - \delta) K_T$, and $\underline{H}^f = D^{-1}(\underline{K}^f)$.

Similarly, let $\overline{K} = D_M - \overline{K}^d$ be the peak demand minus the dominant firm's capacity in the least-efficient plants ($\overline{K}^d$). Given that $D_M = K_T$, then we assume that $\overline{K} = (1 - \delta\overline{\mu}^d) K_T$, and $\overline{H} = D^{-1}(\overline{K})$.

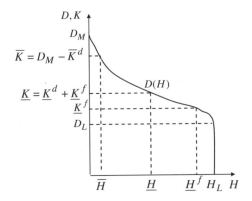

Figure 8.1   An example of supply configuration

Finally, $\underline{K} = [\underline{\mu}^d\delta + \underline{\mu}^f(1-\delta)]K_T$ is the total capacity in the most-efficient plants, already introduced in the previous section.

It is important to note that δ determines not only the degree of market concentration but also the total share of the most-efficient plants in the market, $\underline{K}$. In particular, increasing δ implies increasing $\underline{K}$ if $\underline{\mu}^d > \underline{\mu}^f$, and vice versa if $\underline{\mu}^d < \underline{\mu}^f$.

Figure 8.1 shows a (generic) example of possible power supply configuration.

The following proposition describes the shape of the price duration curve:

Proposition 8.1   There exists $]\hat{D} \in \overline{K}; \underline{K}^f]$ such that the system marginal prices equal the price threshold $\hat{p}$ when $D \geq \hat{D}$ and the marginal cost of the least-efficient plants $(\overline{MC})$ when $D < \hat{D}$. When $D < \underline{K}^f$, pure Bertrand equilibria (first marginal cost pricing) arise and prices equal the marginal cost of the most-efficient plants $(\underline{MC})$, where:

$$\hat{D} = \begin{cases} \tilde{D}(\delta, \underline{\mu}^d, \zeta) = [\delta\underline{\mu}^d\,\zeta + (1-\delta)]K_T & \text{for } \hat{D} > \underline{K} \\[2mm] \tilde{\tilde{D}}(\delta, \underline{\mu}^f, \zeta) = (1-\delta)\left[\dfrac{(1-\underline{\mu}^f)}{(1-\zeta)} + \underline{\mu}^f\right]K_T & \text{for } \hat{D} \leq \underline{K} \end{cases}$$

and

$$\zeta = \frac{(\overline{MC} - MC)}{\hat{p} - MC} \quad \text{with } \hat{p} = \begin{cases} \overline{p} & \text{for } K_c = 0 \\ MC_c & \text{for } K_c = \overline{K}_c. \end{cases}$$

Proof   See Appendix 8A.

Therefore, two price duration curves are possible, depending on whether the discontinuity is at $\tilde{H} = D^{-1}(\tilde{D})$ or $\tilde{\tilde{H}} = D^{-1}(\tilde{\tilde{D}})$.

Table 8.3   *Number of hours in which each technology sets prices in the*
              Italian sub-markets, 2005 (%)

	North	Macro-South	Macro-Sicily	Sardinia
Gas turbine	1	1	0	0
Hydro	29	16	11	18
Oil fired steam cycle	8	34	49	36
Gas-fired steam cycle	26	32	14	22
CCGT	30	12	26	11
Coal	5	4	0	13
Other	1	1	0	0
Total	100	100	100	100

MPTR Curve Estimation

In this subsection we use the simulation model previously described in order to estimate the marginal pass-through rate (MPTR) in each sub-market. The MPTR is the ETS impact on electricity prices (change in price) divided by the difference between the marginal production costs of the marginal unit (under perfect competition) after and before the ETS. Note that, under perfect competition and low allowance prices, this difference is equal to the marginal carbon opportunity cost (carbon cost).

In order to be consistent with the theoretical analysis, we restrict our simulation to the sub-markets, which are best suited to be described by the dominant firm competition model (that is, the North and macro-South sub-markets) and use the load duration curve approach consisting of the following steps.

First we have to derive the real load duration curves and estimate the corresponding price, carbon cost and spread (price minus fuel cost of the marginal unit) curves (before and after the carbon price internalization) by ordering price and spreads by decreasing levels of demand. Then, the MPTR is obtained by dividing the change in spread by the carbon cost. This approach implicitly assumes that factors other than CO_2 and fuel costs do not change from one year to another. Accordingly, the difference in the electricity price corresponding to a specific level of demand after (2005 or 2006) and before (2004) the introduction of the ETS would be explained by the corresponding difference in fuel prices, the impact of the CO_2 price and by an error term.[13]

In order to approximate the real plant mix in both sub-markets, the price and carbon cost curves have been derived by assuming the operation of the following technologies (Tables 8.2 and 8.3): (i) hydro and gas-fired steam-

Table 8.4   Technical parameters of the power generating plants

	Oil-fired steam cycle	Gas-fired steam cycle	CCGT	Coal plant	CMP-CCGT
Variable / cost (v), €/MWh	60	56	42	25	33
CO_2 / emission rate (e), kg/MWh	790	500	400	840	550
Efficiency (η)	0.35	0.40	0.50	0.40	0.70*

Note: *Including heat (that is, useful heat plus power divided by fuel consumption).

cycle plants (*gsc*), CCGT plants (*cc*) and CCGT-CHP plants (*chp*), in the North sub-market; (ii) oil-fired steam-cycle plants (*oil*), hydro and gas-fired steam-cycle plants (*gsc*) and CCGT-CHP plants (*chp*), in the macro-South sub-market. Afterwards, it was necessary to calculate (i) the total capacity and the fringe's installed capacity in *cc* and *chp* plants ($\underline{K}_1$ and $\underline{K}_1^f$, respectively) and (ii) the total capacity and the fringe's installed capacity in *chp* plants ($\underline{K}_2$ and $\underline{K}_2^f$, respectively). The technical parameters of these technologies are reported in Table 8.4. Note that the dominant firm does not operate CCGT-CHP plants. Thus $\mu_{chp}^d = 0$ and consequently $\underline{K}_2 = \underline{K}_2^f$ ($\underline{H}_2 = \underline{H}_2^f$).

The estimated price and carbon cost curves are illustrated in Figures 8.2 and 8.3. Note that we use the superscript star (*) in order to address $\hat{D}$ and $\hat{H}$ after the ETS.[14]

Figure 8.2 shows that in the North sub-market, where excess capacity is combined with a relatively low degree of market concentration, the MPTR should be much more than 1 in a relatively limited number of peak hours whereas the MPTR converges to 1 (or just below or above) in the remaining hours. This outcome is obtained by assuming that storage hydro plants bid prices equal to the marginal cost of the gas-fired steam cycle plants.[15]

In the macro-South sub-market, where a high degree of market concentration is combined with scarcity of generation capacity, power firms do not pass through any CO_2 cost in a large number of peak hours[16] whereas the MPTR should be much more than 1 in the mid-merit hours before converging to 1 in the (very) off-peak hours.[17]

8.4   EMPIRICAL ANALYSIS

In order to calculate the pass-through rate, we use the load duration curve approach (already described in the previous section) whose main advantage

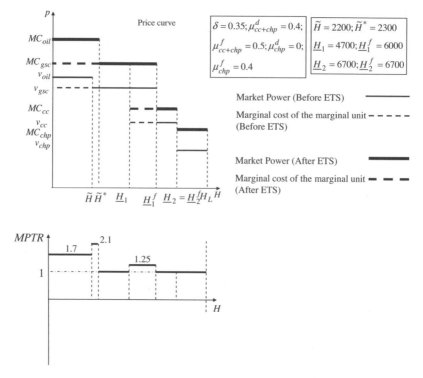

Note: *chp* = combined heat and power plants; *cc* = combined cycle plants; *gsc* = gas–fired steam cycle–plants; *oil* = oil–fired steam–cycle plants.

Figure 8.2   MPTR curves (North sub-market): model simulation

is that it allows us to know how the MPTR varies continuously over time (on an hour-by-hour basis). Thus it is well suited to study the relationship between the pass-through and the structural features of the power market (including the degree of market power whose extent depends on the level of power demand). The main disadvantage is that it does not provide a precise estimate of the pass-through but only ranges of its variability.[18]

Adopting this approach would imply that we should calculate the relevant spread (that is, the difference between the electricity price and the cost of fuel to produce a unit of electricity of the marginal plant) for each level of demand of the year (each hour of the load duration curve) in 2005 and 2006 and compare it with the corresponding spread in 2004.

Fuel costs are calculated by using the information provided by the Italian market operator regarding data on the marginal technology hour by hour (Table 8.3). The CO_2 costs[19] are assessed by accounting for the real plant

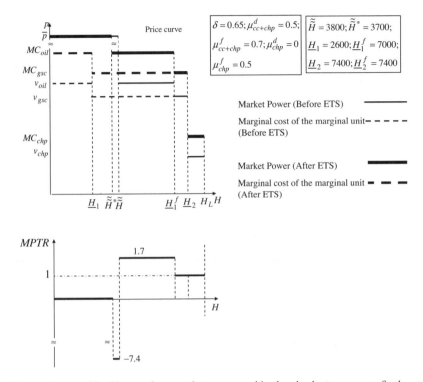

Note: *chp*=combined heat and power plants; *cc*=combined cycle plants; *gsc* = gas-fired steam cycle-plants; *oil*=oil–fired steam–cycle plants.

Figure 8.3   MPTR curves (macro-South sub-market): model simulation

mix in each sub-market (Table 8.2) and estimating which kind of technology is able to set prices in each hour under perfect competition. In particular, in the North sub-market it is very likely that hydro plants (in Italy, mainly storage and pumped storage hydro plants) could be the marginal units in the peak hours,[20] the CCGT plants in the peak and mid-merit hours and the cogeneration plants (based on the CCGT technology) in the (very) off-peak hours.[21] In contrast, in the macro-South sub-market, oil- and gas-fired steam-cycle plants set prices for most hours of the year, and in the macro-Sicily and Sardinia sub-markets, prices are set by oil-fired steam-cycle and CCGT plants, and oil- and gas-fired steam-cycle and coal plants, respectively.

In order to check whether the carbon price was passed through into power prices, we begin by comparing 2005 with 2004. The results are illustrated in Figure 8.4.

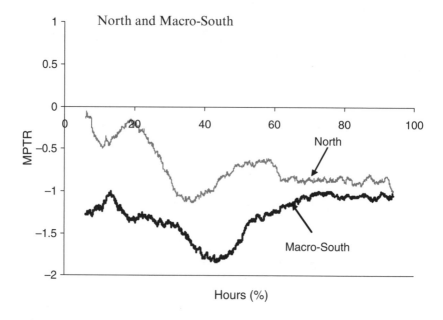

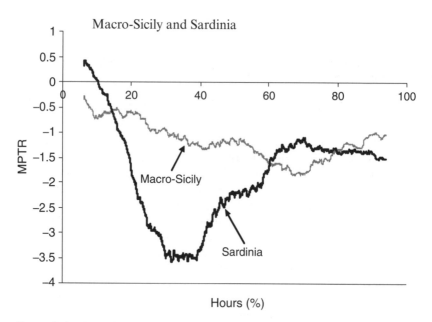

Figure 8.4   MPTR curves: 2005 versus 2004

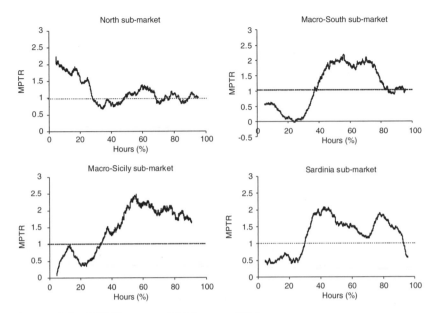

Figure 8.5   MPTR curves: 2006 versus 2005

As can be noted, in all sub-markets the MPTR is negative almost every-where, indicating that it is unlikely that power prices included the CO_2 cost in 2005. This result may be explained by the fact that in Italy the CO_2 emission allowances were allocated only at the beginning of 2006. Consequently, it is likely that power firms began to pass through the CO_2 cost in that year, that is, they decided not to pass through the CO_2 cost during 2005 (before the allocation), possibly to avoid more-restrictive reg-ulations (allowance underallocation).

The empirical analysis seems to support this latter hypothesis (Figure 8.5). In the North sub-market, the MPTR (2006 versus 2005) is much higher than 1 in a relatively limited number of hours (up to about 2,000, that is, up to 23 per cent) in the peak period while in some of the mid-merit hours (between 50 and 70 per cent) it is just above 1. In contrast, in the (very) off-peak period, the change in spread is more or less equal to the carbon cost. The shape of the MPTR curve, therefore, is similar enough to that predicted by the model.

In the macro-South the pass-through rate is much lower than 1 (and even negative) in a large number of hours (up to 4,000, around 40 per cent) according to the model simulation, while it converges to 1 only in the (very) off-peak hours. In contrast, between 45 and 75 per cent, it is much more than 1. According to the model estimates, in this period the dominant firm

Empirical analyses

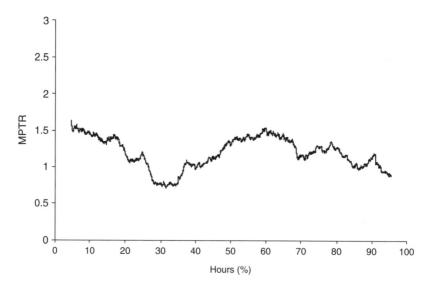

Figure 8.6   MPTR curve: Italy, 2006 versus 2005

would set prices by bidding the marginal cost of the oil-fired plants (second marginal cost pricing). Once again, the observed MPTR curve closely matches the simulated one. This latter, however, does not explain what occurs in the (very) peak hours (up to 15 per cent) where it seems to under-estimate the MPTR.[22]

In the macro-Sicily sub-market the change in spread is lower than the carbon cost in the peak hours (MPTR below 1) and much more than the carbon cost in the remaining hours. Although we have not carried out a specific simulation analysis for this context, we note that the shape of the MPTR curve is close to that of the macro-South sub-market. Indeed, these two sub-markets show a similar technology mix and can be characterized by a dominant firm competition model. Furthermore, even though in the macro-Sicily case there is excess capacity, this is mostly due to inefficient plants operated by the dominant firm. This implies that the leader might behave as if there were a scarcity of generation capacity in the market, that is, the dominant firm can bid the price cap without risking not to be dispatched.

In the case of the Sardinia sub-market, where there is excess capacity, the MPTR is just less than 1 in the peak hours and much more than 1 in the off-peak hours. Thus, the simulation (for the case of excess capacity) does not match the empirical outcome. This result clearly confirms that the dominant firm model is not well suited to describe the mode of competition in this sub-market. The market structure, in fact, seems to be similar to a typical duopolistic framework where coordination between firms is likely.

Finally, by using the partial results of each sub-market we have derived the MPTR curve for the Italian market as a whole. This curve has been obtained by calculating the sub-market volume-weighted average MPTR in each hour of the load duration curve. Figure 8.6 highlights not only that the MPTR can be much more than 1 but also that the corresponding curve is almost flat. In both the peak and off-peak hours the MPTR is between 1 and 1.5.

8.5   CONCLUSIONS

The empirical analysis of the Italian market carried out in this chapter highlights that the extent of passing through the carbon cost into power prices depends on the time of consumption (peak or off-peak hours) and varies significantly between the different Italian sub-markets.

In the North sub-market, where there is excess capacity and a relatively low degree of market concentration, electricity prices include more than the CO_2 cost (MPTR much more than 1) in a relatively limited number of peak hours whereas the MPTR converges to 1 (or just below or above) in the remaining hours.

In the macro-South sub-market, where there is no excess capacity and the degree of market concentration is high, power firms pass through much less than the CO_2 cost in a large number of peak hours whereas the MPTR is much more than 1 in the mid-merit hours before converging to 1 in the (very) off-peak hours.

The macro-Sicily sub-market shows a behaviour similar to that of the macro-South. The change in spread is lower than the carbon cost in the peak hours and much more than the carbon cost in the remaining hours.

In the Sardinia case, in contrast, the MPTR is just less than 1 in the peak hours and much more than 1 in the off-peak hours.

By using these partial results we have estimated the MPTR curve for the Italian market as a whole. The outcome contradicts those who say that there was no carbon cost pass-through in Italy. In fact, we find that power firms pass through into power prices the full carbon cost and sometimes even more (at least in 2006). Furthermore, the pass-through was very similar in the peak and off-peak hours, namely between 1.1 and 1.5 in the peak hours, 1.2 and 1.5 in the mid-merit hours, and 0.9 and 1.1 in the hours of very low demand (off-peak hours).

APPENDIX 8A

Proof of Proposition 1

It is immediately intuitive that when $D \geq \overline{K}$ the system marginal price equals $\overline{p}$ (for $K_c = 0$) or MC_c (for $K_c = \overline{K}_c$). When $D < \underline{K^f}$, pure Bertrand equilibria (first marginal cost pricing) arise and prices equal the marginal cost of the most-efficient plants ($\underline{MC}$). In fact, on the one hand, whenever the demand is so high that both the leader's and the fringe's least-efficient units can enter the market, the dominant firm would not gain any advantage by competing *à la* Bertrand, that is, by attempting to undercut rivals. Therefore, it will maximize its profit by bidding the price threshold.[23] On the other hand, whenever the power demand is lower than the fringe's power capacity in the most-efficient plants, competing *à la* Bertrand is the leader's only available strategy in order to have a positive probability of being dispatched. As a consequence, prices will converge to the marginal cost of the most-efficient plants.

It remains to identify the leader's optimal choice on $D \in]\overline{K}; \underline{K^f}]$.[24] Under the assumptions of the model, each generator in the competitive fringe has a unique dominant strategy whatever the market demand: bidding according to its own marginal cost of production (which, after the implementation of the ETS, includes the carbon opportunity cost). Conversely, the best choice of the dominant firm might consist in (i) bidding the price cap ($\overline{p}$, if there is no excess capacity, that is, $K_c = 0$) or the backstop price (MC_c, if there is excess capacity, that is, $K_c = \overline{K}_c$) or in (ii) bidding $\overline{MC}$.[25]

Let π_1^d and π_2^d be the profits corresponding to the first and second strategies above, respectively. Whenever the least-efficient units can enter the market (that is, $D(H) > \underline{K}$), the profit the dominant firm earns by choosing the first strategy (that is, $\forall H \in]\overline{H}; \underline{H}]$) is:

$$\pi_1^d = (\hat{p} - \underline{MC})[D(H) - K_T(1 - \delta)] - \sum_{i=1}^{z}\sum_{j=a,b}(k_j^i f_j^i - p^{tp}\overline{E}_j^i), \quad (8A.1)$$

where f_j^i is the capital cost per unit of installed capacity of the i-th unit belonging to group j of plants and $\overline{E}_j^i$ the amount of allowance allocated (free of charge) to the generic plant i belonging to group j.

If the dominant firm chooses the second strategy, it earns:

$$\pi_2^d = (\overline{MC} - \underline{MC})\,\underline{\mu}^d\,\delta K_T - \sum_{i=1}^{z}\sum_{j=a,b}(k_j^i f_j^i - p^{tp}\overline{E}_j^i) \quad (8A.2)$$

where:
$$\hat{p} = \begin{cases} \bar{p} & \text{for } K_c = 0 \\ MC_c & \text{for } K_c = \bar{K}_c. \end{cases}$$

Therefore the leader's optimal strategy is bidding $\hat{p}$ if and only if $\pi_1^d \geq \pi_2^d$ that is, if and only if:

$$D \geq [\underline{\mu}^d \delta \zeta + (1-\delta)] K_T = \tilde{D}(\delta, \underline{\mu}^d, \zeta), \qquad (8A.3)$$

where

$$\zeta = \frac{(\overline{MC} - \underline{MC})}{\hat{p} - \underline{MC}}.$$

When $D \in]\underline{K}; \underline{K}^f]$ (that is, $H \in]\underline{H}; \underline{H}^f]$) the profit the dominant firm earns by choosing the first strategy is:

$$\pi_3^d = (\hat{p} - \underline{MC})[D(H) - K_T(1 - \delta)] - \sum_{i=1}^{z} \sum_{j=a,b}(k_j^i f_j^i - p^{tp}\overline{E}_j^i) \ (8A.4)$$

and by choosing the second strategy, the profit is:

$$\pi_4^d = (\overline{MC} - \underline{MC})[D(H) - K_T(1 - \delta)] - \sum_{i=1}^{z}\sum_{j=a,b}(k_j^i f_j^i - p^{tp}\overline{E}_j^i).$$
$$(8A.5)$$

Thus the dominant firm will choose the first strategy (bidding the price cap or the backstop price) if and only if $\pi_3^d \geq \pi_4^d$, that is, if and only if:

$$D \geq (1-\delta)\left[\frac{(1-\underline{\mu}^f)}{(1-\zeta)} + \underline{\mu}^f\right]K_T = \tilde{\tilde{D}}(\delta, \underline{\mu}^f, \zeta). \qquad (8A.6)$$

NOTES

1. See Newbery (2005), Honkatukia et al. (2006) and Sijm et al. (2006).
2. This is the case, for example, of Sijm et al. (2005) and Bunn and Fezzi (2007).
3. See Levy (2005).
4. For a detailed presentation of this model, see Bonacina and Gullì (2007) and Gullì (this volume, Chapter 3).
5. Generally, security of supply needs a reserve margin in peaking technologies around 5–10 per cent of the total installed capacity. Conventionally, above (below) this threshold we face excess capacity (scarcity of capacity).
6. Most contributions using auction models assume inelastic demand (for example, von der Fehr and Harbord, 1993; Crampes and Creti, 2005; von der Fehr et al., 2006). In this chapter, this hypothesis mainly reflects the fact that hourly demand forecasts announced by the market operator are fixed quantities. Indeed, the aggregate demand should exhibit some elasticity, to the extent that eligible customers are allowed to announce demand

bids. Nevertheless, actual observation highlights that the price elasticity of demand is very low.

7. Assuming that each group includes the same number n of units implies that k_j depends on K_i. This is an arbitrary assumption, however, which does not undermine the significance of the analysis.

8. The electricity sector accounts for basically 50 per cent of the EU ETS. Therefore, in principle it has a certain power to influence prices in the carbon market. However, in our analysis, what is important is the ability to do this in the single electricity firm. This ability is relatively low if we consider the entire European carbon market. Moreover, most studies on carbon ETS assume that the firms behave as price takers in the carbon market. This assumption is acceptable when there are other firms outside the oligopolistic industry (other output industries or other power industries) that operate on the same permit market (Requate, 2005). This is the case for the European carbon market, which is the largest multi-country and multi-sector ETS.

9. For a comparative analysis of the different allocation methods, see Burtraw et al. (2001) and Harrison and Radov (2002).

10. Underallocation and change in firms' taxation (for example, taxing windfall profits) are some of the options taken into consideration for the second phase of the EU ETS in some countries in order to reduce the so-called (and supposed), 'windfall profits'.

11. In this case, $v_a < v_b$ and $e_a > e_b$. A typical relevant example is given by coal plants (a) versus CCGT technologies (b).

12. Throughout this chapter, we consider that there is market power when firms are able to set prices above the level which would arise under perfect competition.

13. See Sijm et al. (2006).

14. The price curves are estimated by using a specific carbon price (20 €/tCO$_2$ which is consistent with the average carbon prices in 2005 and 2006) and specific fuel prices (corresponding to the variable costs of the different technologies reported in Table 8.4). However, this choice has only a marginal impact on the shape of the MPTR curve. In fact, $\hat{D}$ and $\hat{H}$ are very low sensitive to the carbon and fuel prices. For instance, moving from 0 to 30 €/tCO$_2$ (the range of carbon price variability from 2005 to 2007) and considering the North sub-market, $\hat{D}$ varies from 0.75 to 0.73 and $\hat{H}$ from 2200 to 2350 hours. Also, the MPTR depends on the carbon and fuel prices only in a few hours (less than 2 per cent of the total), in the interval between $\hat{H}$ and $\hat{H}^*$ (or between $\tilde{\hat{H}}$ and $\tilde{\hat{H}}^*$). Consequently, the MPTR curves, described in Figure 8.2, could be considered as simulations of the real MPTR in 2005, 2006 and 2007 although the carbon and fuel prices change significantly over time (during each year and from one year to another). Moreover, assuming that the fuel prices do not change over time implies that the change in spread is equal to the change in price.

15. Note that hydro plants bid prices equal to the marginal costs of the peaking technologies (for example, gas turbine or gas- or oil-fired steam-cycle plants). The variable cost of hydro plants is virtually zero. However, because of the scarcity of water supplies, a shadow price arises, which can be viewed as a variable cost. In fact, generating one megawatt-hour in a given hour implies not being able to generate one megawatt-hour in some future hour, so determining an opportunity cost.

16. In the macro-South sub-market, we assume that storage hydro plants bid prices equal to the marginal cost of the oil-fired steam-cycle plants.

17. Note that it is widely recognized that Enel, the dominant firm in Italy, sets prices in order to pursue a given profit target. In our model, this would imply that the price cap changed over time (depending on H) whereas in Figure 8.3 we assume a fixed price cap, $\bar{p}$. However, in principle this assumption is not relevant for the MPTR as long as the profit target does not substantially change from one year to the next.

18. However, it can be used to interpret the results of the econometric models and/or to improve their design. In this sense, it should not be considered as alternative but complementary to the statistical analysis. For a detailed comparison of the two approaches (econometric and non-econometric), see Chernyavs'ka and Gullì (2007).

19. With regard to the fuel price dynamic, we use data provided by the Italian Energy Authority for each month of the year. For the CO_2 price, we use the carbon index of the EEX (European Energy Exchange) market. The other European carbon markets show very similar prices.
20. Note that hydro plants bid prices equal to the marginal costs of the peaking technologies (for example, gas turbine or gas- or oil-fired steam-cycle plants). See note 17.
21. In the (very) off-peak hours, prices are set by the CHP-CCGT plants which are CCGT plants providing combined heat and power generation. The overall efficiency (heat plus power divided by fuel consumption) of these plants is around 70–80 per cent. Their marginal cost of power production is generally calculated by sharing the total cost between power and heat, on the basis of the energy or the exergy content (or by subtracting the revenue from heat from the total cost). Thus the marginal cost of power production is lower than that of the simple CCGT. With regard to the CO_2 cost of the CHP plants, we have to take into account that the Italian public authority allocates the allowances on the basis of the total CO_2 emissions without distinguishing between power and heat. Since the amount of emissions from CHP-CCGT plants is larger than that from a simple CCGT (Table 8.4), the CO_2 cost (per unit of electricity) will be significantly higher.
22. This might be due to a particular event that occurred in the beginning of 2006 in Italy. From January to April 2006, in fact, there was a shortage of gas importation from Russia. In order to conserve natural gas storage, the public authorities allowed power firms to increase their use of heavy fuel oil (highly polluting and costly, given the very low electrical efficiency of the old oil-fired power plants). This might have led to a change (increase) in the perceived price cap.
23. Strictly speaking, only offer prices of units that may become marginal units (that is, units belonging to the group b) need to equal the price cap or the backstop price.
24. Note that assuming a dominant firm of the competitive fringe model, rather than an oligopolistic framework, ensures that equilibria in a pure strategy do exist. For an explanation of why equilibria in pure strategies do not exist in the case of oligopolistic competition, see von der Fehr and Harbord (1993).
25. Strictly speaking, bidding $\overline{MC}$ for units of kind b and $p \le \overline{MC} - \epsilon$ (where $\epsilon \approx 0^+$) for units of kind a.

REFERENCES

Autorità per l'Energia Elettrica e il Gas (AEEG) (2005), *Indagine Conoscitiva sullo Stato della Liberalizzazione dei Settori dell'Energia Elettrica e del Gas Naturale*, Milan.

Bonacina, M. and Gullì, F. (2007), 'Electricity pricing under "carbon emission trading": a dominant firm with competitive fringe model', *Energy Policy*, **35**, 4200–220.

Bunn, D.W. and Fezzi, C. (2007), 'Interaction of European carbon trading and energy prices, EMG (Energy Market Group) Working Paper, London Business School.

Burtraw, D., Palmer, K., Bharvirkar, R. and Paul, A. (2001), 'The effect of allowance allocation on the cost of carbon emission trading', Resources for the Future, Discussion Paper 01–30, August.

Chernyavs'ka, L. and Gullì, F. (2007), 'Interaction of carbon and electricity prices under imperfect competition', IEFE (Instituto di Economia e politica dell'Energia) WP 2, Bocconi University.

Crampes, C. and Creti, A. (2005), 'Capacity competition in electricity markets', *Economia Delle Fonti di Energia e dell'Ambiente*, **2**, 59–83.

Harrison, D. and Radov, D. (2002), *Evaluation of Alternative Initial Allocation*

Mechanisms in a European Union Greenhouse Gases Emissions Allowance Trading Scheme, NERA Economic Consulting, Boston, MA, Prepared for DG Environment, European Union, March.

Honkatukia, J., Malkonen, V. and Perrels, A. (2006), 'Impacts of the European Emissions Trading Scheme on Finnish wholesale electricity prices', VATT (Government Institute for Economic Research) Discussion Paper 405, Helsinki.

Levy, C. (2005), 'Impact of emission trading on power prices. A case study from the European Emissions Trading Scheme', DEA d'Économie Industrielle, Université Paris Dauphine, November.

Newbery, D. (2005), 'Emission trading and the impact on electricity prices', mimeo, Department of Applied Economics, University of Cambridge, 14 December.

Requate, T. (2005), 'Environmental policy under imperfect competition – a survey', CAU Christian Albrechts Universität, Kiel, Economics Working Paper 2005–12.

Sijm, J., Bakker, S., Chen, Y. and Harmsen, H. (2005), CO_2 *Price Dynamics: The Implications of EU Emissions Trading for the Price of Electricity*, ECN Report, Energy Research Centre of the Netherlands, ECN-C-05-081, September.

Sijm, J., Neuhoff, K. and Chen, Y. (2006), 'CO_2 cost pass-through and windfall profits in the power sector', *Climate Policy*, **6**, 49–72.

von der Fehr, N., Fabra N. and Harbord, D. (2006), 'Designing electricity auctions', *RAND Journal of Economics*, **37**, 23–46.

von der Fehr N. and Harbord D. (1993), 'Spot market competition in the UK electricity industry', *Economic Journal*, **103** (418), 531–46.

9. The joint impact of carbon emissions trading and tradable green certificates on the evolution of liberalized electricity markets: the Spanish case

Pedro Linares and Francisco J. Santos[1]

9.1 INTRODUCTION

Climate change policies have clearly been escalating in the political agenda in recent years. The growing concern for the impacts of climate change, as recently updated by the Intergovernmental Panel on Climate Change (IPCC, 2007) is driving many governments to take action on reducing greenhouse gas emissions. Among the many policies available for achieving reductions, the most popular up to now have been setting up emissions trading markets, carbon taxes, and also the promotion of renewable energies.

Emissions trading was contemplated under the Kyoto Protocol as one of the mechanisms available to reduce the cost of complying with reduction targets. However, it was not until the European Union implemented its Emissions Trading Scheme or ETS (EU Directive 2003/87/EC) that these markets really took flight. The relatively successful European experience has also prompted other countries to consider this mechanism: the US Senate, for instance, is currently considering several bills for the introduction of such a scheme, and other countries are doing the same. The implementation of these markets is also making carbon taxes redundant, and so the countries which featured them are abandoning this instrument.

Renewable energy (RE) promotion policies, on the other hand, have a longer history. In fact, they were devised as a way to reduce energy dependency, and consideration was first given to them around 1973. However, the subsequent decrease in oil prices in the 1980s rendered them unnecessary to the policy maker, and it was not until the 1990s that they made a strong comeback. Since then, these policies have been used extensively, not only in the US and Europe, but also in many other countries, as a multi-purpose instrument: renewable promotion helps to reduce carbon emissions, but also energy dependency, and contributes to the development of local industry.

The relevance of these two policies has attracted a lot of attention from researchers and policy makers, and has resulted in many studies. The impact of emissions trading policies has been analysed from a macro point of view (see, for example, Huntington and Weyant (2004) for a comprehensive review), and also from the point of view of the electricity sector (which is one of the most relevant players in the carbon emissions market). Here, studies such as the GETS initiative by Eurelectric (2004), Linares et al. (2006), Sijm et al. (2006) and Smale et al. (2006) have produced very interesting insights. More examples of these studies are included in this volume.

The impact of RE promotion policies has also been closely examined. However, because of space limitations, we shall cite only the studies by Amundsen and Mortensen (2001), Menanteau et al. (2003), Fischer (2006) and Ford et al. (2007).

Since both types of policies address the same type of issues, there may be important interactions between them, and therefore their impact may have to be assessed jointly in order to account for that. Indeed, an emissions trading scheme will indirectly encourage investments in 'clean' technologies such as gas, nuclear energy and renewables, while penalizing investments in other 'dirtier' technologies such as coal. This indirect incentive for renewables may interact significantly with current support schemes for REs. Although it is debatable whether the support for renewables accounts for their carbon reduction benefits or for their local positive externalities (which most of the time is not so clear; see, for example, Komor and Bazilian, 2005 or Bergmann et al., 2006), it is possible that the implicit carbon tax may in fact be double-counting the carbon externality of renewables, because of the slow adjustment of support schemes. This raises the problem of how to avoid this double-counting and how to combine regional regulations such as the ETS directive and national ones such as RE support schemes.

Some analyses have already been carried out on the expected consequences of carbon trading mechanisms on renewable support schemes. For instance, Boots (2001) and Jensen and Skytte (2003) have assessed the interaction between carbon trading and tradable green certificates using analytical models. Del Río et al. (2005) have looked at the impact of clean development mechanisms and joint implementation on the deployment of renewable electricity in Europe, although again from an analytical point of view. Hindsberger et al. (2003) and Unger and Ahlgren (2006) used a simulation model to obtain quantitative results for the Nordic electricity and energy sectors, respectively, also under a tradable green certificate system.

The objective of this chapter is to contribute to this analysis, by simulating the joint impact of carbon emissions trading and renewable electricity promotion policies on a liberalized electricity market. Compared to the previously mentioned studies, our approach offers two clear advantages: on the one hand, it is expected to be more realistic, by being able to simulate the oligopolistic behaviour of the players in the electricity market; on the other, it provides a long-term view, since it simulates the evolution of the electricity system up to 2020.

An earlier paper (Linares et al., 2008b) used this approach for the Spanish electricity sector. However, the description of the sector was too stylized, since the focus was much more on the theoretical interactions than on the real impact. Here we try to present much more realistic results, by incorporating as much as possible all the current existing policies and conditions affecting the sector. Of these, the major one may be the regulation of SO_2, NO_x and particulate emissions, which is expected to drastically affect the evolution of the sector in the medium term.

Section 9.2 describes briefly the model used for the analysis. Section 9.3 presents the scenarios considered for the simulation, and Section 9.4 shows the major results. Finally, Section 9.5 provides the conclusions and recommendations from the study.

9.2 THE SIMULATION MODEL

The simulation model used for this study is an oligopolistic, long-term generation expansion model developed at the Instituto de Investigación Tecnológica, Comillas University. Here only a brief overview is provided. For a full mathematical formulation, see Linares et al. (2008a).

The electricity market is modelled as one in which, in the short term, firms compete in quantity of output as in the conjectural variations (CV) approach wherein generators are expected to change their conjectures about their competitors' strategic decisions, in terms of the possibility of future reactions (Day et al., 2002; García-Alcalde et al., 2002). In the long-term electricity market, firms compete in generating capacity as in the Nash game. Conceptually, the structure of this model corresponds to various simultaneous optimizations – for each firm, the maximization of its profits subject to its particular technical constraints. These optimization problems are linked together through the electricity price and the emissions permit price resulting from the interaction of all of them. The general structure of the model is shown in Figure 9.1.

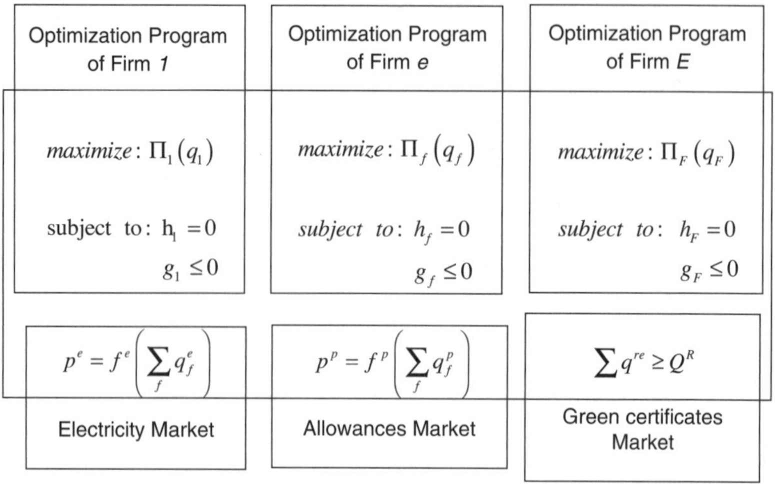

Optimization Program of Firm *1*	Optimization Program of Firm *e*	Optimization Program of Firm *E*
maximize: $\Pi_1(q_1)$	*maximize*: $\Pi_f(q_f)$	*maximize*: $\Pi_F(q_F)$
subject to: $h_1 = 0$	*subject to*: $h_f = 0$	*subject to*: $h_F = 0$
$g_1 \leq 0$	$g_f \leq 0$	$g_F \leq 0$
$p^e = f^e\left(\sum_f q^e_f\right)$	$p^p = f^p\left(\sum_f q^p_f\right)$	$\sum q^{re} \geq Q^R$
Electricity Market	Allowances Market	Green certificates Market

Figure 9.1   Mathematical structure of the market equilibrium model

The figure shows that the objective of each generation firm f is to maximize its profit Π defined as market revenues minus operating costs, investment costs and cost of purchasing emission allowances, the decision variable being the amount of electricity generated q, and the new capacity investments. The sets of constraints h and g ensure that each company's optimization programme provides decisions q that will be technically feasible. For the sake of clarity and computational tractability, generating units have been grouped into equivalent plants according to their technology.

The link between the electricity market and every firm's optimization programme is the demand function that relates the demand supplied by every generator q^e_f to the electricity price p^e. It is assumed in this model that the electricity market price at each load level is a linear function $f^e(\cdot)$ of the total demand (see left-hand side of Figure 9.1).

The carbon allowance market is modelled as a perfectly competitive one. Hence, the clearing price of the market p^p will be the point where the allowances' aggregated demand curve intersects with the whole supply curve. The whole supply curve is set to be a constant quantity of allowances determined by the government, while the aggregated demand curve is the sum of demands of all sectors covered by the ETS at every allowance price.

Part of the aggregated demand function is unknown, since for the electricity sector, this demand will depend on the utility from emission allowances (which in turn depends on electricity prices and costs, and therefore is endogenous to the model). The remaining sectors are much more difficult to model in the same way, because of their disaggregation and the lack of data. However, this same disaggregation allows us to assume that they will behave as price takers in the emissions market, and therefore they may be modelled as a competitive fringe, with a demand function corresponding to their marginal abatement costs. Therefore, the residual supply curve considered in the emission allowance market is obtained by subtracting the total demand function for all these sectors from the whole supply curve (total amount offered by the government).

Then the emission allowance market is modelled by the residual supply function that relates the allowances purchased by every firm q_f^p to the allowance price p^p. It is assumed that the price is a linear function $f^p(\cdot)$ of the purchases (see allowances market box in Figure 9.1).

Finally, the green certificate market is also modelled as a perfectly competitive one, and therefore is represented by a global restriction on the amount of renewable electricity that has to be produced: the sum of all renewable electricity produced by all firms q^{re} has to be larger than the quota set by the government Q^R (see right-hand side of Figure 9.1).

The model assumes that firms make their capacity-expansion decisions as in a Nash equilibrium. Formally, the investment market equilibrium defines a set of capacities such that no firm, taking its competitors' capacities as given, wishes to change its own capacity unilaterally (Ventosa et al., 2002). Thereby, each firm chooses its new maximum capacity so that its own profit is maximized. The Nash assumption implies that firms' investment decision making occurs at the same time that it is modelled.

To summarize, the whole model, which is a CV-market sub-model plus a Nash-expansion planning sub-model, subject to the environmental restriction of the carbon allowances and tradable green certificate markets, defines the operation, the investment, allowance purchases and pricing of both electricity, allowances and green certificates that simultaneously satisfy the first-order optimality conditions of all firms.

This market equilibrium problem can be stated in terms of a linear complementarity problem (Rivier et al., 2001) by means of setting the first-order optimality Karush–Kuhn–Tucker conditions associated with the set of maximization programmes.

9.3   DESCRIPTION OF SCENARIOS

In order to analyse the joint impact of carbon emissions trading and RE promotion policies on the electricity sector, we shall run the model for four different scenarios: (i) a base or reference case; (ii) a case in which emissions trading but no RE promotion policy is simulated; (iii) a case in which

RE promotion policies but no emissions trading is considered; and finally, (iv) a case in which both policies are modelled together.

Reference Case

The reference case consists in simulating the operation and investment in the Spanish electricity market, under oligopolistic conditions, and without any renewable promotion or carbon emission reduction mechanisms (we have considered the existing premiums for renewable generation, but only for already existing facilities).

The basic parameters which define the base case are described below. For a more extensive description of the Spanish electricity system, see, for example, Crampes and Fabra (2005).

Temporal scope

The simulation is carried out for a 20-year period (2005–25). However, in order to avoid unstable results due to tail and start-up effects, only the middle 13 years are considered (2008–20), each of which is disaggregated into five demand levels. The duration of these levels is defined in the following sub-section.

For modelling the emissions market, super-periods are defined, corresponding to the periods set by the European ETS. The first super-period then is 2005–07, and the rest are five-year periods.

Electricity demand

The duration of each demand level, as well as the demand for year 1 of the simulation and its price are shown in Table 9.1. Demand for 2005 was taken from REE (2005).

The slope of the demand curve is 60 c€/MWh×MW, and the demand growth rate is 2.5 per cent. This growth rate is lower than that experienced in the last years (around 5–6 per cent). However, it seems reasonable to assume that this rate will probably be moderated when the long term is considered, and in fact those are the assumptions of the Spanish Ministry of Industry (MINER, 2002).

Firm structure

We have represented the six major firms participating in the Spanish electricity market, plus an additional firm representing new entrants and also another firm which represents the special regime existing in Spain in 2004 (basically, renewables and cogeneration).

Large firms are characterized by a certain slope in their supply curve, which represents the variation of price as a function of the power generated

Table 9.1 Demand characteristics per level

	n1	n2	n3	n4	n5
Duration (hours)	192	1,118	3,037	2,666	1,747
Demand 2005 (MW)	38,724	36,589	32,802	26,908	21,650
Price (€/MWh)	43.63	39.85	35.76	22.72	17.19
Energy (GWh)	7,435	40,907	99,620	71,737	37,823

by the firm (or, to put it in an other way, the capability of the firm to influence market prices by modifying its offered power). These values were obtained from García-Alcalde et al. (2002).

Electricity generation technologies
All the power plants belonging to the generators are aggregated into one group per technology and firm, in order to reduce the size of the model. The existing technologies considered are nuclear (NCL), fuel-oil (FO), natural gas (GN), gas combined cycles (ECCGT), domestic coal (HLL), imported coal (CI), brown lignite (BRL), black lignite (BLL), regulating hydro (REG), run-of-the-river hydro (FLU), pumping units (BOMB), biomass (EBIO), cogeneration (ECOG), mini hydro (EMINH), wind (EEOL) and solar (ESOL).

In addition, future technologies have been considered for the new investments: supercritical coal (CSC), advanced nuclear (NCLAV), gas combined cycles (CCGT), three types of biomass (BIO1: energy crops, BIO2: agricultural waste, and BIO3: forest waste), three types of wind depending on the wind speed of the site (EOL1, EOL2, EOL3), offshore wind (EOLOFF), mini hydro (MINH), cogeneration (COG) and solar thermal (SOLT). Their parameters are presented in Tables 9.2–5. Note that costs for the different technologies may be a bit out of date, but, since the focus of the chapter is not on prediction of prices but on interaction of policies, this is not critical.

The cost function used in the model is a binomial function ($c = ax + bx^2$), where a corresponds to the linear variable cost and b to the quadratic variable cost.

Note that, under the base case, no new nuclear investments are allowed due to the current problems with public acceptance and financing.

Investment-related data
Related to the investment decisions of firms, two relevant factors exist beside the investment cost: the discount rate and the maximum investment capacity.

Table 9.2 Parameters for current thermal power plants

Firm	Technology	Linear variable cost (c€/MWh)	Quadratic variable cost (c€/MW²h)	Installed power (MW)	CO_2 (t/MWh)	SO_2 (g/kWh)	NO_X (g/kWh)	TSP (g/kWh)
1	NCL-1	1,190	0	3,358	0	0	0	0
	HLL-1	1,500	0.41	1,021	0.95	6.800	3.90	0.60
	CI-1	1,560	0	220	0.90	5.000	3.10	0.20
	FO-1	4,140	0.13	2,337	0.78	2.600	1.10	0.10
	GN-1	3,930	0.35	830	0.79	0.600	1.10	0.02
	CCGT-1	2,173	0.16	5,200	0.40	0.007	1.20	0.02
2	NCL-2	1,190	0	3,641	0	0	0	0
	HLL-2	1,767	0.06	1,462	0.95	6.800	1.95	0.60
	BLL-1	1,966	0	1,100	0.92	22.900	2.05	0.30
	CI-2	1,366	0.02	3,181	0.91	5.000	1.50	0.20
	FO-2	4,396	2.10	400	0.76	2.600	0.55	0.1
	GN-2	4,024	0.16	1,543	0.71	0.600	0.55	0.02
	CCGT-2	1,978	0.13	1,200	0.40	0.007	1.20	0.02
3	NCL-3	1,190	0	592	0	0	0	0
	HLL-3	1,530	0.23	1,498	0.90	6.800	3.90	0.60
	BRL-1	1,725	0	583	1.27	25.200	2.00	0.40
	FO-3	4,140	0.74	447	0.76	2.600	1.10	0.10
	GN-3	4,218	0	155	0.99	0.600	1.10	0.02
4	HLL-4	1,881	0.06	544	0.90	6.800	3.90	0.60
	BLL-2	1,788	0.52	400	0.94	22.900	4.10	0.30
	FO-4	3,690	0.35	682	0.76	2.600	1.10	0.10
5	NCL-4	1,190	0	165	0	0	0	0
	HLL-5	1,470	0.41	1,588	0.92	6.800	3.90	0.60
	CCGT-3	2,554	0	450	0.40	0.007	1.20	0.02
6	CCGT-4	1,978	0.20	800	0.40	0.007	1.20	0.02
Other	CCGT-5	2,304	0	400	0.40	0.007	1.20	0.02

Source: Own elaboration based on CSEN (1997).

Table 9.3 *Parameters for renewables and cogeneration power plants*

Firm	Technology	Linear variable cost (c€/MWh)	Installed power (MW)	Use ratio (p.u.)	Premium (c€/MWh)	CO_2 (t/MWh)	SO_2 (g/kWh)	NO_X (g/kWh)	TSP (g/kWh)
Special regime	EBIO	781	1,439	0.509	2,919	0	1.5	0.3	0.50
	ECOG	2,887	5,877	0.374	2,128	0.55	0.6	1.1	0.02
	EMINH	0	1,649	0.324	2,946	0	0	0	0
	EEOL	0	8,152	0.224	2,664	0	0	0	0
	ESOL	0	21	0.098	12,020	0	0	0	0

Note: Use ratio expresses the relationship between the installed power and the energy produced; Premium is the amount paid by the government to renewables and cogeneration over the market price.

Source: Own elaboration.

Table 9.4   Parameters for current hydro power plants

Firm	REG		FLU		BOMB	
	Maximum power (MW)	Annual inflows (GWH)	Maximum power (MW)	Maximum power (MW)	Pumping yield (%)	Maximum capacity (GWH)
1	3,150	8,930	360	628	70	300
2	2,100	2,839	390	1,409	70	515
3	850	1,538	188	208	70	90
4	475	243	41	340	70	50
5	270	264	38	0	70	0
6	0	0	0	0	70	0
Other	0	0	0	0	70	0

Source: Own elaboration based on CSEN (1997).

The discount rate considered has been at 9 per cent. As for the maximum investment, we have assumed that for each super-period the investment capacity of each firm is limited to a quantity equivalent to a number of gas combined cycles, which depends on the size of the firm (from three to five for the existing firms, and only one for the new entrants).

Limits for SO_2, NO_x and TSP emissions
As mentioned before, because it is highly relevant, we have also modelled the European directive 2001/80 on atmospheric emission limits from large combustion plants. This directive has been translated into Spanish legislation by Royal Decree 430/2004.

This Royal Decree establishes that there will not be individual limits for power plants, but rather a National Reduction Plan. Existing power plants must comply with a global annual emissions limit from 2008 onwards (although those plants operating for less than 20,000 hours up to 2015 are exempted). There are limits for SO_2, NO_x and particulate matter.

The precise limits and the implementation methodology have not yet been fixed, so some assumptions had to be made. For our simulation we have considered that all fuel-oil and gas power plants, plus 477 MW of domestic coal and 320 MW of black lignite will be exempted, since they will operate for less than 20,000h (that is, they will not be required to reduce their pollutant emissions). The rest of the existing plants will be incorporated into the National Reduction Plan, for which the global caps listed in Table 9.6 have been assumed. This means that, for most of the existing power plants, the total amount of pollutants emitted cannot exceed those reflected in the table.

Table 9.5 *Parameters for new technologies*

Technology	Linear variable cost	Investment cost	Max installed power	Use ratio	CO_2	SO_2	NO_X	TSP
	(c€/MWh)	(€/kW)	(MW)	(p.u.)	(t/MWh)	(g/kWh)	(g/kWh)	(g/kWh)
CCGT	2,100	466		1	0.40	0.007	1.2	0.02
CSC	1,500	992		1	0.80	0.2	0.3	0.2
BIO1	5,017	1,272	1,131	0.799	0	1.6	0.3	0.50
BIO2	1,003	1,406	1,212	0.799	0	1.2	0.3	0.35
BIO3	6,688	1,142	687	0.799	0	0.3	0.3	0.15
MINH	0	1,700	743	0.267	0	0	0	0
COG	4,700	600	1,315	0.426	0.63	0.6	1.1	0.02
EOL1	0	900	4,000	0.247	0	0	0	0
EOL2	0	900	6,000	0.212	0	0	0	0
EOL3	0	900	10,000	0.159	0	0	0	0
EOLOFF	0	1,600	5,000	0.320	0	0	0	0
SOLT	0	2,500	500	0.109	0	0	0	0

Source: Own elaboration based on European Commission (2004).

Table 9.6   Emission limits for existing power plants

Years	SO$_2$ (kt)	NO$_X$ (kt)	TSP (kt)
2008–12	118.65	175.46	11.87
2013–17	118.65	133.87	11.87
2018–20	118.65	48.24	11.87

For new power plants, the emission limits will be set for each individual power plant. We have assumed that the future power plants to be installed will comply with these limits.

It should be noted that the implementation of the Directive has not strongly influenced the evolution of emissions, because it has not started yet, but it will exert a large influence when it does.

Alternative Scenarios

As already mentioned, in order to analyse the joint impact of carbon emissions trading and RE promotion policies on the Spanish electricity sector, we have built scenarios in which these policies are modelled, both separately and jointly.

Carbon emissions trading policies

The carbon emissions trading policy simulated is the European ETS. Therefore, there is a cap on the total amount of carbon emissions, translated into a certain amount of tradable allowances. The price for the allowances is generated endogenously by the model.

The amount of allowances distributed is that established by the Spanish National Allocation Plan (RD 60/2005), that is, 160 Mt. However, the plan covers only the 2005–07 period. From 2008, the government envisages that emissions should not be higher than those of 1990 incremented at a rate of 24 per cent, so the total amount of allowances from 2008 to 2014 will be 147.8 Mt. This 24 per cent increment is larger than the 15 per cent increase allowed by the Kyoto commitments. However, the Spanish government assumes that the differential will be covered by certified reduction units from clean development mechanisms (7 per cent), and by carbon sinks (2 per cent).

Note that this is the whole amount of allowances distributed among all sectors covered by the directive. However, only the electricity sector has been modelled in detail. The remaining sectors have been modelled, as described in Section 9.2, as a competitive fringe, where their demand function is the aggregated marginal abatement cost curve for all these sectors in Spain, and has been obtained from the PRIMES model (Capros et al., 2001). Of course, since the Directive sets up a European market, allowing trade between countries (and from 2008 on, the emissions market will become global rather than European), the expected results for the allowance price may be different from those simulated here. Since the size of the market when enlarged to a European or global scale will be much larger, abatement opportunities may increase and therefore the expected price of the allowance should be lower.

However, the precise modelling of this European or global market (by including many sectors and countries in the model) conflicts with the detailed specification of the electricity system provided by our model, because of computing requirements, and therefore a compromise had to be made. Consequently, this exercise has veered towards an examination of the electricity sector, assuming that some detail will be lost in the emission permit market. However, we would not expect very large differences between Spanish and European allowance prices, since the Spanish energy technologies and the energy mix are similar to the European average, so we would expect the marginal abatement costs curves (which ultimately define the price of the allowance) to be similar. Therefore, we consider it more advisable to simulate just the Spanish market with no trade, assuming that the real allowance price may be somewhat lower.

A final point to be made about the allocation of allowances is that it is not the objective of this chapter to look at the distribution of costs and benefits among firms, so allocation is therefore not relevant.

Renewable energy promotion policies
With respect to RE promotion policies, two options are generally used: price systems (premiums) and quota systems (usually associated with tradable green certificates). Although the first are more widespread, due to their seemingly better performance (Menanteau et al., 2003), their modelling as an exogenous premium for deciding on generation expansion is somewhat short-sighted. Indeed, premiums are not static, but rather based on implicit quota objectives set by regulators. Therefore, we consider that they should be modelled anyway as quota systems, since that allows for an endogenous generation of the premium.

Therefore, the renewable energy policy considered has been a tradable green certificate system, through which a renewable quota of 17.5 per cent of the total electricity production will be reached in 2010 and maintained, according to European Directive 2001/77 on renewables.

9.4   RESULTS

In this section, the major results for the scenarios described above are presented. The scenarios are: REF (reference case), ETS (only emissions trading), TGC (only tradable green certificates) and ETSTGC (both emissions trading and tradable green certificates) (see Table 9.7).

Again, we must underline that the prices and costs as such are not indicative, since they are based on assumptions that are not necessarily realistic. The focus of the chapter is on the comparison of the different policies, and therefore figures should be considered on a relative, not on an absolute, basis. This is especially relevant for electricity market prices and green certificate prices, and also for the costs of the system.

As expected, prices increase with the introduction of an ETS, and decrease with a TGC scheme (since the amount of 'conventional' energy bid into the system decreases, and so does the marginal price). However, we see that this latter effect is not very pronounced, possibly due to the fact that it is always the same technology which sets the marginal price.

The increase in prices due to the introduction of an ETS is significant: up to 40 per cent in 2012, and more than 300 per cent in 2020. This can be explained by the large increase in demand considered, while the amount of allowances is held constant.

As for the joint impact, we see that the combination of ETS and TGC policies results in significantly lower prices than under the ETS alone (Table 9.8). This may be explained by two factors: first, the decrease in marginal prices by the introduction of more renewable energy, which has already been mentioned; and second, the decrease in emission allowance prices again because of the increase in renewables. The two factors combined produce a significant price reduction compared to the ETS-only case, which as we shall see will have consequences on costs for the consumers.

Note that there are significant jumps in prices in 2013 and 2018. This is due to the jump in carbon prices, which will be explained below.

Emission allowance prices increase over time, basically due to the increase in electricity demand, which makes it harder to meet the constant emission constraint. But, as we mentioned before, we see that when the two policies are combined, there is a reduction in allowance prices. This effect has already been identified in the literature (see, for example, Linares et al., 2007b), and is basically due to the fact that when renewables are forced into the system, they contribute to emission reductions at a zero cost (since they are already paid for by the tradable green certificate), and hence reduce the marginal cost of emissions reduction (which is where the emission allowance price comes from). Another way of explaining this is that part of the permit price is being incorporated into the green certificate price.

Table 9.7 Electricity market price (€/MWh)

Year	REF	ETS	TGC	ETSTGC
2008	26.06	30.70	26.06	27.95
2009	26.07	31.12	26.07	28.12
2010	26.07	31.58	26.07	28.32
2011	26.08	32.08	26.07	28.53
2012	26.08	32.62	26.08	28.75
2013	26.09	36.79	26.08	32.22
2014	26.09	37.75	26.08	32.76
2015	26.10	38.80	26.09	33.36
2016	26.11	39.97	26.09	34.08
2017	26.12	42.34	26.10	34.85
2018	26.17	74.84	26.07	65.07
2019	26.17	79.68	26.13	68.59
2020	26.18	84.98	26.16	72.43

Table 9.8 Emission allowance price (€/t)

Year	ETS	ETSTGC
2008	13.72	5.65
2009	13.72	5.65
2010	13.72	5.65
2011	13.72	5.65
2012	13.72	5.65
2013	30.20	18.20
2014	30.20	18.20
2015	30.20	18.20
2016	30.20	18.20
2017	30.20	18.20
2018	134.37	115.00
2019	134.37	115.00
2020	134.37	115.00

Although it is not the objective of our exercise to simulate allowance prices precisely, it is interesting to note that prices reflect quite well the current behaviour of the allowance market in the short term.

We may also note that there are significant jumps in the allowance prices between trading periods (2013, 2018). This is due to our consideration of different trading periods (which of course may be modified), and to the fact

Table 9.9   *Green certificate price (€/MWh)*

Year	TGC	ETSTGC
2008	13.95	12.07
2009	13.95	11.89
2010	13.94	11.70
2011	13.94	11.49
2012	13.94	11.26
2013	13.93	7.79
2014	21.04	14.37
2015	21.04	13.77
2016	21.03	13.05
2017	39.08	30.32
2018	39.10	0.11
2019	39.05	−3.41
2020	39.02	−7.26

that we do not consider banking between them. Banking would produce smoother price increases, as well as longer trading periods.

The green certificate price (Table 9.9), as previously explained, is the difference between the renewable energy marginal cost and the electricity market price, that is, the degree of support required by the marginal renewable energy producer to recover its long-term costs. It only appears when associated with a renewable quota. Here green certificate prices are lower than current ones, based on two facts: first, we are considering quite low investment costs for new renewables; and second, we are not introducing a risk premium into the certificate price. Again, since our focus here is on a stylized comparison of policies, we do not find these assumptions too critical. The interesting effect to be observed is that, when an emissions trading system is implemented, the certificate price is reduced, because the electricity price increases and therefore there is less need for external support. This even results in negative prices for the certificate around 2018 (when the allowance price increases considerably and so does the electricity price).

We should point out that the evolution of CO_2 emissions under the reference scenario, although significant, is probably much lower than that corresponding to the increase in demand (Table 9.10). This is basically due to the impact of the Large Combustion Plant Directive, which implies the decommissioning of most of the most-polluting (and CO_2-emitting) plants in Spain. Therefore, there is already a large reduction implied in that reference scenario.

Table 9.10 CO_2 emissions in the electricity sector (Mt)

Year	REF	ETS	TGC	ETSTGC
2012	110	86	100	84
2020	124	88	105	87
Total 2005–2020	1,480	1,076	1,318	1,067

Table 9.11   Installed power in 2020 per technology (MW)

	REF	ETS	TGC	ETSTGC
Gas combined cycles	23,860	22,240	19,523	22,499
Supercritical coal	3,593	–	2,087	–
Energy crops	–	1,131	827	827
Agricultural residues	–	1,212	1,212	1,212
Wind-good	–	4,000	4,000	4,000
Wind-average	–	6,000	6,000	6,000
Wind-offshore	–	–	1,459	1,459

With regard to the impact of the different policies, we see that an ETS has a significant impact, keeping emissions around 85 Mt per year, while a TGC does not really reduce to that level (indeed, a TGC policy alone such as the one considered here would not be able to achieve the goals set under the Kyoto Protocol for Spain). When the two policies are combined, again we see an interesting effect: on the one hand, we should see a reduction compared to the ETS case, because of the larger participation of renewables in the system. But on the other hand, let us not forget that the combination of policies also produced a reduction in the price of the carbon allowance (and therefore a reduction in the incentive to abate emissions). So the final effect is not, as might have been expected, a larger abatement than the one under ETS, but rather a similar one (although of course there will be differences in costs and renewable energy development, which will be analysed later).

Table 9.11 shows the evolution of installed power. We see that under an ETS, there is a large investment in gas combined cycles, but also some investment in renewables, in order to achieve the reductions required. These technologies basically replace coal power plants (both new and existing). When a TGC is introduced alone, the investment in gas decreases compared to the reference case, since most of the effort goes into complying with the renewable obligation. And, what happens when we combine both policies?

Table 9.12   Production and consumer costs, and generating firms' profits
(M€, net present value 2005–20)

Costs	REF	ETS	TGC	ETSTGC
Production costs	48,300	67,793	52,330	64,731
Consumer costs	80,600	114,015	88,830	107,630
Firms' profits	32,300	46,222	36,500	42,899

We see here that the result is a mixture of ETS and TGC. The investment in gas is a bit higher, as well as the investment in renewables, but only marginally. This explains why emissions are only marginally reduced compared to the ETS-only case.

Finally, the cost of the different policies is a very interesting issue. We shall compare here production and consumer costs (Table 9.12). Production costs are those borne by generating units (basically, investment, operation and maintenance, and fuel costs) and consumer costs are those paid by consumers for their electricity (we use here as a proxy the wholesale price rather than the tariff or retail price, since it will vary, depending on the policy). We also calculate firms' profits as the difference between consumer and producer costs (although this is of course an approximation, it gives a hint about the increase or decrease of profits from one case to another).

We can see that production costs increase when the different policies are introduced. The introduction of ETS increases production costs by 40 per cent, as well as consumer costs by 41 per cent (thus also increasing firms' profits). The introduction of green certificates also increases costs, but to a lesser extent (around 10 per cent). This is clearly because the reduction in marginal prices compensates for the increase in costs due to the larger introduction of renewables. This is why some authors have proposed that TGCs alone might be a cheaper alternative for emissions reduction. However, we should take into account: first, that renewable promotion policies also have a cost (the green certificate cost); and second, that they are not enough for achieving significant carbon reductions. Therefore, it seems that this mechanism cannot be considered alone for that purpose.

Finally, the combination of both reduces costs compared to the ETS-only case. Therefore, it seems that the combination is an interesting option, given that, as just mentioned, renewables promotion systems by themselves, which are cheaper than the emissions trading system, are not able to achieve the required emission reductions.

9.5   CONCLUSIONS

This chapter has analysed the joint impact of carbon reduction and RE promotion policies on liberalized electricity markets, and has shown some interesting results from which some conclusions may be drawn.

But first, recall that the analysis has been carried out at a national level, due to the difficulties in modelling in detail the European electricity market and its environmental policies, as already mentioned in the introduction. However, the conclusions can easily be generalized to the regional level.

With regard to the interaction of instruments, we see that the reduction of carbon emissions only through renewables promotion is very complicated under the current growth of demand, even in a high-renewable-potential country such as Spain. On the other hand, carbon trading systems, although able to stimulate renewables growth, are quite costly for consumers.

However, we observe that the combination of policies produces a reduction in electricity market prices compared to the ETS system alone, which is ultimately translated into a global reduction in the costs paid by the consumer (including the green certificate costs), while still producing significant emission reductions and renewable electricity deployment.

This also reduces the windfall profits received by producers due to the introduction of the ETS system. However, this assertion should be treated with caution, since in different contexts there may be difficulties in effecting this pass-through (for example, in countries with regulated tariffs). Therefore, it will be the regulator who is ultimately responsible for adjusting firms' benefits by modifying the tariff. This of course depends on the allocation method chosen (see Linares et al., 2006 for an analysis of the effect of allocation on profits).

Therefore, we may conclude that the combination of carbon reduction and renewable promotion policies is very promising, in that it helps to achieve the required carbon reductions at a lower cost, while at the same time promoting renewable development. Therefore, there may be a sort of double-dividend in this combination which could be exploited.

The only drawback of this combination is that, since consumer costs decrease there will be a lower long-term signal for consumers to reduce energy consumption, and this is clearly a negative outcome for the long-term sustainability of the system.

As a final comment, this exercise has been carried out under the assumption that the electricity sector is a closed one (except for the exchange of emission permits), and therefore, real effects may be somewhat different from those shown here. For instance, there may be substitution effects between energy sources when their relative prices are modified. In order to simulate these effects, a general equilibrium model would be required.

NOTE

1. The authors are grateful to Fundación BBVA and to the European Commission (Contract 4.1030/C/02 004/2002) for their economic support. Pedro Linares also acknowledges the hospitality of the Harvard Electricity Policy Group, and support from Fundacion Repsol YPF, Unión Fenosa, and the Spanish Ministry of Education (SEJ2006-1239/ECON).

REFERENCES

Amundsen, E.S. and J.B. Mortensen (2001), 'The Danish green certificate system: some simple analytical results', *Energy Economics*, **23**, 489–509.

Bergmann, A., N. Hanley and R. Wright (2006), 'Valuing the attributes of renewable energy investments', *Energy Policy*, **34**, 1004–14.

Boots, M. (2001), 'Green certificates and carbon trading in the Netherlands', *Energy Policy*, **31**, 43–50.

Capros, P., N. Kouvaritakis and L. Mantzos (2001), *Economic Evaluation of Sectoral Emission Reduction Objectives for Climate Change. Top-down Analysis of Greenhouse Gas Emission Reduction Possibilities in the European Union*, Athens: National Technical University of Athens.

Crampes, C. and N. Fabra (2005), 'The Spanish electricity industry: *plus ça change . . .*', *The Energy Journal*, Special Edition on European Electricity Liberalization, **26**, 127–53.

CSEN (1997), *Una simulación del funcionamiento del Pool de Energía Eléctrica en España* (A simulation of the Spanish electricity market pool), Dirección de Regulación, Comisión del Sistema Eléctrico Nacional, Madrid.

Day, C. J., B.F. Hobbs and J.-S. Pang (2002), 'Oligopolistic competition in power networks: a conjectured supply function approach', *IEEE Transactions on Power Systems*, **17**, 597–607.

Del Río, P., F. Hernández and M. Gual (2005), 'The implications of the Kyoto project mechanisms for the deployment of renewable electricity in Europe', *Energy Policy*, **33**, 2010–22.

Eurelectric (2004), *GETS 4 – Greenhouse gas and energy trading simulations*, Final Report, November.

European Commission (2004), *Sustainable Energy Technology Reference Information System (SETRIS)*, Joint Research Centre, European Commission.

Fischer, C. (2006), 'How can renewable portfolio standards lower electricity prices?', RFF Discussion Paper 06–20, Washington, DC.

Ford, A., K. Vogstad and H. Flynn (2007), 'Simulating price patterns for tradable green certificates to promote electricity generation from wind', *Energy Policy*, **35**, 91–111.

García-Alcalde, A., M. Ventosa, M. Rivier, A. Ramos and G. Relaño (2002), 'Fitting electricity market models: a conjectural variations approach', Proceedings of the 14th PSCC Conference, Seville, June 24–28.

Hindsberger, M., M.H. Nybroe, H.F. Ravn and R. Schmidt (2003), 'Co-existence of electricity, TEP and TGC markets in the Baltic Sea Region', *Energy Policy*, **31**, 85–96.

Huntington, H.G. and J.P. Weyant (2004), 'Modeling energy markets and climate change policy', in C.J. Cleveland (ed.), *Encyclopedia of Energy*, Amsterdam: Elsevier Science, 41–53.

Intergovernmental Panel on Climate Change (IPCC) (2007), 'Climate Change 2007: *Synthesis Report. Contributions of Working Groups I, II and III to the Fourth Assessment Report of the Intergovernmental Panel on Climate Change*, IPCC, Geneva, Switzerland, p. 104.

Jensen, S.G. and K. Skytte (2003), 'Simultaneous attainment of energy goals by means of green certificates and emissions permits', *Energy Policy*, **31**, 63–71.

Komor, P. and M. Bazilian (2005), 'Renewable energy policy goals, programs, and technologies', *Energy Policy*, **33**, 1873–81.

Linares, P., F.J. Santos and M. Ventosa (2007b), 'Coordination of carbon reduction and renewable energy support policies', *Climate Policy*, forthcoming.

Linares, P., F.J. Santos, M. Ventosa and L. Lapiedra (2006), 'Estimated impacts of the European Emissions Trading Scheme Directive and permit assignment methods on the Spanish electricity sector', *The Energy Journal*, **27**, 79–98.

Linares, P., F.J. Santos, M. Ventosa and L. Lapiedra (2008a), 'Incorporating oligopoly, CO_2 emissions trading and green certificates into a power generation expansion model', *Automatica*, **44**, 1608–1620.

Linares, P., F.J. Santos and M. Ventosa (2008b), 'Coordination of carbon reduction and renewable energy support policies', *Climate Policy*, **8**, 377–94.

Menanteau, P., D. Finon and M.-L. Lamy (2003), 'Prices versus quantities: choosing policies for promoting the development of renewable energy', *Energy Policy*, **31**, 799–812.

MINER (2002), *Planificación de los sectores de electricidad y gas* (Electricity and gas sectors planning), Madrid: Ministerio de Economía y Hacienda.

REE (2005), *Informe del Sistema Eléctrico 2005*, Madrid: Red Eléctrica de España.

Rivier, M., M. Ventosa and A. Ramos (2001), 'A generation operation planning model in deregulated electricity markets based on the complementarity problem', in M. Ferris, O. Mangasarian and J. Pang (eds), *Applications and Algorithms of Complementarity*, Boston, MA: Kluwer Academic, pp. 273–298.

Sijm, J., K. Neuhoff and Y. Chen (2006), 'CO_2 cost pass-through and windfall profits in the power sector', *Climate Policy*, **6**, 49–72.

Smale, R., M. Hartley, C. Hepburn, J. Ward and M. Grubb (2006), 'The impact of CO_2 emissions trading on firm profits and market prices', *Climate Policy*, **6**, 31–48.

Unger, T. and E.O. Ahlgren (2006), 'Impacts of a common green certificate market on electricity and CO_2-emission markets in the Nordic countries', *Energy Policy*, **33**, 2152–63.

Ventosa, M., R. Denis and C. Redondo (2002), 'Expansion planning in electricity markets. Two different approaches', Proceedings of the 14th PSCC Conference, Seville.

Index